LET IT ALL FALL

LET IT ALL FALL

UNDERGROUND MUSIC AND THE CULTURE OF REBELLION IN NEWFOUNDLAND · 1977–95

MIKE HEFFERNAN

Breakwater Books
P.O. Box 2188, St. John's, NL, Canada, A1C 6E6
www.breakwaterbooks.com

A CIP catalogue record for this book is available
from Library and Archives Canada.

ISBN 9781550819779
Copyright © 2023 Mike Heffernan

This book is a compilation of interviews and statements made by a variety of individuals, often many years after the events being described. Memories and opinions may differ. We have chosen to remain faithful to the voices represented here rather than to impose a single narrative on this rich and complex history.

All rights reserved. No part of this publication may be reproduced, stored in a retrieval system or transmitted, in any form or by any means, without the prior written consent of the publisher or a licence from the Canadian Copyright Licensing Agency (Access Copyright). For an Access Copyright licence, visit www.accesscopyright.ca or call toll free 1-800-893-5777.

We acknowledge the support of the Canada Council for the Arts. We acknowledge the financial support of the Government of Canada through the Department of Heritage and the Government of Newfoundland and Labrador through the Department of Tourism, Culture, Arts and Recreation for our publishing activities.

Printed and bound in Canada.

Breakwater Books is committed to choosing papers and materials for our books that help to protect our environment. This book is printed on Forest Stewardship Council® certified paper.

for
Charlotte Jane O'Brien
April 11, 1970 – March 23, 1993

"Only yesterday, Newfoundland stood for cod and Joey Smallwood. Now it stands for some of the freshest, brashest, most compelling art in the country. Suddenly, all of this rock—'this poor, bald rock,' as Joey used to say in his eloquent, long-ago prime—painters and actors and poets are popping up in sweet and splendid profusion."
— Sandra Gwyn, "The Newfoundland Renaissance," *Saturday Night*, April 1976

"We have so much here [in Newfoundland], and then we have so little."
— Lois Brown, actor and playwright

"This town ain't no place to cash in."
— Ron Hynes, musician

"Be everything this society hates."
— Malcolm McLaren, Sex Pistols manager

"Let it all fall, let it all fall down."
— Mike Wade, actor and musician

CONTENTS

The Rock Ain't Always Stable: An Introduction **xi**

PART 1

This is What Happens When You Play Punk Rock **3**
The Dark Corners **16**
Sounds like a Revolution **23**
Stand Tall and Act Tough **38**
Stirring Things Up **48**
Unsuitable for Public Consumption **55**
The House of Dreams **63**
The Gang of Four: Peace-A-Chord Part 1 **72**

PART 2

The Fleming Street Massacre **89**
Everything is Possible: or, Have Some Guts and Quit School **105**
Youth Crusaders: Schizoid Part 1 **124**
Relentless: Thomas Trio and the Red Albino Part 1 **135**
World Domination: Schizoid Part 2 **146**
No One Goes to Newfoundland by Accident **167**
If I Can't Dance, I Don't Want to be Part of Your Revolution **171**
One Nation Under a Groove: Thomas Trio and the Red Albino Part 2 **179**

PART 3

Animal Energy: Bung Part 1   **203**
Blowing Smoke (up Your Ass)   **213**
Halfway to Hell   **224**
A Scrappy Esthetic   **228**
Danger: Falling Rock   **244**
The Queen of Punk Rock   **248**
The Most Dangerous Band in the World: Bung Part 2   **252**
Scruffy-Looking Teenagers Playing Punk Rock in the Park:
    Peace-A-Chord Part 2   **262**
A Hard-Volume Experience: or, the End of the Century   **271**

Epilogue: A Moving Target   **285**
Cast of Characters   **293**
Acknowledgements   **297**

THE ROCK AIN'T ALWAYS STABLE
AN INTRODUCTION

The etymological origin of "rebellion" is easy enough to trace. The word has its roots in mid-fourteenth-century France. According to Merriam-Webster, it means "war waged against a government by some portion of its subjects." Newfoundlanders don't have to look too far in the past to see examples in their own history. On April 5, 1932, an angry mob of thousands stormed the steps of the Colonial Building in St. John's to protest the corruption and ineptitude of the Squires government. In July 1992, the unthinkable happened. What had been the most abundant cod population in the world had been fished out of existence. John Crosbie, then federal Minister of Fisheries and Oceans, held a press conference at Atlantic Place on Water Street. Anger and resentment spilled over as a throng of fishermen stormed the building, pushing and shoving at the conference room door, the few police on hand lost in the violent melee. Protests, riots, and confrontations with politicians filled the news.

Music historians celebrate being in the right place at the right time—those critical moments and locations when and where cultural revolutions are spawned. Every significant underground music scene from London to Liverpool, from Washington to Wisconsin, has its "zero hour"—that lightning-rod moment that galvanizes a generation. For punk rock, it was the Sex Pistols' gig at Manchester's Lesser Free Trade Hall in front of thirty-five people and the Ramones' twelve-minute blistering set at CBGB in the bowels of Manhattan. With grunge, it was Seattle's U-Men and their notorious 1985 performance at the Bumbershoot Festival when an ill-conceived prank set the stage ablaze. Those events were the catalysts that took underground music out of dingy basements and back-alley dive bars and brought it to the masses.

During the 1980s, St. John's had few bands and even fewer venues for them to play in. Then, in May 1986, in a little house on Fleming Street, a single party changed all that. The seeds had been planted the year before at Peace-A-Chord—a one-day festival held in Bannerman Park that transformed a ragtag bunch of teenagers into social activists. Known as a hangout and party den with a history of noise complaints, 15 Fleming Street was on police radar. Official attention to the location culminated in a violent episode infamously known as the "Fleming Street Massacre." Thirteen people were arrested on a variety of charges, including resisting arrest and belligerence. The event and the court battles it generated imbued the fledgling punk rock community with a profound sense of purpose. In just a few years, the scene would grow to encompass dozens of bands and hundreds of people, and garner the attention of national television shows and major record labels. At the heart of this book, then, is the marriage between the progressive protest movement and the underground music scene.

Let It All Fall: Underground Music and the Culture of Rebellion in Newfoundland, 1977–95 explores an important era in our socio-cultural history. As a member of the subculture discussed in the book, I had the advantage of perspective that comes from being a participant-observer. I have spent the better part of a decade conducting interviews and poring over archival material, newspapers, and magazines. *Let It All Fall* is a collection of first-person monologues based on oral history interviews. It's a qualitative approach to historical writing that seeks to gain a close familiarity with a group of people in their cultural environment. That's the academic definition. Ultimately, though, it's a rock and roll oral history, like *Everybody Loves Our Town: An Oral History of Grunge* by Mark Yarm (2011) and *Please Kill Me: The Uncensored Oral History of Punk* by Legs McNeil and Gillian McCain (1996).

Shaping a narrative from the rhythms and tones of speech—and often chaotic and conflicting memories—the interviews are organized and edited together as free-flowing conversations among multiple subjects. In some instances, the text has been culled from other sources, including court documents and unpublished interviews. Those excerpts are sourced within the text. The informants' words are verbatim; they have been edited for consistency and length but otherwise maintain the original language, including slang commonly used in the era.

The musicians and activists featured in this book challenged conservative culture during one of the province's most turbulent times. *Let It All Fall* is by no means a complete history; some bands, informants, and anecdotes were included, and others were not. Otherwise, the book would be an encyclopedia—or at least a multi-volume work. The timeline is not arbitrary, either. It begins with the creation of seminal punk band Da Slyme, and it ends with the death of local musician and promoter Fred Gamberg in July 1995. As one St. John's musician said, "It felt like the end of the century."

Those two events provide appropriate bookends to a period of astonishing artistic output. The unity of sound couldn't last forever and maybe, having served its purpose, it didn't need to.

THIS IS WHAT HAPPENS WHEN YOU PLAY PUNK ROCK

Wallace Hammond *(musician/sound engineer)*: Peter Morris proposed that we put a band together and play a MUN [Memorial University of Newfoundland] Radio beer bash. Beer bashes happened quite regularly at the university. I'm sure fundraisers still work the same way. You would approach the beer companies, whether you were the soccer team, the radio station, or the student newspaper, and promise to sell their product for a discount and make some money.

How it all happened in about a month was a minor miracle. Peter knew Justin Hall. Justin was hanging around the *Muse* [student-run newspaper]. I didn't hang around there, but a lot of us radio guys drifted between both. CHMR was on the second floor of the student centre. Student organizations were on the second and third floor. Peter invited Justin up to jam with the intent of playing the beer bash.

With Da Slyme, the version that played the beer bash, it started with a drummer. There was a review in the *Muse* of some show at MUN. I think Bob Hallett wrote it. The review said, "It just goes to show what you can get away with when you have a good drummer." Justin showed up with this very motley drum kit, but he knew how to play the thing better than we could have imagined. George Smith filled in on bass. He had a little bit of guitar experience and maybe some piano lessons.

A week before the gig, we put up four different posters. We had eight hundred of the various versions printed off. There were blurbs [on them]: "The Ramones could've written this song if they'd had teenage lobotomies.

These punks really know where it's at, or where it isn't." The quotes were from these fake magazines: *Swillboard, Miss Cattleaine,* the *Earlobe,* and *Snail.* "Finally, a band that doesn't write like a bunch of bloody classical composers. Hurrah! Simple-minded people need more simple-minded songs."

There was a full-page ad on the back of the *Muse.* Basically, rumours went around that CHMR was bringing in a punk band from England.

Nobody had any experience whatsoever with punk, including us. We all had fake punk names. I was "Kirt Sic-o-via." Justin was "Dead Beat." Butler was "Snotty Slyme." George was "Stig Stiletto." Then there was "Goohaw Groon" and "Pig Filthy." Some of the guys were dressed outrageously. I had on my jean jacket and a pair of shades. Gary Day, who passed away a few years ago, had a coat hanger through his hat and blonde pigtails. Justin looked pretty wild. He had his face painted white. He had on a leather jacket with no shirt underneath. Butler had his hair done up in curlers and a pair of pantyhose pulled up over his jeans.

The beer bash started on Friday at four o'clock. People were in there as soon as the doors opened, and it was definitely blocked by six o'clock. There was a lineup out by the door. Apparently, there were fights outside. I think Peter said that his younger brother was into one. Craig later ran into some guy who claimed that he got laid in the elevator. We played at ten o'clock. You're talking about six hours of people drinking fifty-cent beer. It was a drunken, rowdy mess.

People were really sort of out of it. They were throwing beer bottles because beer was so cheap and they were so drunk. There were reports in the papers and in the news of Sex Pistols shows down in Texas where the audience threw beer bottles at them. I guess people thought, *Well, this a punk band, and this is what you do.* It wasn't so much fun, but it's the stuff of legend. There was student security, but they were so busy controlling the crowds outside that they never got inside.

To me, it's sort of a blur. You're onstage concentrating on the songs. I mean, I'm dyslexic, at best. Even playing two- and three-chord songs requires some effort. So I didn't really notice what was going on. I certainly didn't notice the amount of beer bottles smashed behind our amps. I don't think there was any serious violence, but there was certainly the potential for that to happen.

Peter ended up getting into a match with some guys who were spraying him with beer. I remember he got very upset because he was holding an electric guitar. He was afraid he was going to get electrocuted. Peter lashed out and kicked the guy's chair. The next day, he ended up in the hospital with a badly swollen foot. Butler slipped because he had on the pantyhose and went down into the glass and cut himself. When he got to the hospital, the nurse said, "Sir, you're going to have to remove your pantyhose." It's been a standing joke since forever.

Gary Clark was in charge of student security, and he managed the Breezeway. At the end of the show, after Butler went to the hospital, we were all sitting around. Gary said, "This is what happens when you play punk rock."

The next week, we convened with my four-track and recorded all the songs for posterity. It was mastered down to cassette. That was to be it—lesson learned. We felt that we had unleashed forces that we couldn't control. We didn't do it to make money, and there was simply nowhere to play. We played the university, but we certainly wouldn't have been looked upon favourably to do it again. That was February 3, 1978.

* * *

Wallace Hammond: I got into this whole music racket in a weird way. In about 1975, I spent a thousand dollars on a four-track console. It's long since bit the dust. I had that machine, but I didn't have much in the way of microphones. I recorded one of Mike Fisher's early bands, Hammingwell. They had a whole pile of original stuff, which most bands didn't, at the time. They were an art rock band. I must've recorded close to two hours of material. We got together whatever microphones we could find and went down into Mike's basement in Mount Pearl. Some of those guys later became the Reaction.

Craig [Squires] and I met in 1973, I think. I was at CHMR; he walked in, and we started talking about music. We both had radio shows. I was the station manager in 1975. I think it was the shortest stint ever for a station manager. It was a hard time for CHMR. Everyone was more interested in drinking and smoking dope. CHMR was in the old Thompson Centre. The signal went to the cafeteria, to the *Muse* offices, our offices, and to a transmitter down in residence through what they used to call "carrier current." We didn't even know if anyone was listening.

Terry Carter, the guy who wrote "Newfie Rastaman," was also around. Terry didn't have any musical skills that we knew of, but he was interested in forming a band. He'd run into people in bars, musicians, and invite them up to the radio station to play.

Terry was really into punk and proto-punk bands. You got to remember, there wasn't a whole load [of] those bands at the time. There was bands like Jonathan Richman and the Modern Lovers. There were the New York

Dolls. There was the MC5. Peter was definitely into Lou Reed and the Velvet Underground.

There's a guy down in Italy who bought a Da Slyme album. He's some kind of professor and an art rock musician. He's a punk rock record collector. He bought a Da Slyme album for something like seven hundred dollars back before those prices weren't even hinted at. He bought another album from us for four hundred and fifty bucks Canadian. That four hundred and fifty dollars helped pay for the Da Slyme CD. I said to him, "Some people don't realize the connection between art rock and the punk movement." It was an element Da Slyme definitely embraced.

Wallace Hammond: In terms of original music, Denis Parker had a band back in England called the Panama Limited Jug Band. They did two records on Harvest EMI, the same label as Pink Floyd. Denis lived in swinging London. He saw the Who at the Marquee, and he saw the Rolling Stones. He saw the Beatles. He used to go down and watch Pink Floyd perform at the UFO Club.

Denis plays a big role here. In about the mid-'70s, Denis and Neil Bishop started this band called Mantis. It was all original material. During university orientation week, Brave Belt opened up for them. Brave Belt was Randy Bachman before he formed Bachman-Turner Overdrive. They got booed off the stage. That's how good Parker and them were. For all the guys at CHMR and the *Muse*, they were our rock stars.

Denis said that, basically, the reason why he came over to Newfoundland—I mean, he had just put out two records on Harvest Records, but they weren't making any money—was that Neil Bishop enticed him here. Back then, you could make two thousand bucks a weekend playing places like the Old Mill and the Circle. Denis and his drummer got on a plane and landed in Gander in the middle of a snowstorm. Denis has been here ever since. That's how Denis ended up in Newfoundland, for the two thousand bucks a weekend, and he was sitting in London with a record contract. Older musicians remind me all the time about how much money you could make.

People still went out to the Strand to see bands. The Strand was a weird amalgamation of stuff. They'd have cover bands coming in to do all the latest hits. I did a week-long sound gig for Figgy Duff at the Strand in the Avalon Mall. I didn't even know those guys at the time. That was the thing that drew the most people into the clubs. When Ryan's Fancy played, I'm sure it was the biggest thing that they would have in there. On the one hand, you had at the Strand Ryan's Fancy and the cover bands. Then, up to the university, you had Denis Parker. I think it's important to talk about what went on here musically before the punk scene. That's why I mention Parker. They opened our eyes to what we perceived as possible.

In the meantime, Peter Morris went on a work term to Calgary and sent us a letter. He'd gone to a Halloween party dressed as Tooloose from the band Tooloose and Da Slyme. He had a broomstick fashioned into a Gibson Les Paul. That was his costume, the front man for a made-up band.

Carter was away up in Nova Scotia, and he came back for Christmas. We knew he was hot to trot about playing something. Because we had the drum kit, we broached the subject with the boys: "Why don't we do this Tooloose and Da Slyme that you were talking about?"

The guys showed up the next day. Carter played drums. Craig played bass. Peter and I played guitar. George Smith was the station manager at that time, and he was there. It was Sunday; it was a holiday. I don't think the station was running. While we were setting up the gear, George and Terry sat on the window ledge and wrote "Piss-Eyed Sleezoid," the first song on the album. [...] That second day, we wrote three or four more. At the end of Christmas break, Carter went back to Halifax, and Craig went back to Toronto.

Wallace Hammond: I was running the sound board at the university. The entertainment director, Len Penton, was in the cafeteria. I was standing by the board talking to him, and he said, "Why don't you try this? You could probably do it better than me." Because of that, I ended up going on the road with Figgy Duff. Who was in the band? Dave Panting, Pam Morgan, Art Stoyles, Phil and Noel Dinn. Then there was me and Doug Warren. Later on, he started the Corner Stone. There was us and Noel's younger brother, Brian, who was living in Toronto. Their mother let Noel take him out west to get him away from the hard cases that he was hanging around with.

Figgy Duff were sort of contenders. They had already spent a year up in Toronto. They had a manager, which wasn't something bands had around here. They had never been further west than Toronto. They wanted somebody doing sound, and they asked me and Doug Warren if we were interested. We went to Grand Falls. I remember the monitors were cutting in and out. They had this old ten-channel Traynor board. I had some tools and a soldering iron with me.

I fixed the board, and then it was on.

During the summer of 1978, I accompanied Figgy Duff on a tour they had lined up to go across the country. The first gig they had was three nights at the Horseshoe in Toronto.

When we got to the club, there were posters on the wall for Thursday night: Richard Hell and the Voidoids, the B-Girls, and two other Toronto punk bands. Thursday was the layover day, and Friday we went out west.

Me, Doug Warren, and Brian Dinn went to the show. They were selling draft for eighty cents in plastic cups—no bottles. They knew more than Da Slyme did. We saw the B-Girls, who are quite celebrated as an early punk band in Toronto. We maybe saw one other band that was quite forgettable, including their name, and we saw Richard Hell and the Voidoids. I'd heard *Blank Generation* before I'd gone to Toronto because the record was at MUN Radio. We saw the band that played on the record: the Puerto Rican guy, Ivan—I don't think they give him a last name—and Robert Quine, who is famous for having played with Lou Reed on some of Lou Reed's great '80s records. These two guys were riffing back and forth off each other. Richard Hell wasn't playing bass; they had a bass player, the original bass player for Television. The drummer was Marc Bell, who later played with the Ramones.

We had sort of agreed never to do the Da Slyme thing again. But then I saw Richard Hell and the Voidoids, and I realized how good a punk band could be. I also realized how chaotic and crazy it could get. It was like letting the genie out of the bottle. I got home and bought the Richard Hell album. Some of the other bands I saw on that tour were good, and some were not so good. I realized what we were doing was pretty chaotic, but I had something to compare it to. Until then, none of us had seen a real live punk band before. But after seeing Richard Hell, I was a little more interested.

Terry Carter *(musician)*: I was born and raised in the east end of St. John's. I spent most of my life on Cochrane Street. I got a transistor radio when I was seven years old and kept that constantly glued to my ear. I was always a big rock and roll fan and wondered about putting a band together. Not being much of a musician, I was very intimidated. When I heard the first Ramones album, I immediately got it. The Ramones started getting talked about in *CREEM*. Television and Blondie were being written about. So was Richard Hell. I got a guitar [...] and quickly realized that I'm one of the world's worst guitarists. But drumming did seem to come naturally. I wasn't ambidextrous or anything like that. I was good at straight beats with the snare and the kick and playing hard and fast. Those were the only rules. I bought a second-hand Rogers drum kit from my dentist's son. I still have the Ludwig snare.

I distinctly remember myself and a friend sitting in the control room of CHMR and reading the current *Melody Maker* and *NME* [*New Musical Express*], and there was a review of one of the Sex Pistols' first gigs where they were interacting with the audience in their own inimitable way. I said, "These guys come out, and they insult the audience. They throw bottles at them, and they spit back at them." Obviously, it was more than just a novelty.

Da Slyme never had any big blueprint or any strategy. We sort of made it up as we went along. We really didn't know what we were doing, honestly. There were no forerunners in St. John's or anywhere else in the province. All we had were the records.

Wallace Hammond: Terry had the advantage of not having been at the original show with all the chaos and bloodshed. Obviously, the word was out, and he'd heard about it. We were trying to get something on the go, and we had Justin's drums. Craig wasn't around, either. He drifted in and out because he was going to university in Toronto.

At one time, there was a club right across the street from the old fire station on the east end of Duckworth Street called the Cabaret. It was on the second floor of the building, and it had a balcony that overlooked the harbour. It was a great place to drink a beer and watch the harbour lights flicker. It was down there that Terry ran into Tony Richards. He got Tony to come up for a jam at CHMR, and that's how Tony became the singer in Da Slyme.

By Halloween, we did a show on Carpasian Road [at a house party]. We played down next to the furnace in the basement. I guess it's significant, because we actually played when we had vowed never to do it again. This would have been towards the end of 1978, a year after Peter came up with the concept in Calgary and wrote us the letter.

Terry Carter: The Middle Earth was a sort of Lord of the Rings–themed bar right across from the courthouse on Water Street. We just happened to be downtown for an afternoon beer. There was hardly anybody else in the room besides us. It looked like the kind of place where we could play. We ended up approaching the manager, and it turned out that they had nothing to lose by booking us. I think we ended up playing for free beer.

Wallace Hammond: As it turned out, the bartender was my buddy's soon-to-be ex-brother-in-law. I looked around and thought, Da Slyme could play here.

We played the Middle Earth almost every weekend or every second weekend. By that time, something else happened: the second punk band. Carter somehow teamed up with Rick Harbin and Mike Fisher to form the Reaction.

Terry Carter: In the spring of '78, I was walking down the stairs of the third floor of the Thompson Centre [at MUN], and I saw a "Drummer Wanted" sign. I remember it said something about punk and new-wave influences—everything from the Sex Pistols to Cheap Trick. I called the number. We got talking, and I went out for an audition. I think the first song we did was "[Do] Anything You Wanna Do" by Eddie and the Hot Rods. We kind of bonded over a shared love of Irish hard rock. We had the basement of Mike's parents' house. He was living at home, and he had a fairly big space for us to set up in [...]. That's where we practised and wrote songs.

Mike Fisher *(musician)*: My mom is a Newfoundlander. My dad was in the air force. I grew up in Trenton, Ontario, and I moved to St. John's in 1972. In '78, I was living in Toronto, and I heard from Rick Harbin that Wallace's band was happening. I said, "If I go back to Newfoundland, there might be a bit of a market there."

There was a vibrant punk scene in Toronto. I saw the Viletones with Steve Leckie. They were Canada's Sex Pistols, I guess. [Steve Leckie] was a bit of a nutcase.

I wanted to try something new. I was tired of Toronto. I was working in bars, and I was in a cover band that really just bottomed out. I came back home, and I connected with Rick Harbin. We were looking at a couple drummers, and Terry Carter came into the picture. We were doing the Clash and Sex Pistols and a lot of British stuff like the Jam. There was some Ramones. I don't recall writing right away.

Wallace Hammond: They were better musicians than we were, certainly. By that time, Justin would have been back, too. When we did those gigs at the Middle Earth, he was behind the drum kit. Carter had this other thing on the go anyway. After we did sound check, I remember missus behind the bar said, "There's going to be a crowd here tonight." I don't know how she knew that, but we drank the bar dry.

There [were] three girls sitting at a table next to the stage. We always started off with "Piss-Eyed Sleezoid." Before we got to the four-count, the girls downed their drinks, grabbed their purses, and ran out the door.

Terry Carter: I don't know about exact numbers. There must've been fifty people there. The Middle Earth wasn't a very big place. The tables were all jammed together, and there were people standing along the walls.

Wallace Hammond: We played a number of gigs there through January and February. They may have even paid the Reaction some money because they were the more finessed of the two bands.

Terry Carter: The essential difference between then and now is that there was no infrastructure. You were pretty much on your own, making it up as you went along. We were the scene, the two bands.

Mike Fisher: The Reaction recorded a lot of stuff at Echo Music at the top of Long's Hill. It was Jack Winsor's music store. That's where we recorded "The Kid's Arrived (On the Beach)." Hammingwell had done a few recordings there. Jack had no experience that we knew of. But when the Reaction started, it was the logical place to go. By that time, Jack had gone to eight-track. Echo Music and CBC were the only places a band could record. Echo was the only private studio.

Terry Carter: Recording singles just seemed like the thing new-wave and punk bands were doing. We certainly didn't have enough material for anything beyond that. There might have been two other songs kicking around in half-finished form, but that was about it. We had our own independent label, Neutron label. I think we pressed five hundred forty-fives. That single is now extremely rare and passing for stupid amounts of money among punk collectors.

Wallace Hammond: The boys in the band soon got tired of playing the Middle Earth. After a while, what seemed to be fun wasn't much fun any longer. In the meantime, we'd written a bunch of songs. Me and Craig were moving gear into the studio, and the boys were in the bar drinking, and they wrote "Tanya, Whatcha Doing with That Seal?"

Terry Carter: The Browned Off was another place down on its luck. Coincidentally, I needed a job because my unemployment had run out. I just happened to be walking along Duckworth Street, went in, asked for a job, and got one right on the spot with little to no experience. I thought, You could put a sound system in here and make it a new-wave disco. The owners were agreeable to that. They fitted the place out, and I started making up compilation tapes. Through word of mouth, things took off. I guess it started around 1979. Bands played periodically. The Browned Off actually burned down. That's what ended that scene.

Wallace Hammond: There was a weird couple managing the Browned Off. They were always fighting, this fat missus and a skinny guy. After a while, the owner got rid of the couple. The guy who replaced them was nice enough but not the type of person you'd want managing your bar. I remember when the Browns finally fired him. I was renting a room in the same boarding house where he was living, and Mrs. Brown came up the stairs demanding the keys to the car that he bought with company money.

Mike Fisher: We used to drive around the island finding bars. "Do you have live music? Can we play here in two months?" We'd give them a couple copies of our band photos and maybe the record.

Terry Carter: That was our mission, to bring punk and new wave to the people out beyond the overpass.

Mike Fisher: We came up with all kinds of gimmicks. We'd cut a Pepsi can in half and put gunpowder in it, introduce a song, light a cigarette, and drop it in. With my Toronto band, the Ritz, we'd go to Malabar, which was a makeup store. I bought leopard-print tops and spandex pants, and I took that stuff back with me to Newfoundland. There was a mixed reception. But the girls liked it.

Terry Carter: Even now, those places [around the bay] are still probably pretty conservative. We got away with being a novelty.

Mike Fisher: In Colliers, some guy bought our record and […] broke it in half right in front of us.

Terry Carter: We played Bonavista and Dildo. Those shows went over really well. We played Marystown. It was one of the final gasps of disco, and the club was being refitted as a dance bar. I think we were the last actual band to play there.

Mike Fisher: The Old Shop Army was our fan base. Old Shop is north of Dildo. Old Shop had maybe two hundred or four hundred people. But guys would drive down from the top of Trinity Bay and come in from Whitbourne. It was one of the few live venues in the area. The problem was we'd have to drive back the same night because there was no accommodations.

The last version of the Reaction was with Steve Jackson, when we were influenced by Eurobeat—stuff like Ultravox and Gary Numan. Steve brought in keyboards. We'd play some Rolling Stones covers and the punk stuff and the originals. [We] played Whitbourne a few times at [the Moorland Motel]. Once I was sitting on the sink, it broke, and water spewed out. Word got out that the Reaction destroyed washrooms. The Old Shop guys would follow us around and smash the toilets. It kind of killed our prospects.

Even though we were doing the punk thing, we wanted to expand our sound: "Let's do a really polished commercial product that would maybe get a record deal." That caused a split between myself and Terry. Terry and Vaughn Whalen did not get along at all. Terry was more into an authentic type of rock sound.

Terry Carter: Vaughn was a guitar player. He had the look and the clothes and all that down, but he didn't have a great sense of rhythm. His personality could rub some people the wrong way. You either liked him or you didn't. I certainly didn't. I also kind of wanted the group to go in a tougher direction.

Wallace Hammond: The Da Slyme record [self-titled, 1980] cost around sixteen hundred dollars. We got five hundred and thirty-five pressed. We raised the money for the record between friends and the band.

Mike Fisher: While Terry was in [the Reaction], we recorded another three songs: "In Tune with the Times," "Trials in Error," and "Til Midnight." We got interest from Aquarius Records, April Wine's label. But it never resulted in anything. I heard they were interested [in] the Pinups with Sass Jordan, but then they signed Corey Hart instead.

Wallace Hammond: The band wanted to get a proper cover done, but it was more expensive than the record. There were various ideas kicking around. The prevailing idea was to print a poster and fold it in half. There was also an eight-page booklet.

Justin was working at Fred's Records. When a big record came out, the record stores would get a number of covers to put up as advertising. Fred's had a pile of that stuff lying around, and Justin made a deal with his manager. It caused a lot of consternation because the money was spent without getting a consensus. It was decided we would somehow print Da Slyme on them. I think we bought eighty religious records for a dollar each that were still in the plastic. They got a pile of empty jackets from various groups. That's why you see so many different covers.

I might have come up with the solution. I know I did the work. I made a stencil, laid it on the records, and spray-painted our band name on them. I used auto primer because it dried quickly. The first numbers were grey; I ran out of grey, and then I bought red. I sprayed them down in my parents' basement on a ping-pong table. Everybody acknowledged that it was probably the best thing that could have happened. The cover is one of the main reasons why the record is a collector's item. I have Tanya Tucker's first record. She's looking all of fifteen or sixteen, and it says "Da Slyme" right across it.

★ ★ ★

Terry Carter: There was another winter of our discontent. Da Slyme wasn't doing very much. They just tended to have periods of inactivity. Wallace had some songs lying around. Wallace, Craig, and I put together the A-Tones, aka the Infideltones, aka the Semi-Tones. Craig had the brilliant idea that we should rename the band every week and give people in town the impression that there was a scene happening. I thought it was genius. We did a special for a local cable company of close to an hour of music. The A-Tones didn't do very many gigs outside the university. There was one at Martha's. We just sort of thrashed our way through [a set]. Some people thought it was brilliant, but they were in the minority.

Mike O'Brien *(singer)*: The frustrations of the post–Da Slyme bands was that the university crowd liked the comedy aspect and the costumes but couldn't connect with the other bands who were a little more serious and a little less parody. They would come to shows and say, "Why isn't this more fun? Why is it so loud?"

Terry Carter: There really was no year-zero mentality like other punk scenes. There was no real moment that bonded us together. With other scenes, there was a lot of posturing going on with that sort of mentality. But going back to the basics had to be done. We had to remember what was great about rock and roll. Some quarters were more ideological than others. We were the longhairs. We had as much a progressive influence as a punk influence. Bubonic Plague was a neat little hybrid of those styles. We got a better reception in Toronto than we did in St. John's. They were more receptive to our weird brand of punk rock.

We moved to Toronto because there was no scene in Newfoundland. There was nowhere to play. There were no prospects.

THE DARK CORNERS

Sheilagh O'Leary *(photographer/activist)*: I grew up in Churchill Square on Smithville Crescent. I was a middle-class Catholic girl. I was the youngest of five kids. We were a very sports-oriented family. Music in my family was school choirs and concerts. I was a competitive swimmer, and my brothers were baseball and basketball players. I had a sister who was a runner and played volleyball and basketball. My parents were hard-working people. My mom was a nurse, and my dad was a salesman. They were one of the first people to build on the street. It was a really privileged area. There were lots of doctors and lawyers living around us. There were lots and lots of kids. It was a great neighbourhood to grow up in.

I did everything I was supposed to do. I was a bright student. But I always questioned things, and that sometimes got me into trouble. I went to Holy Heart [and] graduated in 1981. I remember being in Holy Heart and [questioning] things. I felt like something was seriously missing, but I had no idea what it was. When I graduated from high school, I went right into MUN. But then everything kind of went flatline, and I pulled out.

That first year of university, everyone was partying. I had this new-found freedom. What kind of started me with music was my brothers moved to Florida. My brother was a big baseball star, and he had a tryout in Fort Lauderdale when he was seventeen. My brothers went down to party and to get away from Mom and Dad. That's when the whole Latin hustle and disco movement went wild. It had come right out of Cuba and into south Florida and into the Miami area. They were entrenched in it, these boys from Gonzaga. Of course, when they'd come home, they'd bring all the music with them.

I always loved to dance. In high school, me and my girlfriend used to sneak off at night, not because we wanted to drink but because we wanted to dance. We used to go downtown to Friends, which was the gay bar. It was a very different scene. To be gay at that time was not cool like it is today. People were getting pounded every time they turned around. Gay bashing happened all the time.

Barry Newhook *(musician)*: There was violence, and there was harassment. I remember leaving Friends with a friend who was openly gay. Seeing an openly young gay man was a rarity, and he looked different. It was nothing outrageous, but he looked different than the norm. My friend got beaten up pretty badly right outside of our apartment. He was followed; they knew he was gay. I remember somebody running up to the apartment to tell me. I went outside, and my friend was covered in blood. I was truly fucking angry. I wanted to look for whoever the fuck did it.

Sheilagh O'Leary: They used to call Friends "the Zoo." Friends was a gay bar, but it was really for anyone who was alternative, fringe, or freaky. It was for anyone who loved to dance. At the start, it was members only. I'm sure they knew we were underage, but they let us in. We'd buy an obligatory drink, probably never drink it, and dance all night. We did a lot of that throughout high school.

Then I went to university, and I started losing interest in studies and just not really paying much attention and not knowing what was going on because I'd always done well. I wasn't getting along with my father, who was a very old-school Catholic conservative type. I knew there was something waiting—I could just feel it. I just didn't know what it was, and I decided to move out of my parents' house.

A friend of my sister's helped me get a job at a group home. I had no experience in social work, but I was a natural. In many ways, I've had a lifetime of social work since then. There were five residents who were mentally disabled. Some had psychoses. They weren't troubled kids; they just needed to be watched.

I rented an apartment on Queen's Road from my cousin. It was a little flat with a bar. I thought I was in absolute heaven. I worked at the group home, and I used to party at the bar. That was my little circuit.

I've always been a freak magnet. If there's anybody out there that's got those tendencies, they find me. I had the apartment, and the next thing I know, there's a whole bunch of punk rockers on my floor: Mike Buhler, John

Pastore, Sean Doran. They were out tearing up the town, the little rot bags. I had a couple of friends at the gay bar that I went to school with, and they kind of hung around, too. My flat became the hub of God only knows what.

There was a huge relationship between that gay bar and the live music scene. How I grew as a person was right out of that whole community. What I was starving for was somewhere that I could actually express myself. I wanted to be around people who didn't care what anyone thought and who were totally cool about expressing themselves in any way that they wanted. I found that at Friends.

Somehow, in my world, there was this fusion between this kind of downtown gay bar and the young punks out beating the streets. Some of it was because—I would now say this in retrospect—people were probably experimenting sexually [and] testing the waters. It was kind of this weird fusion time. People just wanted to explore.

Punk rock was happening. I got a mohawk and shaved my eyebrows, and I was an absolute anomaly. There were very few people who were visibly into that scene at the time. I think that's what drew some of the punk rock community to me. My dad never talked to me for a year; he must've nearly had a stroke. I'm sure my parents were very worried and concerned. They knew I was hanging out at this gay bar. But it was a beautiful time for me.

I remember trying to get a job at Fred's, and Terry Reilly wouldn't hire me because I had a mohawk. Terry and I are now great buddies, but he didn't know quite what to make of me. This is all before punk went off. Newfoundland has always been ten years behind the rest of Canada.

I went to university for about a year, and I had my first serious relationship. He was [a] kind of straight guy, and we all hung out and partied. It was great, but I knew it just wasn't what I wanted to do. So we split up, and I went full-tilt boogie. I didn't worry about boys. I wanted to party and dance. That's all that was on my mind. I was comfortable in a gay scene as a straight woman. It was a completely non-threatening environment. It was exactly what I needed to prepare me for what was coming next.

There were a lot of gay people and misfits who kind of hung around. All of a sudden, there was Duncan Snowden sleeping in his mother's Valiant. She went on sabbatical, and he never got it together to find a place to live. My roommate really liked Duncan and ended up bringing him home: "Can we keep him? Can he stay here with us?" He ended up staying, and out of that came Barry Newhook and Simon Dingle.

My roommate and I decided we were going to move to Toronto. When I came home, Barry Newhook and I started seeing each other. We were together for six years. It was a very tumultuous relationship, and we went through lots. We lived together in all kinds of apartments and through all kinds of situations. It was crazy growing-up times, but we had a real community around us. Barry had been friends with Jennifer Dick, who was also one of the original organizers of Peace-A-Chord. There was another crowd: Tim Angel, the Thomas boys [Danny, Lil, and Louis Thomas], Duncan Cowan, and Jon Whalen. Barry was my key into a whole other bunch of different worlds. There was the dance club community, the gay bar scene, and the punk rockers.

There were people you'd find in the dark corners of the bar. Remember, this was all when [the scandal-plagued orphanage] Mount Cashel was still open. Down in the gay bar, you had businessmen, lawyers, and judges all down picking up young men, and in the daylight, they were different people. It was a place where people would go wild. I gelled because I was extremely social and never tolerated anyone thinking they were better than anyone else. That was always the philosophy inside of me.

Jennifer Dick *(activist)*: I had two lives: my downtown life and my dance and family life. [...] My older sister was an athlete, and she was also a big girl. I was this tiny, skinny, frail thing. The gym teacher, who knew my sister, said, "Get on the trampoline." She bounced me into kingdom come, and I landed with my foot around my neck and tore my knee. But it was misdiagnosed at the time and never properly taken care of. When I went to ballet school, I went down, and my knee had to be reconstructed.

It was good that I left ballet school because it wasn't a healthy place for me. It was a great break at a crucial time for me to go home and get strong. I borrowed my mother's clothes to go in and apply for a job at the Second Page Bookstore on Water Street. They basically hired me right on the spot. When I showed up for work, I had on a leather jacket and boots. I brought in a whole other clientele with me. It became a place where a lot of people who were interested in books but who wouldn't go to the library or who couldn't really afford books came.

I would finish up at the bookstore and go meet Sheilagh [O'Leary] at Friends. I was there because I was definitely an outsider.

Natalie Spracklin *(musician)*: I can relate to the whole Arcade Fire concept of suburban wasteland culture. That's what I grew up in. It was a little bit bleak and a little bit too quiet. In comparison, downtown was a lot more of an active place. You could find a community more readily than you could on the outskirts of town, where you could smell the cow shit coming from Kilbride.

Right from the start, all of my friends were weirdos, freaks, and punk rockers. I had a lot of gay friends who were outside of the punk rock circle. We used to do a little bit of clubbing when I was still in high school. Really, what was being offered to you in terms of a scene wasn't very much. I mean, there was the gay bar, Friends. That was a subversive scene, which I identified with because you could push the boundaries of what was considered acceptable or appropriate. You could listen to some interesting music that you would never hear on the radio, and you could dance and feel safe. You could seek solace in your weirdo friends that nobody else wanted.

Barry Newhook: I always wanted to get into a bar. I went to see a band in a bar, and it was no problem getting in. I was there really late, and there was a guy there who I knew from St. Philip's. The bar was closing, and I remember he said, "I know a place where we can go to, but it's kind of weird. You might not be into it. It's a gay bar."

I said, "That doesn't mean anything to me."

I guess, being young, I was completely devoted to the night life. Friends was a place to stay up until dawn and drink. I remember being in there and covering up all the windows. I never really examined what the attraction was. Maybe it was an alternative to everything you had encountered in the outside world. All the pressures and all the things that kept you down, all the sort of things that made you feel bad about yourself for not fitting in with the world outside disappeared in that place.

John Pastore *(musician)*: I grew up in the Battery. The first or second house when you drive out there was ours. It was a beautiful old Victorian that we bought for eleven thousand dollars. Life was cheap and easy in St. John's. They've since built matching Victorians on either side of it, these new, sort of fake houses. They're using them as B&Bs. My parents got divorced when I was about eleven or twelve. My father moved to Barnes Road. In my punk rock years, I split my time between there and the Battery.

St. John's was a different city then. It was pretty rundown. My memories of 1970s St. John's is not how it seems today. Right on the corner of the Battery, there was a grocery store. It burned down, and then it became a park full of drunk old men. I think Barnes Road was tougher, but the Battery was drunker, at least through a teenager's eyes. There was a lot of fighting. People liked to fight, for some reason. Maybe it was because alcohol was thrown into the mix. I could only walk one way home to Barnes Road. I couldn't come up from Military Road because there was this row of rough-looking houses. I'd never be able to make past them without getting chased.

Mike Buhler *(showgoer/scene supporter)*: My parents had both come out of the US. They were academics; they taught at the university. My father really cared about teaching and sharing his knowledge. If you look at the drama community here today, he has absolutely left a legacy. His students were people like Robert Chafe, Jill Keiley, and Danielle Irvine, who have all gone on to very successful careers. They're all protegés of my father.

In those days, I was living in Portugal Cove, but I spent all my time in town. Everyone got shipped out for school. I went [to school in the] United States for two years, and then I went to Macpherson for Grade 9. That was in 1980. That's when Sean Doran and I started kicking around together. I think it might have been John Pastore who brought us into the fold. Our parents were friends because both of them came out of the US at the same time and taught at the university.

Clark Hancock *(musician)*: We were all freaks who hung out around downtown. We weren't great kids, by any means. I was born in 1969. I guess I started getting into the scene when I was eleven. So, whenever that was—1980 or '81. I grew up in the East End, in Virginia Park—the projects. I hung out with the wrong crowd. I used to get into trouble and steal from the rich and give to myself. I finally got caught and had to do nine months in the correctional institution. Whitbourne [juvenile detention centre] had just closed down because some kid had died on the train tracks trying to escape. They shut it down after an investigation and revamped the whole system. In the meantime, it was temporarily set up in White Hills. Not a word of a lie, I could look out the window and down into my house and see what was on the table for supper.

Arthur Haynes *(musician)*: As a teenager, I was a downtown car-park attendant. I would see these strange guys with leather jackets, chains, and torn-up clothes. They were hanging around the roofs and sneaking around the backs of building, especially on the top of Bowring's. There was a heat-exhaust vent up there which, if you sat within a couple feet of it, you could stay warm and dry all winter.

Mike Buhler: Sean Doran and I had a level of anger and angst that led us to punk rock. I don't know if I had any good reason to be angry. I grew up in a loving family who were supportive. I didn't suffer the kind of abuse that so many other people suffered. I didn't want for anything. I knew there was going to be a meal for me every evening. I knew I had clothes to wear. My mother was into her career, and my dad was doing his teaching. Maybe, in some respects, I wanted more attention. It was easy to be an angry kid.

Chris Jerrett *(musician)*: There was a gang of us: me, Johnny Pastore, Peter Martin, Sean Doran, and Mike Buhler. We spent all of our time downtown, skipping school and causing trouble. We used to hang around Atlantic Place and the games arcade, walking back and forth between those places. We used to spend a lot of time on the building tops.

John Pastore: It's a miracle I'm here to do this interview. I guess it was probably me and Buhler and Doran who […] found "the jump." It was on the back of an abandoned department store on Water Street. We climbed up onto the roof, and there was a little one-room utility shed, which we turned into a hangout. Then we started doing "the jump" between two buildings. It was at least ten or twelve feet wide with a forty-foot drop to the ground below. I can't remember who did it first, but Chris didn't think for a second. Chris stepped back and just leaped right off the building. It was like something out of a movie. I remember Sean came the closest to not making it. I think his toes just caught the edge and sort of slipped off, and we grabbed him before he fell.

Natalie Spracklin: Chris is still totally into pushing himself physically and doing things that keep him on the edge. He was one of the ringleaders. He used to kind of inspire people to do stupid stuff like that. He's always been into riding BMX bikes. He was kind of athletic and able to handle himself.

Mike Buhler: We got nicknamed "the Original Six." There were only six people who ever did the jump: Mark Northcott, Johnny Pastore, Chris Jerrett, Jack Lanphear, Sean Doran, and me.

Clark Hancock: "The jump" was the initiation into the punk rock hangout.

Natalie Spracklin: I liked those guys because they made me laugh. They had a really great sense of humour, and they didn't particularly care about what other people thought. There was a certain bravery about that.

SOUNDS LIKE A REVOLUTION

Barry Newhook: I never thought music was open to me. None of my friends were exposed to learning music. I thought it was a special thing. Records were made by people who were not like us and who lived away in this magical world.

My cousin was six years older than me. I was a kid at this point, and he was my favourite cousin. I idolized him. He was a fantastic guitar player. [He] had personal issues that probably got in the way of him doing anything with it, […] but he was a really smart guy and incredibly talented. So I guess there was some musical talent in the family. That was about my only exposure to music until I became a punk rocker. […]

I started listening to the Clash. If you listen to their earlier records, they fairly well describe what it was to be a punk rocker. I saw pictures of the Clash in magazines, and I started dressing like them. I started doing the Johnny Rotten haircuts and the ripped jeans and T-shirts. I didn't know anyone else who dressed like that.

I met a guy at the bus stop. He said, "Are you a punk rocker?" I was wearing a torn-up Mickey Mouse T-shirt, really skinny jeans, and combat boots. It's the uniform I still wear, I guess. But at the time, it was punk.

Dave Sweetapple *(musician/promotor)*: I wonder if kids could even relate to how we grew up. I was at the Mall one day. There was an A&A Records [store] there. I was looking through the Clash section. Barry leaned across and went, "You need that one." He pointed to *Give 'Em Enough Rope*. I can't imagine that these days young people identify with someone based on musical tastes. […] I think that's mostly all gone now.

Natalie Spracklin: I think that we identified with each other as being slightly subversive and not really fitting the mainstream mould. It wasn't about politics or anything like that. The music is what ultimately connected people. It's a small population here. You connect with the people who are most similar to you, and you make the best with what you have. But if we didn't genuinely like and appreciate each other, then none of that would have ever worked. I think it's got to do with that common shared experience. Whenever you ran into somebody at school and you made some obscure punk reference and they got it—and you were just testing them to see if they were one of you—then they were in. If you connect with someone who likes the same music, […] then you've found a kindred spirit.

Barry Newhook: A few of us were walking along Rennie's Mill Road on this miserable kind of day. I was with John Crane and Dave Sweetapple. There was snow on the ground, but it was raining. I may have been sixteen at this point. Duncan Snowden was out shovelling his driveway. We were laughing at him. It was kind of derisive but yet friends going, "Duncan, there's a new Cars record out. We saw it in the record store."

He said, "Hang on." He ran in the house, came back out with these ridiculous stacked-heel boots on his feet like something KISS was wearing.

We got in his mother's car, and she came out the door: "You're not allowed to take that car. You don't have a licence!"

Duncan pulled out of the driveway, and we went to the Mall. The next time I met him, he's got a band on the go with Dave Sweetapple and Simon Dingle. It's in the basement of his mother's house, and they're playing punk rock songs.

Dave Sweetapple: Duncan lived by Bannerman Park. He played guitar. He'd taken a few lessons from some blues guys in town, but he was into English punk rock. Just through meeting him on the street, he was like, "Do you play anything?"

I said, "I'm thinking about getting a bass."

I went down to Hutton's because I really wanted a Rickenbacker, couldn't afford one, and bought a Washburn instead. That thing traded hands so many times with people in other bands. Stuff in Newfoundland was expensive. You simply couldn't find deals on classic guitars.

I started practising with Duncan, and we formed a band. I had just turned fifteen. Duncan was a couple of years older than me. It was pretty much covers and one original. It was mostly rotating drummers. I remember one guy in particular. My parents said they ran into him the other day: Simon Dingle. He was a complete lunatic. He would always flip out and start throwing stuff around the room. He was kind of short-tempered and loosely wired. But he was a great drummer. I don't know where he came from. Someone said they knew a drummer, and he showed up. He had some knowledge of punk rock. I remember him dazzling us with stories of his brother seeing Motörhead in London in 1977 and that the show was full of Hells Angels.

The Riot would have started in, like, 1981.

Barry Newhook: Music, at that age, feels like a revolution. You're identified with what you listen to, and you're disparaged for it. You're singled out, which makes it even better. You're singled out as an object of derision by people who you feel superior to because of your music and what you adhere to.

Dave Sweetapple: Anyone who had a green army coat or a leather jacket and a pair of combat boots, or any kind of military clothing, was instantly recognized as a "punk faggot." That was the thing in high school, the constant hassle from the jocks. [...] It wasn't just in St. John's, Newfoundland. It was in London, England. It was in Vancouver. It was like that everywhere.

Natalie Spracklin: Johnny Pastore, who now does record distribution in Brooklyn—his mom was a visual artist and a jewellery maker. She was a craftsperson. She was doing a show at the museum on youth culture. My friends and I [...] were always such weirdos. I don't think she thought we were weirdos—I think she liked our style—but we definitely stood out. She took a bunch of photos of us on the courthouse steps as examples of what "punk rock" was all about. Some of us had mohawks. Some of us had no hair. Some had piercings through their face. In my little subculture, the people who I hung out with looked very menacing. But once you really connected with them, you realized that they were caring and intelligent and creative. We just really didn't fit in with the mainstream norm. And that was perfectly fine by me.

Danny Thomas *(musician)*: Sean Doran had spiked hair and a piece of chain around his waist. He looked like Sid Vicious. It never went well for him walking home. We'd basically have to pass through four Catholic schools to get to his house. There was just no saving grace for him whatsoever. But no one ever never laid a finger on me. The hard cases in Chalker Place would beat the shit out of him, and I'd stand there and try to talk them out of it. "Boys, are you going to keep doing this? You must be getting bored of beating up Sean Doran." It seemed just so ridiculous.

"Shut up, Thomas, or we'll have to beat the shit out of you, too."

They'd beat up Sean because he was a "punk faggot." The funny thing was, about three years later, they were all listening to Stiff Little Fingers, the Clash, and the Sex Pistols, too. These were the same guys that, by '84 or '85, took off their Rolling Stones patches from the back of their jackets and put on the Clash patches, after spending two years beating up Sean for liking punk rock.

John Pastore: Chris Jerrett was always a hothead. We stepped out of my house, and there was a crowd of guys standing on the corner. They said something saucy to antagonize us. Chris was eating an apple. I could see him getting angrier and angrier. I thought, *Oh, God. Don't do anything stupid*. Chris turned around and threw the apple at one guy's head. Then, of course, we had to run for our lives because there was seven or eight of them chasing after us.

Dave Sweetapple: Back in the early '80s, St. John's got a huge influx of boat people from Vietnam. A bunch of them started going to Booth Memorial High School. There were four of them who got into punk rock. For whatever reason, they really identified with the Ramones. They pegged their jeans, got cheap leather jackets from the army surplus store on Water Street, and had one-length bobbed haircuts.

It seemed like they were all completely trained in martial arts. Having them around, I used to equate it with a teen movie where there's some huge jock, like in *Revenge of the Nerds*, that's about to beat on some guy, and then these Vietnamese would clean house. So many times they jumped in and saved somebody's ass. People were really afraid of them because, I guess, they were used to tons of violence. They would just go nuts.

One time, this hockey player hit me in gym class, and I pushed him back. We got into the locker room, and he took a swing at me. Out of nowhere, one of the Vietnamese levelled him across the chest with a leg kick and drove him into the lockers. He went, "Don't fuck with Dave." And then that was the end of that.

Barry Newhook: Punk rock was so new that it was totally outside of anything that had ever happened up to that point, other than maybe the first real rock and roll revolution.

We'd dress in punk rock clothes and go down to Duncan's basement and hang out. We'd listen to punk rock and reggae. It was sort of exclusive. It was sixteen-year-old boys smoking lots of dope. Duncan and Dave and Simon had their band, the Riot. They did covers, but they had one original song called "Protest." Dave came up with the lyrics; Duncan came up with the music. Duncan had a really great voice and a wonderful sense of melody, and they were absolutely competent in a punk rock kind of way.

Everyone who talks about hearing early punk talks about the most inspiring thing [being] the ability to create something that's really exciting and without having unattainable decades of practice. If you stick with music, it changes and evolves, but real punk, the real stuff—and I don't mean the really good musicians who pass themselves off as punk and pass themselves off as playing not as well as they really can—was new and full of excitement.

There was one huge moment for the Riot. It happened during the annual OZFM concert in Bannerman Park.

John Pastore: The concert must've been why I was there; 12 Gauge were playing. They were a popular local band, and they got a lot of airplay. You know what's funny about their song "I Saw You on the Telephone"? It's "Hold On Loosely" by .38 Special. Not only did they steal the song, but they called themselves 12 Gauge. It wasn't very imaginative.

Barry Newhook: We took all of the gear and ran extension cords outside. We took the guitar amp, the bass amp, the drum kit, and set up in the back yard. Duncan and Dave sang through stereo speakers. I wasn't in the band at this point, but I was there helping out.

They started playing [in] his mother's backyard, which was directly adjacent [to] Bannerman Park. People started leaving the concert, coming up and standing outside the fence. The announcer stopped the concert and said, "Will the guys in the backyard please shut up?"

There was a sense of excitement. It felt like something real and amazing. It wasn't intentional to fuck up what was going on in the park. When you're a teenager, you don't mind doing that sort of stuff. But there was an audience right there. If we didn't do it, we would've missed a great opportunity. The guys from Da Slyme were there, people like Wallace Hammond and Justin Hall, and they told me later that they liked it. I guess it sort of suited their anarchistic kind of ideas of what rock and roll was really about.

John Pastore: It was a pretty ballsy move to just set up and start playing. I didn't know what was happening. I was just as surprised as everybody else. I guess that was the first local show I ever saw. I can't really think of anything before then.

Dave Sweetapple: On the other side of the fence, this massive crowd of people had gathered to watch. Then the police came. They're like, "Shut this down, or you'll all be arrested." We argued with them. I remember playing "Police on My Back" by the Clash.

Thom Thorne (*musician*): Seventy or so people ran over and surrounded the fence. The 12 Gauge guys got pissed off and stopped playing. The cops showed up and made everyone leave. Did they arrest Duncan? They definitely made him shut it down. The cops asked Duncan his name. He went, "Johnny Rotten."

Wallace Hammond: Then it started to rain, and the show ended.

Dave Sweetapple: That was a weird time. We were too young to do a proper show in a club. The first real time we played out was at Uncle Albert's. They used to do a Saturday afternoon open mic where anyone could get up. Duncan, Simon, and I dragged all our gear down. We had on army clothes, camouflage, and berets, and we looked like complete assholes. We hauled in our stuff and set up. The bartender was like, "What are you guys doing?"

I looked at him and said, "We're going to play."

Terry Carter: Uncle Albert's was across from the courthouse. Back in the '60s, it used to be called "Fogo-A-Gogo," and then it got a makeover. I remember seeing the Riot there for the first time and being wowed. Scott Goudie and some guys were there doing their usual blues jam. Duncan got up onstage, plugged in, hit an E chord, and Scott made some snotty comment like, "We got a guy here from the McCulloch chainsaw school of guitar playing."

Dave Sweetapple: We broke into "Guns of Brixton" by the Clash, and people went apeshit. There were these British sailors in the audience who were into the punk scene back home. Here they were in this weird little town, and there are these kids up onstage playing punk rock. They were all over us: "You guys are fucking brilliant, man!"

Some other guys came up to us. "Where did you come from?"

I said, "We've just been practising in the basement and playing our favourite tunes." Terry Carter was in the audience. Terry played in Da Slyme. He was part of that whole Wallace Hammond–Vikki-Beat crowd who were making cassettes. He was like, "We can't believe you guys exist. Do you have anything recorded?"

We got invited to Jon Heald's house. Jon had a four-track set up in the basement. We mostly recorded covers, but there were a couple of originals. We thought we'd completely made it.

Barry Newhook: The Riot were going to play another gig at Uncle Albert's, but Dave left the band, and Duncan asked me if I wanted to play bass. Of course, I said yes. The idea of being in that basement and actually rehearsing was really appealing to me.

Duncan said, "We're going to play in a bar." I always wanted to see a band in a bar. We had a week, and Duncan would teach me all the songs. I crashed at his house, and we stayed up really late learning the songs by playing the records over and over again.

When we got to the club, I remember shaking and not wanting to do it: "Can we leave? Let's just leave."

Chris Jerrett: Dave Sweetapple was a little older than us, and he knew Bob [Armstrong] because they both went to Booth. Me and Peter [Martin] went to Bishops College, which was only across the field. It was a pretty small world. This city was so small that we'd walk all over. We'd cover the core of St. John's, no problem: the Mall, MUN, downtown, the East End. We walked everywhere.

John Pastore: Pete Martin and Chris Jerrett were skateboard and BMX guys. I remember seeing them at the Avalon Mall. It was me and Mike Buhler and Sean Doran. We're wearing Converse, and they're wearing Vans. Chris is largely responsible for the whole BMX and skate thing in St. John's. But at that point, it was just him. There was no scene. I do have this memory of us circling each other. Chris and Pete weren't into punk rock, but they were made for it. We're like, "This is the music that goes with skateboarding." They took to it instantly. It's like they were waiting for it to happen.

Dave Sweetapple: While we were into Minor Threat, I kind of got away from the British stuff, while Duncan was still stuck in Sex Pistols, Sham 69, and the Clash—that kind of influence. Then Bob had started this thing called Public Enemy. Pastore played bass; I played guitar. It was straight-up hardcore. It was our first inkling of a real scene.

John Pastore: We gave ourselves fake punk names. Bob was "Bob Average." I was "Johnny Sputum." Craig Murray was "Verbal Damage."

Bob Armstrong (musician/promoter): My punk name was kind of stolen. There was a guy by the name of Joe Average in the Toronto band Young Lions. I had this tape, *T.O. Hardcore '83*, with a bunch of Toronto bands on it. I was with Thom Thorne. I said, "That guy's name is Joe Average."

Thom looks at me and goes, "That's perfect. That's you, Bob." Thom was sitting there with his spiked hair and his Stiff Little Fingers shirt on, and I had bangs and an Adidas sweatshirt. "You're Bob Average." It just stuck.

Dave Sweetapple: Bob went to high school with me at Booth. He opened his locker one day, and he had some Sex Pistols posters cut out of a magazine and stuck up. Mike Buhler looked like something straight from the streets of London. He had a mohawk and was dressed in camouflage. But Bob was just a dude in jeans and a sweatshirt. When he opened up the locker, I was like, *What is this guy doing with all this stuff?* The next thing you know, there are shows going on at the Grad House.

Barry Newhook: Duncan always had instruments lying around his house. I don't know who owned them, but they were there. He had his guitar, which I guess he's still playing. It was a Stratocaster he got from Paul Monahan, a great guitar player known around the city for decades and decades. At some point, Duncan went to visit his relatives in England. When he came back, he had this great Fender Precision Bass. That's what I played my entire time with the Riot. Even afterwards, I always borrowed that Precision.

Bob Armstrong: The Catholic school board provided a lot of gear, in one way or the other. I remember Murray saying, "I don't know if I should sing into this mic, man. It might catch fire." It was a hot mic from a Catholic school. I don't know what was going on at Brother Rice Junior High. Where were they getting the gear? For some reason, they had all kinds of stuff. Booth had nothing. PWC [Prince of Wales Collegiate] had nothing. But Brother Rice got everything from the Catholic school board.

Barry Newhook: For me, the Riot would have been on the go from around '82 until maybe '86. It went through a bunch of incarnations. Our drummer, Simon, was kind of leaving. He got bored with it, I think, and he wanted to do other things. Myself and Duncan spent all of our time together sort of planning revolution. We went to see Da Slyme once, and I remember saying, "Imagine if we had that guy playing drums with us." It was Justin Hall. We were really impressed by how fast he could do a snare roll. As you can imagine, our drumming was pretty rudimentary. I guess we pursued him. He said that he'd seen the thing in the backyard, and that was the only reason he came over in that first practice.

I was living at home on Vinnicombe Street. In the backyard, there was a shed. My father built it, and he put a wood stove in. Dad was handy; he worked for the civil service. That shed became a focal point for a lot of bands. WAFUT [What a Fuckin Ugly Truck] was born there. Schizoid practised there. But that was later. Initially, the Riot practised there. By this point, it was me, Duncan, and Justin. I got Duncan to show me a bit of guitar. I was playing guitar for a month. We figured I should play guitar and Justin should play bass.

Des Walsh was interested in drumming for the Riot. Des had played with Tickle Harbour and some traditional bands. When he was really young, he played with a proto-punk band, Ash Wednesday. Mike Wade formed that band. They went to Montreal to record those great Mike Wade songs "God Bless You, Miss Rosewater" and "Hollywood Farm." I think Brian Best might have played some bass with them. They were probably kicked out of every bar in town. They'd play once and would thus be removed. They'd try anything onstage. They would attempt levitations—all kinds of bizarre stuff. They were anarchistic, to say the least.

Natalie Spracklin: Somehow, gigs got booked in bars. We were in high school. We certainly weren't old enough to drink, but it was never an issue.

John Pastore: Public Enemy did a few bar shows [at] an old restaurant on Duckworth Street called the Gilbert. But most of them were at the Grad

House on Military Road. There'd be one aging hippie in charge who was going to grad school. He'd say, "The place is yours until midnight." I guess he hoped that there was a couple of people in our crew who were old enough to drink.

Barry Newhook: Duncan and I would go down to the used-book stores, and we'd find all these magazines—images and stuff. Then we would arrange them together on a piece of cardboard. It was always a big deal to make show posters. We'd put a lot of effort into them. We'd run them off at Afterwords [bookstore] and then plaster downtown.

The first poster we made had this great image of a Russian tank with explosions and fires and people running around screaming. It was my first real experience with DIY.

Dave Sweetapple: Roger Howse came up to us downtown: "You guys are punk. Would you mind if I interviewed you?" He was going to university, and he was writing some kind of paper for a folklore class. He was drawing comparisons between blues and what he'd read about punk. "Bring as many examples as you can. I want to hear what the music is, and then you can describe it to me."

He lived in an apartment out by the Mall. A bunch of us showed up with a stack of records. We played some Sex Pistols. We put on Minor Threat. He just sat there for hours, writing down what we were telling him about the history of punk. We were like, "The problem is we don't have anywhere to play."

Roger said, "My wife [...] is involved in the Grad House. You can do shows there. They have people perform there all the time."

The Grad House was one of the best times I remember from the St. John's music scene.

John Pastore: People would beat the shit out of each other and dive off the pool table.

Dave Sweetapple: There was a point where this new guy showed up, and he started hitting on Peter Martin's girlfriend. Pete went over and punched him right in the back of the head. The guy fell down, and he ended up suing Pete for assault. Pete said, "You can't sue me, because we were dancing." We all had to give depositions about slam-dancing. It seemed like an episode of *Quincy*. Pete got away with it because he said he was flailing his arms on the dance floor. This new thing called slam-dancing was taking place, and Pete had accidentally struck him.

Natalie Spracklin: It was pretty much sweaty young men flailing around. It really wasn't a mosh pit, and I wouldn't really call it "moshing" either. It was very aggressive in its appearance. I mean, it looked terrifying when you saw someone fall down. There's combat boots and fists flying. I saw a guy go down on the ground. I saw what I would describe as our community sort of very quickly identify that he was down and immediately get him up off the ground. People really took care of each other within that chaos. Nobody ever wanted to see anybody get hurt. People played around with the idea of anarchy, but when it came right down to it, they always had each other's backs.

Barry Newhook: The Riot and Public Enemy would have been the only punk bands playing the Grad House. Public Enemy was a more traditional Canadian hardcore band.

Chris Jerrett: For me, the '80s was the highest point of creativity [...] when we were just getting things off the ground.

Public Enemy deserves a lot more credit. They jump-started the scene. They were the first band to organize independent shows. We knew that bars weren't going to work for our fan base. Before you know it, we got a couple hundred people in a room. That's a major accomplishment, without even trying too hard. We were the guys who started doing it ourselves, the punk guys. In the beginning, Public Enemy couldn't really play in a club because our clientele were too young. No one would show up.

Dave Sweetapple: I wasn't playing in Public Enemy at that point. I joined right after the D.O.A. show. I was still in the Riot. I think Public Enemy was a four-piece at that point. Then I joined and became the second guitarist. Drummers were so hard to find that you would pick up anyone who was available. Many of them weren't even into punk rock. Public Enemy had like four drummers. It would be random guys. "You play drums, and can you play fast? You're in."

Bob Armstrong: Me and Craig Murray started hanging out and watching the Riot practise. We said, "Let's try to do something ourselves." I guess John Pastore was around by then. We picked him up to play bass, and we started practising our favourite songs. The Riot was doing Clash covers, and we were doing Exploited covers. To get to the gigs, Craig had this old Chevette, and we packed it with everything, the PA, the amps, the instruments. [It was all] borrowed from Duncan.

John Pastore: I bought Dave's old bass in the summer of '83. We were practising at my house in the Battery. I don't know who was drumming. I don't think Dave was playing with us yet. I do remember that "No Government" by Anti-Pasti was the first song I ever learned how to play. At that point, we didn't know how to write our own songs.

Bob Armstrong: A Booth High School variety show would have been our first live performance. We only played a few songs: Quiet Riot, D.O.A., and "Someone's Going to Die [Tonight]" by Blitz. I know my parents hated the whole thing. They thought it was useless, and I couldn't convince them otherwise.

Bob Armstrong: There was a book called the *International Discography of the New Wave*. It documented every punk record. In the back, it had a whole pile of phone numbers for musicians. Labels and record stores. We called Jello Biafra's place once, and we got this woman. I don't know who she was—his mother, his girlfriend, a friend. But she sounded old. She said, "No, Jello is not at home." That was pretty thrilling. At least we got the right number.

John Pastore: When I was a teenager, I used to play soccer for Feildian Gardens. In the off-season, which was from September through May, we would break into the clubhouse because there was a phone in there and the line was active. We would go down, usually in the winter, jump the fence and break into the clubhouse, and call all these bands and record stores. We did that for a couple of years. I can't believe nobody ever noticed [on the phone bill] these random calls to American record labels. It would have cost a small fortune for a long-distance phone call. Then Danny stole the telephone.

Dave Sweetapple: Bob and I used to write to Joey Shithead all the time, and he would send us D.O.A. singles. I still have tons of those old letters. He would write on the back of band posters, talking about how his friends were arrested for doing this and that—punk rock war stories. It was weird having these pen pals on the other side of the country, knowing that they already had legendary status.

Bob Armstrong: We got on the phone and tried to find out when D.O.A. was on tour. We had this stupid idea about getting them to play St. John's. Their manager, Ken Lester, said, "They're in Europe. They're coming back to Toronto, and then they're going to do Canada. Let me talk to them."

The venue they were supposed to play backed out at the last second. We always had our ear to the ground, looking for different places. There was this place in Pleasantville called the Village Inn or something like that. It could easily pack in two hundred people.

John Pastore: Bob called Joey Shithead. I remember listening in on the other line. It seems crazy that a bunch of fifteen- and sixteen-year-old kids called up D.O.A. and got them to drive all the way to Newfoundland from Toronto.

The first time that Public Enemy played an actual live show was with D.O.A. That was in April 1984. We played both D.O.A. and the Subhumans when we opened for D.O.A. We definitely did "Nazi Training Camp."

Bob Armstrong: At the last second, the club owner bailed. It was supposed to be an all-ages show, but the owner didn't have the right licensing. He chickened out. Maybe he thought everybody was going to be over nineteen. Maybe he thought we were all adults. So then we scrambled.

Barry Newhook: It might have been Mike O'Brien who led us to the eventual venue, and I don't know if it was the Admiral's Keg or the Oil Patch. Maybe it was Smitty's Piano Bar. Over the years, it had a hundred different names. Mike woke up the guy who ran the place and made him open the doors. It was all very rushed.

Bob Armstrong: We had to go in and clear all the bottles out of the place. The bar owner just let us run with it. In that way, he was our great saviour.

Barry Newhook: Wimpy, the bass player, was shaving in the bathroom. The band got out of the van, went in, and we were crowded around him in the bathroom, asking them all these stupid questions, this real punk rocker. I thought, *These people are the coolest thing I've ever seen. That guy can fucking shave, man.* I'm sure I couldn't, at that time.

John Pastore: There was an article in *The Newfoundland Herald* where the reporter didn't believe D.O.A.'s press kit that the band had toured all over the world and had been in riots: "Their press release is impressive, but not necessarily believable."

Touring and putting out a bunch of records seemed pretty impossible. By mainstream standards, you had to be Van Halen to do that.

Dave Sweetapple: The show wasn't anything people really cared about other than our crowd of friends. Plus, we had switched venues at the last minute. By this point, D.O.A. were playing huge halls with Black Flag and the Dead Kennedys. But they wanted the experience of driving to Newfoundland. They drove through snowstorms and took the ferry after they landed back in Toronto from Germany to play for fifty kids halfway across the country.

Johnny Fisher *(musician)*: I don't want to get my mom into any trouble because she passed away a few years ago. Before I was in Tough Justice, she would take me to bar shows. I was thirteen and fourteen going into bars with my mom. But I didn't get to see D.O.A.; she wouldn't let me. I was still listening to her back then. Rod Locke was fourteen, and he went downtown and there was a lineup of people trying to get into the show going from Smitty's Piano Bar up past the Silver Spur.

Dave Sweetapple: D.O.A. wanted a thousand-dollar guarantee. Kenny Lester wrote us saying, "All we want is a thousand dollars and a place to sleep." Maybe the tickets were twelve bucks, so there must've been sixty people. I think, at the end of the night, there was something like seven hundred and fifty dollars—that's it. We said, "This is all the money we have."

D.O.A. were like, "Whatever. It was a good time." They went back to Murray's mother's house on MacDonald Drive and stayed up all night watching NTV.

Clark Hancock: D.O.A. was the first punk band to come from away. I think they legitimized […] our scene at the time. It made what we were doing seem more real.

John Pastore: It wasn't even just in Newfoundland. This happened for the whole Maritimes, because they played Saint John [New Brunswick] and then Halifax on the way back to Toronto. That was the first big hardcore band to play anywhere east of Montreal. I feel like it pulled the whole scene together. People in Halifax talk about it as much as they do in St. John's. At least they do in the hardcore scene. Sonic Youth played the same night in Halifax as D.O.A. They flew in and played the art college. There were ten people to see Sonic Youth because nobody knew about them. Everybody in town went to see the hardcore band. They thought Sonic Youth would be this weird art show band, which they were, and nobody went.

Johnny Fisher: After D.O.A., we realized how important it was to network with other scenes. Pretty much right after the D.O.A. show, Dave Sweetapple, Bob Armstrong, and Chris Jerrett started up a fanzine. They interviewed Joey Shithead, and they asked, "What did you think of St. John's?" Joey said it was real, it was fresh, and what we were doing was something new for everybody in town. And that's what they wanted to see. They wanted to help break new ground.

STAND TALL AND ACT TOUGH

Dean Locke *(musician)*: Rod, my brother, and I were born a year apart. We grew up on Bannerman Street. When we first moved there, we were kind of brought up to be decent kids. We weren't really like a lot of the crowd who were beating the streets. You know, like latchkey kids. A lot of the youngsters were rough. We used to get the shit kicked out of us all the time, and I had to learn pretty quickly to pick up for myself. Walking home from school, it was nothing to come around the corner and find five guys waiting for me.

I had another brother about ten years older. He taught me how to fight. He said, "You got to start picking up for yourself."

Around the neighbourhood, kids would be standing in doorways smoking cigarettes, cursing and swearing at you. You'd be afraid—terrified. You'd have to stand tall and act tough. There was always one bigger guy. You had to haul off and give him an uppercut. You looked at another guy and gave him a smack upside the head. Then they all scattered and took off running.

Don Ellis *(musician/sound engineer)*: Rod and Dean were two sweethearts. Rod never had an aggressive bone in his body. His brother, Dean, on the other hand, was a big brute of a guy. He was tough, but he had a great sense of humour.

Dean Locke: High school is always described as the prime of your life. All your reflections, all your friends, all your interactions are supposed come from that time. We had a band [Tough Justice], and our close group of friends partied with us. It was like a community. We took care of each other. If somebody would be going through hard times, we'd look out for them.

Johnny Fisher: I didn't go to high school. I dropped out in Grade 7. I decided I wanted to play guitar and hang out instead.

Dean Locke: Johnny lived with his mom. He didn't have a dad. He never came out much, really. It's probably why, at first, we didn't really know him that well. His mom worked nights, and she'd sleep during the day. Johnny was never at school. For some reason, his mom got to the point where she just gave up. I guess he was being rebellious.

Johnny Fisher: When I was about eleven or twelve, I saw Billy Idol on TV. At that point, something just clicked. I became obsessed. I bought every magazine Billy Idol was in and wallpapered my entire bedroom from floor to ceiling in his posters. I started reading about him and found out that he had come from a punk band called Generation X. I went to Fred's and imported all the Generation X albums. The people at Fred's said, "You'll probably like this, too." It was *London Calling* by the Clash.

Dean Locke: We did a talent show at Macpherson when I was in Grade 3. We did all the makeup. We made outfits. We did platform boots. We put aluminum foil, beads, and chains on our costumes. My dad made guitars cut out of plywood. He even made the bass look like a demon. We had lights and confetti. We did three songs, and the crowd screamed and yelled. It was me and Rod and our friends Neil McKenzie and Scott Locke. They were our buddies from the hood. We thought we were stars. That was the roots of us starting a band.

    Rod said, "I want to get in music club. I want to learn how to play guitar." The music teacher took an interest in him for whatever reason. Mom and Dad didn't have a lot of money, but they bought him a cheap electric guitar. He came home one day, and we were sitting in the room listening to the Clash. "Should I Stay or Should I Go" was sort of a top hit on the radio. Then Rod started playing along. Soon after, he was jamming with Danny Thomas. Danny and his brothers always played. Chris Jerrett had a couple songs written. Rod played guitar, Danny played drums, and Chris sang. They were shagging around after school, but I wasn't involved.

    I can't remember exactly how I got a bass. It was used and cheap; it was a no-name. Rod would come home from Danny's, and I'd be sitting there plucking away by myself. A couple of times we recorded some stuff on cassette. One day after jamming with Danny, Rod brought the tape up to him. He played it, and Danny was just floored. He said, "Get Dean up here now." That sort of sealed the deal.

Danny Thomas: I guess I met all of them—Rod, Dean, and Sean Doran—in junior high. Sean and I were just so bad. The strap didn't work anymore—nothing really worked. We never did nothing too bad, other than selling joints. It was just normal teenager stuff except with my religion teacher. I didn't really like her very much, and I didn't want to be in religion. Let's just say that I could be pretty disruptive. Sean's a couple years older than me. He failed or had been kicked out of school a couple of times. His stepfather was our industrial arts teacher and a complete asshole. I think he failed Sean every year just out of spite.

Dean Locke: Sean was one of the first people to spike his hair. He'd take a safety pin and stick it in his ear or stick it in his nose.

Danny Thomas: You couldn't have put people like us in a worse school than Macpherson. It was terrible planning by the school board. All the really hard tickets from St. Philip's, Portugal Cove, Shea Heights, and the only Anglicans who lived in downtown St. John's went to Macpherson. Macpherson was a reprobate school, much like Booth Memorial. Once you got thrown out of every other school or got pregnant, you ended up at Booth.

The strange thing about Booth was you had this horrible cross-blend of every reprobate from downtown St. John's and the surrounding areas, plus only the finest people from the MacDonald Drive suburb. It was just a complete failure in school zoning.

The fact that me and Sean are still best friends thirty-five years later is astonishing. It's a beautiful thing. I don't know why Sean was in so much trouble. I didn't know him at this point. We [eventually] met at the vice-principal's office. I sat at one desk, and he sat at the other [for detention]. We spent three months together in detention. And that's when we became best friends, and have been ever since.

Barry Newhook: I pipped off school, and I was going to the Village to get Gang of Four's *Entertainment!* I remember seeing this weird kid on the bus and thinking, *Why isn't he in school?* Meanwhile, I was skipping school, too. But this was a kid. *What the fuck is he doing?* Anyway, it was Danny.

Rhonda Pelley *(activist)*: Danny and Sean Doran were inseparable. Sean had black leather pants, and Danny had red leather pants and dog chains. Sean had Sid Vicious hair, and Danny had these incredibly long, beautiful ringlets of hair. They were quite gorgeous, but they would never take off their pants. I remember the stink of sweat off them.

Sean Panting *(musician)*: Danny had on the same leather pants for, like, three years straight. For three years solid, he was shirtless and in leather pants.

Danny Thomas: People see photos of me from back in the Tough Justice days and say, "There used to be a six-pack on you. What happened?"

"Well, I'm pushing fifty. That's what happened. I was fucking starving to death back then." It had nothing to do with staying in shape. It had everything to do with not eating.

Don Ellis: I remember being freaked out and nervous about going to my first punk show. I thought, *I better look like a punk rocker.* I had on a kind of green lumberjacket. I think I had on a pair of Converse sneakers. I never really looked the part. I think I had a rat-tail. That was about as sinister as I ever got.

Dean Locke: Macpherson had a variety show coming up. We wanted to do this band thing. We had three songs: "Should I Stay or Should I Go," "Belsen Was a Gas," and something off of Sid Vicious's solo album. At the time, I was just singing. I wasn't good enough on bass; Danny played bass. Sean Doran learned how to play drums in two weeks. Rod played guitar. That was the beginning of Tough Justice. That was Grade 9.

We did a couple rehearsals in the gym, and our vice-principal, who was Jewish, heard us play "Belsen Was a Gas." Everybody was just so offended. They're like, "You got to change the lyrics." Right before the show, we changed them: "Esso was a gas, I heard the other day/I put five gallons in my Chevrolet/I drove around town all night long/Blasting my stereo to a mean punk song."

We then started skipping school in the afternoon and jamming at Danny's house for three hours: "Mom is working. We'll go down and use my brother's gear. We could use the amps and the drums." Sometimes one of his brothers would come home, and we'd scramble out the back window.

Danny Thomas: Being someone who now knows music on a more professional level, I think we did astonishingly well. Playing was already in our fingers.

Dean Locke: The Grad House was actually the very first formal Tough Justice show [1984]. Rod and Danny and I were the core. Sean didn't really progress. Whatever happened—God bless him, he was trying—but he just couldn't keep up.

Rod and I were walking home from Danny's, and we ran into Duncan Snowden. He lived near Bannerman Park. He had an English accent, and he wore combat boots. "Are you any good? We're doing a show at the Grad House." Their band was the Riot, with Barry and Duncan and Justin Hall. "We want you to play if you're interested."

We phoned Danny right away. The next day we got together and skipped school and tried to learn more songs. I think we ended up with a lot of covers and a couple of originals, believe it or not. We were officially a band.

Johnny Fisher: This was before I was in Tough Justice. I went to see them and Public Enemy at the Grad House. After the show, Rod and Dean asked, "What did you think?"

I said, "Public Enemy were great." Public Enemy played "War," by Edwin Starr. I knew that song because it was in my mother's record collection.

Don Ellis: Tough Justice recorded a strong-sounding demo for a CBC broadcast about the punk rock scene in St. John's.

Dean Locke: Imagine how excited we were, a bunch of dirtbag teenagers. They introduced "Time Bomb," and then it faded into a voiceover of someone talking about punk rock. It was very dry—like CBC.

Don Ellis: There was enough going on with the scene for a story. Wallace's bands had been there since the late '70s. But they were never anywhere close to hardcore.

Danny Thomas: We played Sound Symposium. We did the Oil Patch, which was above Erin's Pub. The Oil Patch was a rock bar at the time. Reg's Pub was on the go. It was sort of next to the Ship Inn at the bottom of the stairs. The owner was just a complete booze bag. He was usually so drunk that he didn't know we were all fifteen or sixteen years old. It was his liquor licence—not ours.

Dean Locke: For some reason, we were able to get our band into those places, and we were never questioned about our age. It was nothing for me to play in a bar at sixteen years old and have beer lined up on the head of my amp. People would bring beer back between songs, and I'd guzzle them down.

Johnny Fisher: Danny convinced the manager of the Corner Stone to give Tough Justice a three-night stand. We got paid fourteen hundred bucks. We were kids. We did three nights, and everyone hated us. But we still got paid. On the third night, there was a nurses' convention.

Sean Panting: I've never been punched, but I had a beer bottle thrown at me. I played at the Corner Stone for Buck-a-Bacardi Tuesday. This was later; this was probably 1987. While the visuals are burned into my mind pretty good, the details are long ago and far away. But I'm sure it was Tough Justice and Cult of Reason. Somebody chucked a beer bottle at my head, and it smashed on the wall behind me. Two bouncers came in, pounded the shit out of the guy, and threw him over the stairs.

Tough Justice played, and some of the rednecks were getting pretty testy by that point. Someone said, "Play some old-time rock and roll."

Dean Locke went, "This is new-time rock and roll, you fat fuck. Now sit down!"

I thought, *We are all going to die tonight.*

Danny Thomas was on acid. He was trying to cheer me up because I was really worried. I wasn't tough. I saw the Tough Justice guys, and they were tough. I was not like that. I was real soft. I could hang out with people who were pretty hard, and I got along with everyone, but that wasn't my basic nature. I was pretty worried that I was going to get killed. In between songs, Danny looked over. "Sean, I'm a walrus." He jammed two drumsticks up his nose, really far up his nose, alarmingly far up his nose. Then Tough Justice started playing with blood seeping down Danny's drumsticks. The next day, he had blood in his hair and all over his clothes. Apparently, he just cut the blood out of his hair instead of washing it.

Dean Locke: I had a Traynor cabinet with two fifteen-inch speakers with a 200-watt Traynor head. The two fifteens were almost shot because we jammed so loud. With the Corner Stone money, we got two new speakers in there, and we got a new JBL speaker for Rod. It improved our sound quite a bit. It was the whole incentive thing. It drove us to practise.

Don Ellis: Rod used to play through a Traynor that was like something he'd hauled out of the garbage. But he ended up getting this great JBL speaker. That's how he got that fantastic guitar sound. Everything [in the '80s] was solid state. You couldn't find a tube in anything. The only guy who had a tube amp was Duncan Snowden.

Dean Locke: We wanted to expand our sound. Up to that point, it was my responsibility to keep the rhythm going on the bass. Johnny had a guitar. He was sort of learning how to play. Rod and I were walking down Bannerman, and I think he wanted us to hear him because he had his front door wide open. We poked our heads in, and Johnny was sitting there smiling. We'd found our rhythm guitar player.

Johnny Fisher: Me and Llewellyn Thomas, who had filled in with Tough Justice a few times, started a band called the Asthmatics in late '83 or early '84. Nothing really took off from it. Tough Justice decided they wanted a second guitar player. They held auditions, and it came down to me and Bob Hallett, [who went on to form] Great Big Sea. Bob was there because he had the exact same guitar as Rod, a Cimar, a Japanese copy of an Ibanez Roadster. I got the gig because I was their friend, I lived in the neighbourhood, and everybody hung out at my house. My mom was really easygoing, and she allowed us to do things that most parents wouldn't.

Dean Locke: Johnny smoked cigarettes with his mom. He had asthma, but he smoked cigarettes. She loved him, and she'd do anything for him. "You want to smoke cigarettes? I guess you're old enough." We could drink beer at Johnny's house. He could have people in after a gig. His mom didn't mind. We could hang out there in the daytime, and Johnny was the king. He even had his "special chair" that nobody could sit in.

Don Ellis: It was at Prince of Wales Collegiate that I sort of started hanging around with Mike Buhler, Rick Mercer, Andrew and Geoff Younghusband, and Ashley Billard. The first exposure to punk, I think, was through my sister, Roberta. In 1984, MUN brought in Teenage Head. I remember she came home and went, "They had this band, and they were awful."

I thought, *Oh, that sounds interesting. I'd probably like them.*

Right around the same time, Mike Buhler gave me this beautiful compilation tape. It's a brilliant mixtape of the Clash, the Ramones, Pistols, D.O.A., Dead Kennedys, a bit of GBH, and a bit of Exploited. My friends in high school were all into ZZ Top, Stevie Ray Vaughan, and blues rock. Stuff like Molly Hatchet and Van Halen. It was hard to get anything halfway decent in '82 or '83. Fred's wouldn't really bring in anything unless they figured it would sell. You had to special-order from them. You kind of had to find this stuff on your own.

It was Llewellyn Thomas who introduced me to the boys, because he had seen me drum. But I can't remember where or when. That's a mystery to me. He thought I'd be a decent candidate to try out for Tough Justice. He said, "Come down to the French Association." The French Association was across from Gower Street United Church, a curved building that's now a condo. Of course, Llewellyn and his family are all fluent French speakers. I went down one night. I'll never forget walking in the door and this smell of fucking sweat hitting me like a ton of bricks. It's that unmistakable foul odour that inhabits jam spaces. I went in, and it was stinking hot down there. Danny: shirt off. Dean: shirt off. Rod: shirt off. Llewellyn: shirt off.

It was really exciting, the blistering speed of the music. But it was really positive energy. It was this great visceral, physical outlet at a time when music was all about Ratt and Quiet Riot. Everyone was getting soft and flabby. The Who was long gone. Led Zeppelin was dead. Everything had a beat box. There was that early British pop sound. I listen to it now, and I don't mind it so much. At the time, it was nauseating. It was really wimpy kind of stuff. I played some drums at that jam, and the boys were gobsmacked: "You're in."

Danny Thomas: When I came back from the mainland, I got severe tendinitis in my arms, severe enough that I couldn't play drums anymore. We added Don Ellis, and I became the singer.

Don Ellis: My folks gave me a set of drums for my tenth birthday, or maybe it was Christmas. They were Maxwins. They cost seven hundred dollars in 1978. Maxwins were dirt-cheap Pearls. In those days, there were no stores that even had Pearl or Tama. Ludwig? Forget it. A set of Ludwigs in '78 would have been close to two thousand dollars. My parents could have bought me a used car for that kind of money. The price of instruments in the 1970s was staggering. No wonder we had to piecemeal stuff together. Only the professional musicians had real instruments, and they guarded them with their lives.

I did a little bit of time with Don Wherry, but it was theoretical, and I was just too young. I couldn't follow it. I couldn't read music. Don was a proper teacher: "You don't touch that set of drums until you can read music."

I'd been going to him for months, and eventually I just kind of broke down. I started to well up and cry. I said, "I just can't do it anymore. I can't tap out of time on a rubber pad anymore." Mom and Dad finally took me out of it.

But I did learn something from Don. I thought, *I'm not going to become a percussionist in the* NSO [Newfoundland Symphony Orchestra]. *I just want to rock.*

Johnny Fisher: Punk rock has a lot of humour in it. There was no humour in Tough Justice. A lot of the songs were about getting beat up. Rod Locke had a song that was called "Headbanger." It was basically about gang violence and getting jumped in the park. There was two or three carloads of rednecks who used to hunt down punk rockers. I think someone within the punk rock scene had gotten busted for stealing car stereos and ratted. There was a ring of them stealing car stereos. From that point on, if we were hanging out at Bannerman Park and a car pulled up, we'd scatter in every direction. Inevitably, one of us would get a turfing. Fortunately, that was never me.

Danny Thomas: We recorded in Don's mother's basement through two sound consoles we linked together. When we played, we needed to take three seconds of silence between songs. We did that for ten songs without tuning a guitar or checking the mics. That's well represented on the record.

Dean appeared with mushroom cookies, which kind of screwed up the process. There's a lot of phase shifter and delay vocals, which you wouldn't normally hear on a punk rock record. But we couldn't afford the sixty-three dollars to do it all again. That's how much it cost to rent the consoles.

Don Ellis: My grandmother, who had a stroke in 1978, was about eighty-five years old. She was totally paralyzed; she couldn't speak. I would come upstairs, and there was this look on her face: *You are a product of Satan.* She was just so pissed off. I used to feel so bad for my grandmother. She must've thought there was something wrong with me.

Johnny Fisher: The demo was released with half the cassettes having a song called "Justice Hammer" and the other half having a song called "Ego."

We couldn't decide which one to use. It's a rare piece of information, I guess, that some people got the tape with "Ego" and some people got the tape with "Justice Hammer."

Don's dad worked for Pfizer Canada. He had all these educational cassette tapes on arthritis. Don commandeered a box. We recorded over them and put sticker labels on the tabs. Then we stamped every cassette with "Tough Justice." With some of the demos, a song would end, and you would hear something like, "One in every five Canadians have arthritis."

Don Ellis: We'd run through the set five times, and I'd be bloodied. We'd do that like four straight nights before a gig. That was our routine. Rehearsing to the point of being completely bloodied was the norm. You hear stories of Black Flag rehearsing all day long. That's what we did. We rehearsed a lot, and we got really tight. All those crappy recordings that we released are all live. There are no overdubs.

Johnny Fisher: We went from playing fast, but not really fast, just kind of up-tempo, basically, and then we started listening to American hardcore. From that point on, everything got faster. We jammed five nights a week for about six months. We never wrote a new song during that entire period. Our only goal was faster.

Public Enemy sort of finished playing because some of the members moved away. John Pastore went to Montreal. Dave Sweetapple went to Toronto. In all actuality, those guys ran the scene. They were doing fanzines, importing records, booking shows. After Public Enemy kind of imploded, Schizoid came along and basically stole the show.

Don Ellis: Chris Jerrett was always a bit of a tough guy. He was always a real shit disturber. He always picked on Duncan Snowden. He always picked on me. I went to kindergarten with Chris. When I went down to the French Association that first time, there he was. I was like, *There's that guy who stole my dinkie when I was six years old.* The next time I saw him, I guess, would have been at the Grad House, and he's thrashing around and fucking killing people on the dance floor. Awesome. We meet again.

A year later, I'm playing with him in Schizoid.

STIRRING THINGS UP

Barry Newhook: As far as live bands go, St. John's has gone through a whole bunch of ebb and flow. When we were kids, nobody wanted live music, and clubs weren't set up for live music. They were still really holding onto the whole disco era.

Danny Thomas: The Grad House used to be a place where everybody played: blues bands, jazz bands, punk bands, folk bands. Every Friday and Saturday night, there was usually a show there. I remember going to see Denis Parker when I was fourteen years old. There used to be a little bar and a dining room with a pool table. We'd rent out that room. Underage people could go there, and people who were old enough could grab a beer at the bar in between sets.

   I'm pretty sure that Roger Howse was in charge of the Grad House. I guess he was sort of like, *How do we make a little more money to keep it running?* I know it was sort of falling into disrepair. [Bands] would play in the little bar that could seat probably thirty people. In the main room, which was the whole front of the house, was the dining hall. It was quite a large room. It had a full-sized billiard table. It was kind of set up like a lounge. People would sort of go in there to study.

Mike O'Brien: We never went to the Grad House to play; we went there to drink. It was the graduate student residence on Military Road, next to Bannerman Park. I guess that I would have first went in there sometime around 1979.

Wallace Hammond: The Graduate Student Union bought the place in the early '70s.

Mike O'Brien: Dog Meat BBQ played there in the '80s. But it took a long time before the management would have us. What put a hell of a lot of people off in a big way was that we cursed onstage at a time when you really didn't do that. It's astounding how freaked out people got when you said "fuck" onstage. I'm probably the first person who ever deliberately said "motherfucker" on a public stage in St. John's. The songs I wrote had swear words in them, and sometimes there was a lot of them. Our music was also loud and abrasive, at a time when people weren't prepared for loud and abrasive.

Dave Sweetapple: In St. John's, there was just us and the handful of bands that we played with. In that way, the city was disconnected from the larger music scene. But as a group, you knew everybody. I went to shows all the time that weren't what I was into. It was a social thing.

Bob Armstrong: Carol Croke [the girlfriend of Public Enemy's Tony Meaney, aka Hardcore Tony] couldn't come to a show. She came up to me downtown. She said, "I'm really sorry I missed the show. Here's six bucks." I think it was three bucks cover. They knew we didn't have any money and that we basically paid to play.

Barry Newhook: I think the early hardcore scene here kind of put me off a bit because it was so narrow-minded. Everyone dressed exactly the same. I found it very restricting. The later hardcore scene, when it started to evolve and there was a more of a crossover metal influence, it kind of broadened. Before that, the punk rock scene, pre-hardcore, was really freaky. When I talk about Da Slyme and the Bubonic Plague, they came from a sort of artistic idea of what punk was about mixed with a lot of satire.

Mike Buhler: Teenagers were in the Grad House drinking beer and totally gone mad slam-dancing. Attendance? I don't know. Maybe a few dozen people. I couldn't imagine seeing more than fifty people there at any given time. We're not talking about a massive room. If you got twenty or thirty people rocking out in your living room, it would be pretty full.

Chris Jerrett: There were all-ages shows at the Grad House in the afternoon. There was no alcohol, and that's when things really started to change. By doing that, we drew a lot more young people to the scene. Public Enemy was the critical link; that band started the all-ages scene. Because Tough Justice and Schizoid began booking all-ages shows, the other bands that came up around that scene started playing with those punk bands, too. Jody Richardson's bands and his crowd were involved in some of those shows. By interlinking all the bands, we were able to build a scene.

Barry Newhook: Jody was around with the Dirt Buffaloes. They were people who could really play. They were kind of peripheral to that scene. They were more into an avant-garde type of music—college rock.

Dave Sweetapple: With Public Enemy, there would be Tough Justice and A-Truce, which was more like the Jam and a lot of those late '70s British bands. Brad Burness and his brother, Gary, did mod-type stuff. It wasn't like the British thing of the punks versus the mods. There was no animosity. None of the bands [we played with] really sounded alike. They were all different in some way.

Mike Buhler: Music was the glue that kept the broader scene together. It was a rallying point. With the zines and stuff, I was never a contributor. I was just out having a good time and living the lifestyle. I wasn't a musician. Stage-diving—that would be me.

Barry Newhook: We would have to move the pool table [at the Grad House] and get it out of the way. That became an issue. People would get up on the pool table and dive off. Management was concerned that as soon as the punk rockers started showing up, things got broken. They said, "You can't play here." We finally lost out on the Grad House.

Johnny Fisher: Somebody stole the cushions off the couch. Tough Justice took the blame for it because we were the band booked to play. Ironically enough, we were asked to play a Grad House benefit at the TSC [Thompson Student Centre] in 1987. There was a lot of traditional bands, Tickle Harbour and all that crowd, and we were stuck in the middle. We got onstage and played seven songs in like five minutes, and then they cut the power on us. People started to get up and slam-dance, and then that was it. The show was over.

Danny Thomas: Whoever took over after Roger Howse [at the Grad House] wasn't open to us putting off shows. I know that some stuff got beaten up. I think Jack Lanphear put his head through a wall. I don't want to throw anyone under the bus here, but there were a couple of incidents that I remember. Actually, I don't think Jack put his head through a wall. I think he put Eugene Leger's head through a wall. That sounds more than likely. Jack was a bit of a scrapper back then.

Dave Sweetapple: There were a group of kids from Long Harbour who drove to the Grad House. They read an article in the *Newfoundland Herald* that there was a show happening.

Dean Locke: If you didn't live in town, you lived in the bay. If you lived out in Conception Bay, you lived in the bay. Pouch Cove was the bay. Torbay was the bay. Long Harbour was definitely the bay.

John Pastore: It must've been September '85 when the kids from Long Harbour wrote us a letter [asking about our bands]. We're like, "Let's drive out and surprise them."

Me, Buhler, Chris, Doran, and Dave piled into Mike's car, and we drove out to their high school. We just walked in the front door and asked for them. Buhler had a huge mohawk back then. It must've looked like we just stepped off of the moon. The principal of the school was terrified. The teachers were terrified. Five punks jump out of a car with leather jackets and mohawks, and Chris cracks open a can of spray paint and starts spray-painting the school. It was literally like we were a biker gang who just rolled into town. While the guys from Long Harbour were cheering us on, the principal and the teachers were peeking out of the windows watching us terrorize.

The school found us through an article in the *Newfoundland Herald*. The police went to Dave's house because he was the only one of us who used his real name. They had no problem finding him. Sweetapple is a pretty unique name. Maybe Mike and Chris had to go back and clean up the graffiti.

Dave Sweetapple: My memory of it is the whole school cowering and hiding except for those guys who were just blown away that these mutants showed up. It was the middle of the afternoon right after lunch. How far is Long Harbour, about an hour? I couldn't even find it on the map.

John Pastore: I have some memory of maybe the police saying they were going to press vandalism charges. Nobody was arrested.

Bob Armstrong: I think it all just gelled around that time. There was the D.O.A. show. We were booking the Grad House. Then we started doing a fanzine, *Wabana Riot*. I think we stirred things up and broke some new ground.

John Pastore: I don't think Fred's would have had *Flipside* or *Maximumrocknroll*. The only magazine you could [get] around St. John's in the early '80s was *Trouser Press*. That was more mainstream. It was new-wave kind of stuff. But they would have scene reports from various other cities, which was always hardcore.

We were already sending letters to bands and going to the post office and getting money orders. We would sit at home writing endless letters to every record label and to every band and to every magazine that we could find an address for. The back of *Trouser Press* would have small ads. I think that must've been how we got started.

Dave Sweetapple: *Wabana Riot* was me, Bob, Chris Jerrett, Pastore, and Craig Murray, who did vocals in Public Enemy. His father had a real estate agency down on Logy Bay Road. We'd wait until everyone left, and Murray would get the key. We'd go down and sit there with glue sticks and scissors at the conference table. We'd sit there with a briefcase full of black-and-white photocopies and use up every bit of toner they had in the place.

On the cover of the first issue of *Wabana Riot* was D.O.A. The magazine covered a lot of Canadian hardcore: Stretch Marks, Death Sentence [...] and Slow Death [...]. There [were] weird scene reports. We would write bands for interviews. I remember writing Suicidal Tendencies, and they wrote back: "Thanks so much for supporting us. Here's a copy of the record to review, and here's a half-page ad for your zine."

Bob Armstrong: It was a great way to get free records.

Dave Sweetapple: It wasn't just bands in Canada and the United States, but it was hardcore bands in Finland and Sweden, too.

Bob Armstrong: We send out like twenty or thirty letters, and most of the time we got responses. I sent Youth Brigade a letter hoping for an interview. They sent back a tape of them sitting around talking, drinking beers, and cracking jokes.

Chris Jerrett: There was the "War in the West End" column about playing war-game scenarios with slingshots. That was with Steve Campbell, my next-door neighbour. I got shot in the eye and spent a week in the hospital. I almost lost my eye from getting hit with a doughball.

Dave Sweetapple: Bob and I opened a P.O. box on Water Street, and every day we would march down to get the mail. Every day would be like Christmas. There would be packages coming back of records to review and interviews. Other zines would want to trade copies. Of course, as kids, you're driving the guys at Fred's nuts because we'd put copies in there on consignment, and we'd stop in every other day. "Did we sell any more?"
"Yeah, we sold three. Here's your $1.50."

Bob Armstrong: We used to fight to get to the mailbox the quickest because there was always going to be stickers and records. We were usually pretty fair. Whoever wrote the letter got the stuff, and then they got to do the review and keep the record. At the time, I was going to MUN. I was up the earliest. I would go to my first class, and I'd beat it down to get to the post office box. I'd grab everything. Hopefully, it was the time that *Maximumrocknroll* was released, and then I'd go read that for three or four hours at Ports of Food. A couple of years ago, I finally fessed up to Tony that I'd ripped open his letter from the Freeze from Boston. It took a while to admit to that.

Dave Sweetapple: We had a "Dear Hardcore Tony" column. It would be fake letters about women who had problems with their husbands. Tony would write the replies. It was stupid kid stuff.

Bob Armstrong: After Craig Murray drifted away from Public Enemy, we got Tony on vocals. He's mostly responsible for getting us into US hardcore. The story on him is he was on a bus wearing a punk shirt, and Doran and Pastore started talking to him. Tony was three or four years older than us and lived in an apartment upstairs from Leo's Fish and Chips [on Freshwater Road].

Dave Sweetapple: I know where the name came from, *Wabana Riot*. We went over to Bell Island to poke around, trying to see if we could get into one of the mines. We were thinking, *What would happen if people started a riot over here? It's an island. It would be this self-contained thing.* We were trying to come up with a name. We just said, "Let's call it *Wabana Riot*."

When you're a teenager and your life is consumed with music it seems to last forever. On the last page of *Wabana Riot* #3, Bob did this blurb that read, "Tony joins the band. Dave moves to Toronto." I was only up in Toronto for like six months. The next thing, we're all there. Schizoid formed, and the band moved up to try and make it. Instead, they moved into an apartment and got on welfare.

UNSUITABLE FOR PUBLIC CONSUMPTION

Mike O'Brien: I got involved in the music scene in the late '70s with a whole bunch of forgettable bands. I didn't really get serious until the early '80s, when I hooked up with Wallace Hammond and formed the Bubonic Plague.

Making music was something I just fell into. Sometime in about '77 or '78, a couple of people I knew said, "Let's form a punk band." They wanted me to be the singer because they figured I had stage presence. That was just at parties drinking and making up stuff as we went along. Writing songs was not something I did as a teenager. I quickly realized I couldn't write anything that would have passed as semi-normal. There has got to be something abrasive or in your face about it.

In those years, really from the time I finished high school right up through the '80s, I wasn't always in St. John's. I never actually had a real job here. I used to work the door at bars downtown for cash, but that's about it. I always had to go away to work construction up in Alberta and Toronto. It was typical migrant labour. I'd spend at least part of every year up on the mainland, and then I would come home again and go on unemployment.

Wallace Hammond: How did I get involved with Mike O'Brien? Part of it was John Heald. The band the Issue was Carter, Heald, and maybe Mark Oakley on bass. Carter moved away, and they became another band called Ground Zero. When I hooked up with Mike, it was through those guys.

That was about the time Craig Squires bought this house here on Victoria Street. Back then, I was still living on the top of Patrick Street. When I moved in here, I bought two dozen beer and enlisted Mike and John

Heald to help. We got the stereo up and running, and we were drinking beer and talking. I broached the idea of putting some music to Mike's lyrics.

Mike O'Brien: The first thing I did that lasted was with Wallace and a drum machine. I'd been talking about doing something for months, and we finally sat down in Wallace's living room with the drum machine and a guitar and wrote "Angie." I think we might have played it once onstage somewhere, but it was not recordable because we would have been sued for libel by the person we wrote it about. That was a problem with a lot of the early songs. They were just unsuitable for public consumption.

Terry Carter: Mike would just show up with his lyrics, and Wallace would generally have an idea. It was nothing I would really associate with jamming, but there was an organic dynamic between us. We would get a groove going, and Mike would structure his lyrical delivery around that. Songs like "Dancing in a Wasteland" were largely improvised.

Wallace Hammond: Carter was interested in the idea of putting stuff out on cassette. Peter Narvaez made a tape. People are still making tapes today. Peter put his name and the title of the cassette on a [rubber] stamp. We copied all that stuff from him. What he did for the cover was mimeograph a piece of paper with a picture and fold it to fit the cassette case.

I discovered that if you took a picture with a camera and scaled it down, the photo was the same width as a cassette case. There used to be a place on Freshwater Road called Northlight Photography. We photographed the cover and brought it in there.

Mike O'Brien: We were writing songs that we believed in. We thought we were pretty good, and I think a lot of the recordings still hold up. It's definitely competent stuff. We just wanted to document our music and get it into people's hands. We had no money to cut an album.

Over several beers—maybe several more—me and Wallace and Terry got the idea of creating a record label. That's the origin of Vikki-Beat. The reference is to Victoria Street and Wallace's house, the place where we mixed all the stuff. I got my brother to design the logo.

Wallace Hammond: We put out a couple of things right away. *Don't Quit Yer Day Job* [Vikki-Beat, 1984] was the first one. We did one for the Reaction, and the A-Tones too.

Mike O'Brien: We sold the cassettes in Ziploc bags with lyric booklets. We couldn't get the lyrics small enough to put them in a cassette insert, so we'd have lyric booklets stapled together and the tape in a Ziploc bag. We included instructions: "Open bag, insert tape in machine, fill bag with glue, sniff, and play loud."

Terry Carter: The beauty of the Vikki-Beat production method was that we didn't have to make a run bigger than a box of cassettes.

Mike O'Brien: We released the tape in the spring, and shortly thereafter I had to go away. Because of the way unemployment works, you got the clock ticking, and you have to boot it back to the mainland before your claim runs out. I headed up to Alberta and discovered things there were not as booming as they had been. The world price of oil had dropped. After 1982, I couldn't find much work there. I never really liked Alberta, and I kept hearing about all these construction jobs in Toronto. I got to Toronto sometime in early June and spent the first couple of nights sleeping in Allan Gardens. It was warm, and I wasn't a fan of the YMCA. I kept my stuff in a locker at the bus station and crashed in the park for a day or two. I called a friend to go have a beer. [...] He hooked me up with somewhere to crash until I found a place in Scarborough. I actually ended up not working at all for a couple months of the summer. It was the hottest summer anyone could remember, and who the hell felt like working? My unemployment claim was still good for a while.

We ended up hanging out drinking beer and playing crib for a good chunk of the summer. I was grabbing a little bit of casual work here and there. As soon as my claim ran out, I was eligible for a government make-work project and got a really good gig as the supervisor renovating a theatre. When that was done, I opted to come home.

It was Wallace who hit on the idea of campfire stuff. Instead of doing a punk show with a whole band that would involve trying to find a drummer and a bass player, we would just do it with Wallace and John Heald playing acoustic guitars. We rehearsed a whole night of music, the first Bubonic Plague tape, a bunch of Da Slyme songs, and a twenty-minute-long version of "Louie, Louie."

There's an amazing number of songs that can be sung to the tune of "Louie, Louie." "Purple Haze," "Like a Rolling Stone," "Girls Just Want to Have Fun," the theme from *The Carol Burnett Show*, the theme from *The Beverly Hillbillies*. Most infamously, the square-dance fight song from the old Bugs Bunny cartoon: "Grab a fence post, hold it tight, whomp your partner with all your might."

Wallace Hammond: Then, in the spring, the band broke up. They used to practise in [John] Heald's parents' basement up on Portugal Cove Road. That's where they recorded the cassette. I helped them set up, and I think I rented some equipment. Then Heald was going back to England because he had joined the Royal Air Force.

Terry Carter: Big Tears had a very brief existence. [...] We managed to record some of the stuff and put it out as one of the Vikki-Beat tapes. We were good, but we sort of got lost in the shuffle.

Mike O'Brien: We [Bubonic Plague] booked a gig at the Admiral's Keg, which was not the original Admiral's Keg that had been in the Newfoundland Hotel. This was another bar, upstairs from Erin's Pub [on Water Street]. It's gone through a million names. It was the Oil Patch. It was Smitty's Piano Bar. It was the Admiral's Keg. It was a space where nothing ever lasted. Everything was booked when John Heald announced that he was quitting music and going back to join the Royal Air Force. It was parental pressure, mostly, I think. His parents were unimpressed with the drinking and the drugs and the sordid bunch of people he was hanging out with, namely us.

Myself and Wallace decided we were going to go drown our sorrows at the Grad House on Military Road. We ran into Mark [Oakley], who was also drowning his sorrows because his band was gone now, too. At some point, after many beers, Mark said, "Why don't I just take John's place in your band?" The gig was a week later, and we played thirty songs over three sets. It took Mark about two days to learn them.

We went ahead and did this acoustic show. We had a great time, and we found there was this amazing chemistry between us. There was a crowd of a few dozen, which, by our standards, was pretty good. The bar loved us. We would later play in other bands in the same space. It wasn't until years later that I figured out why they loved us so much. Between the guys in the band, we were drinking enough to keep them in business.

We came out of the early punk scene, and people tend to forget how much punk was a drink-beer-as-much-as-you-can-and-as-fast-as-you-can kind of scene. Punk and beer were one and the same thing.

The Admiral's Keg wanted us back the following weekend. We played Friday and Saturday night to a diminishing crowd. People had seen what we were all about and weren't really into doing the same thing again.

Wallace Hammond: We played the Brandy Saloon on Duckworth Street. Some guy in the audience punched Mike's brother. At the end of the song, Mike said, "We're going [to] take a break. We got some business we need to take care of." The next thing you hear on the recording is Mark's wife screaming. Mike walked off the stage, grabbed the guy, belted him one, and threw him down over the stairs.

Mike O'Brien: He smashed the microphone into Mark Oakley's face. At some point, I turned to Wallace: "Play a guitar solo." I got down, smacked the guy around, got back onstage, and started singing again. We got stiffed that night, too. I never did pay my bar tab, which probably amounted to more money than we were going to make in the first place.

Wallace Hammond: Mike was coming back and forth from the mainland. Carter and Oakley were going to Toronto. There was nothing on the go here. There wasn't even much in the way of sound jobs. I spent a year in Toronto, and I probably shouldn't have. […] We played in any place we could. We played maybe a dozen times.

Terry Carter: I think we got a better reception in Toronto than we did at home. We went to Toronto because it was going nowhere fast in St. John's. […] There were no prospects. We'd been around the block there way too many times and thought a move to Toronto might work. I think a couple of the guys were half-hearted about it. I was a little bit more gung-ho. That was the summer of '84, almost forty years ago. I think the guys got a little homesick. I was the only one to stay here and carry on playing with other groups.

Mike O'Brien: I come back from Toronto in '86. Peace-A-Chord had started up the year before. My view was that Peace-A-Chord really transformed the scene here. It was the best thing that ever came along for independent music, in terms of our exposure to younger audiences.

I found out about Peace-A-Chord when I was in Toronto. As soon as I got back, I was talking to Wallace: "Let's get a band together. This Peace-A-Chord would be the perfect time to play." But we didn't have a band because Terry and Mark were still away. […] Justin Hall was into it. But there weren't that many people around who we'd played with before. We decided to do things a bit different and recruit Duncan Snowden. The Riot and Bubonic Plague had played several shows on the same bill.

Duncan was still playing with the Riot, but they were sort of on their last legs. [...] We soon discovered what a brilliant musician he was. Like Mark, he learned nearly all of our songs within a couple of days. He was quick to pick them up. We then wrote a couple more songs and booked the gig at Peace-A-Chord under the name Backstreet Jihad.

The day before, down to Wallace's place, we were running through a few last-minute details, and he mentioned he got this package of propaganda from the National Fund for Animal Welfare, who was trying to get this big protest up and running against people eating dogs in South Korea. We're looking through the pamphlet, and I read out: "You cook the dogs up in a big dog-meat barbecue. That's going to be the band name, Dog Meat BBQ."

The next day, I get up to the microphone: "We are no longer Backstreet Jihad. We are Dog Meat BBQ!"

By the time we were finished, people were chanting, "Dog Meat! Dog Meat!"

I thought, *This is definitely working.*

Don Ellis: Dog Meat was great because they were politically eye-opening and funny. It was a great kind of extension of the Dead Kennedys without the anger. By the *Frankenchrist* record, the Dead Kennedys were so loud and fast. It was very aggressive, which I loved, but what was great about Dog Meat was that they were funny. The lyrics were strong, and you just couldn't deny any of their songs.

We learned a lot about the world by going to their shows and listening to their music. That was really important at that time. The whole world had gone completely vapid. Tune out. Don't worry about stuff. You get your political soul just kind of springing to life at seventeen and eighteen.

Mike O'Brien: Peace-A-Chord was a chance at exposure and a tribute to the fact that we made really good money when we got back together in the '90s. We would pack bars because the young kids who saw us at Peace-A-Chord were then old enough to get into bars. That festival built an audience for a lot of bands. It also got people out of the mindset that infected this place still well into the mid-1980s: the crowd doing original music weren't real bands. The real musicians were the cover bands. In this town, that's the way the vast majority of people thought. If you're a local St. John's band and you're writing and playing your own music, there's something wrong with you. Even the most successful of the original music bands couldn't draw anywhere near what the cover bands were getting.

Peace-A-Chord was a big part of changing people's idea that you can do something different. If you do your own songs, you don't have to pretend you're from America or England somewhere and avoid any mention of Canada. Certainly, you wouldn't mention Newfoundland. At that time, there were people who actually said you can't mention Canada in a song. You don't want it to sound too Canadian. You want it to sound American. What is it they used to say? "You have to be universal in your lyrics." That meant you had to be American or British. Now the bands who play original music get the good gigs and make the good money, and the cover bands play in Mount Pearl.

Sean Panting: Two things struck me the most. Dog Meat BBQ's lyrics were hilarious, but they were not stupid. "Star Kist Tunie" was funny, but it wasn't dumb. Dog Meat BBQ could play "Kiss Me Godzilla" and "Johnny Was a Hero" back to back, and it wouldn't be weird.

Wallace Hammond completely blew my mind and continues to do so. For me, he's one of the top three most influential guitar players ever, on the planet. He gets embarrassed because I'm always getting on this topic of conversation. He's a great guitar player. What I liked about him was: here's a guy with an individual style. What it taught me was I don't need to pretend to be a guy from Los Angeles or London or New York or Toronto. I don't have to be that shit. I can write a song about downtown or the Mall or school or whatever is in my immediate surroundings.

There were two things about Wallace's rig. He had a distortion box made out of a Maxwell House Coffee can. [...] Before I had even heard anything, I see this Maxwell House Coffee can with knobs on it. I'm like, *This guy is awesome. I don't even care if he can play or not.* He had a speaker set up on a trolley your teacher would put the TV and VCR on in school. He was using the speaker to get all this feedback. He'd sort of move around, and he knew exactly where to step to get the right sounds. This is not a guy who had bought *Guitar for the Practicing Musician* and worked out how to play "Living Loving Maid" and Yngwie Malmsteen riffs. This is a guy coming at it from a way different angle. He's completely himself.

Dog Meat BBQ was ugly guys in T-shirts. At the time, hard rock was all frizzy hair and spandex pants. Mike O'Brien was not frizzy hair and spandex pants.

There's theatricality about them, too. They're out there singing "Tanya, Whatcha Doing with That Seal?" while they're clubbing fake baby seals. [...] If you threw these guys in the middle of Andy Warhol's studio, they'd fit right in. It's punk rock, but it's also art. These guys were making art, and they were serious about it, but they were drunk and hilarious, too.

Mike O'Brien: Sometime later in 1986, we started recording another cassette. In the meantime, Wallace had kept Vikki-Beat going and was releasing cassettes by other groups. Wallace was working as the sound man at the Corner Stone. That's where we recorded the basic tracks for *Dead Dogs of the Summer of Love*.

That was the first of the Vikki-Beat tapes that actually sold well. It was the first one people came into Fred's Records looking for.

Sean Panting: Dog Meat BBQ was the game-changer. That's kind of when my brain slipped over [...] to not even caring what's going on outside of the city limits. What was going on in St. John's became the world to me.

THE HOUSE OF DREAMS

Danny Thomas: When Mom and Dad split up, we sold our nice four-bedroom house on Leslie Street to move into a nine-thousand-dollar house at 15 Fleming Street. Back then, Hayward Avenue was one of the drug capitals of St. John's. It was sort of Buckmaster Circle, Chalker Place, and Hayward Avenue. These were places you wouldn't step foot in unless you wanted to get your face beat off, and we lived three doors down from it. Fleming Street was probably more depressed than others. Property was cheap, so a lot of artists lived in the area, too. In downtown St. John's, there was no middle class.

Louis Thomas *(musician)*: My parents are Robbie and Reg Thomas. We emigrated from England in 1972. When we first got to Newfoundland, we lived out of tents on the Manuels River because Dad was out of work. I'm three years older than Danny, so my memory might be a little bit better [than his]. Our family was sort of all over the place: Fitzpatrick Avenue, Warbury Street, Leslie Street. We shuffled around a lot. My parents divorced when I was fourteen. My brothers moved to Fleming Street with my mom, and I went to live with Dad in Cowan Heights.

Danny Thomas: My father spent a lot more time out of the house than he did in the house, and Mom finally said, "Enough is enough." A lot of things changed in our lives. It was just at the point of sensible. Both parents worked. We seemed to be no worse off than any of our friends. And then everything kind of went to shit. It definitely affected us, me probably the most because I was just ten years old. It was sort of like the walls came crashing down around me.

Lil Thomas *(musician)*: Fleming Street was a very small house. It might have been nine hundred square feet, and that's being generous. Money was the main reason Mom bought the place. With just her salary [working at the Maritime History Archive], I'm sure that was all she could afford.

Danny Thomas: I can only describe the house as a complete disaster. There was no running water for most of the winter because the pipes would freeze and burst. On a regular basis, we would have to melt snow from the backyard to wash our hair for school. We had a wood stove to heat the place. There were two electric radiators in the kitchen, but the plywood was so damp that the heat would get sucked out like a vacuum. We just stopped using them altogether. It wasn't uncommon to wake up in the morning with a drink of water frozen next to you on the nightstand. It was pretty perishing. Your odds of staying warm were a little better when other people started staying at the house because they would help keep the wood stove going the whole night. I'm sure there were lots of people who had no hot water and no love. At least we had the important things.

Lil Thomas: My mom was very open to people hanging out and coming over. She was [...] warm and welcoming to the neighbourhood strays that were having troubles at home or who just needed some friendship and a shoulder to cry on. A lot of people certainly gravitated towards my mom and that house. I think people thought they were part of something really special going on there. There was definitely alcohol and drugs involved in that scene. But I wouldn't say anything too heavy, just your typical kind of smoking marijuana and doing mushrooms and drinking. It was the kind of place where people could do that stuff without being judged and still get excited about life and have interesting conversations about how they were going to change the world. For some people, they had to fight through adversity to find a positive outlook on life. I do think people found that kind of haven at Fleming Street.

Danny Thomas: Over the years, the house became a real home for so many of our friends. Even though we had nothing, we shared it with them, and those people will be with us forever. They're still considered our sisters and brothers, and that's what made that house what it was.

My mother's influence on people was astonishing. I guess I knew this all along, but I realized it more and more as she got sick [with cancer], and people were coming out of the woodwork, sort of confessing to us things about her. That house had a real character and a personality. Dreams became reality for a lot of people who stayed there. Their dreams were not to get smacked in the face when they went home or not to get thrown out for the weekend. Fleming Street created a community of dreamers. But they didn't just dream. They actually did it.

Lois Brown *(actor/playwright)*: I used to call it "the Fleming Street Freeschool." I can remember crediting that in my master's thesis. I felt like I learned a lot about teaching from hanging out there. You could see that Robbie tolerated a lot of bullshit. She called everyone on the bullshit, but you didn't have to be punished because of the bullshit. She had a remarkable ability to tolerate kids and allow for them to grow up.

Charlie Tomlinson *(actor)*: When I think of that time, I always think of the group of young people around the Thomases and the great matriarch that was Robbie Thomas. Fuck anybody who doesn't agree with that. Robbie was not an easy person, and nor am I. Who was she? She was a single mother. She was a very practical person. She loved and enjoyed life. She was an eater of life.

Lois Brown: It was good times. It was legendary times. For me, the best times were around the Corey and Wade's Playhouse and Tough Justice stuff. Me, Charlie, and Robbie used to go because she was there to support Danny. This was early, before the boys could really play. I remember walking up and down the Gonzaga gymnasium arm in arm with Charlie and Robbie while the bands played. I used to always find it so weird that the punk bands could even get into a school with that kind of music.

Louis Thomas: Lots of teenage girls came through the house. Maybe they felt that Mom was a good sounding board compared to their own parents. For them, she was someone who was very non-judgmental. I don't know if they were getting advice from her. They were going through puberty and various phases of their lives and difficulties with their parents. Considering we were all in the house smoking dope and there was people staying over all the time playing music, they probably saw Mom as a pretty cool and relaxed person. But I'm just speculating. I suspect Dana Warren or Sheilagh O'Leary would probably give you a better idea.

Danny Thomas: Dana's father had passed away. I don't think her life was going too well. She became very attached to our lives. There was lots of love at Fleming Street, and I think that's what she needed more than anything, and we became extremely close friends. She was friends with Lil through a few of his high school buddies. She became a friend of mine when we started Peace-A-Chord. Louis was the stubborn mule that Dana related to 100 per cent because she's the exact same way. I don't really know when she came into our lives, but she's never left.

Sheilagh O'Leary: When Dana moved out of her parents' house on Gill Place, she was like the adopted daughter. This was before my time; I came along after. She was a sister to those boys. She moved in and learned how to cook and all that stuff through Robbie. [...] She's had a long family history with the Thomases. My experience growing up was very different. I had a sheltered kind of middle-class family life. But Dana grew up in the bowels of downtown.

Lois Brown: It wasn't just the fact that Robbie cared about those kids. It was the way that she cared for them. It wasn't like she just said, "Oh, Dana can live at my house now." I mean, she went and visited with Dana's mother and thought about things and made really conscious decisions.

Dana Warren *(activist)*: High school felt like a river that was rushing by, and I was trying to hang onto the banks. It felt like if you were a teenager, you were a fuck-up. I got very involved in [the] politics of being different than the hockey players and the cheerleaders. I felt like a minority for sure. I think some of that was self-prescribed, looking back on it now.

High school was wicked and hard. My father died when I was fifteen, which was a springboard for me really rejecting a lot of what was going on around me and just really questioning my life and where it was and what mattered. It really set me on the path of thinking, *I'm floating alone in the world*. Teenage angst is, on some levels, a myth. Not every teenager goes through teenage angst. But I was a classic case for sure.

Louis Thomas: Fleming Street was a central hangout point. Some were still in school; some were not in school. Some were definitely in transition from quitting school or trying to leave their parents' house.

Danny Thomas: A lot of people were hanging out at the house and hanging out on the front step and hanging out on the back parking lot. It had definitely turned into a flophouse for the wayward youth of St. John's. And we had a pretty open-door policy about it, too.

THE HOUSE OF DREAMS

Lil Thomas: The second floor of the house was divided into two bedrooms. We basically took it over as our bedroom and jam space. Danny and I came home from school one day, and we literally started kicking the wall down in between the two rooms. It was actually really hard to kick down because the house was about a hundred years old, and it was all this old, petrified spruce. It got so brittle with age that it was almost like fibreglass. It took a bit of an effort to tear the wall down. We got it cleaned up and put a carpet over the crack. There was no thought at all about the structure of the house. The floors were already pretty sloped, and then we kicked out what was probably a significant support wall.

For a while, we actually had two drum kits up there because both Louis and Brian Gregory were playing. People used to come by and listen to the music. That seems to be what we spent most of our time doing. We were pipping off school and playing music in the afternoon and luring in the women from Holy Heart of Mary.

Jon Whalen *(musician)*: Fleming Street was central to a whole whack of different scenes. Robbie ran a little restaurant downtown [the Continental Café] that all the older bohemian types went to. She knew a bunch of them, and her kids were involved in the music scene. They had their own extended gang of friends. You could go to their house and do pretty much whatever the fuck you wanted. Hot knives in the kitchen. Drop acid and stay up. Mom was a steady presence and solid influence on her boys, and they all turned out fine, but she had her own social life and ran a business. Me and Lil Thomas, the middle son, were good buddies from school. There was a large extended crowd of people who showed up for parties. Friday and Saturday nights there might be thirty or forty kids in the house […]. Most nights of the week there would just be a few of us. I would've been in that gang who was there pretty much all the time. Robbie was great to us, man. She put up with a lot.

Lil Thomas: It's hard to talk about my mom because she passed away a few years ago, and it's always a little bit emotional. When I look back at that time, I can see that there was a huge transition taking place in her life. In the few years following her separation from my father, she had to find her independence, her own individuality, her own voice, and her own place in the community. She got involved in the community surrounding the LSPU Hall. Those were the people who she hung out with and partied, the generation of artists who came before us.

Lois Brown: Robbie was my best friend for a long time, and I was really close to Danny when he was growing up. She was really good friends with Anita Best, and she used to go out with Frank Barry, the actor. She was part of the Sheila's Brush crew of people. Robbie would come over for supper, and she would bring Danny with her because he was the youngest. When my partner and I broke up, I started going to her house for supper.

Dana Warren: I worked at the Continental Café, as did Jon Whalen, which was on Water Street. All the boys worked there. It was a coffee shop, but Robbie opened the restaurant in the evenings on Thursdays, Fridays, and Saturdays. She was a trained chef. When the restaurant first started, you could bring your own wine. It was the only place in town where you could do that. It was a great restaurant, and it lasted for a very long time.

Johnny Fisher: Danny robbed the café. He took all the money, went to the airport, bought a ticket, and flew to Toronto.

Danny Thomas: At the time, my mother wasn't running it anymore. There was another woman who had come on as a partner, and she was managing it. Technically, I didn't take the money from my mother. I took the money from somebody who was probably nicer to me than my mother would have been. My mother would've had me thrown in jail.

On Sunday afternoons, Louie would practise his drums, and he would use the pillows off my bed to mute his kick drum. I wrote a letter saying where I'd gone and left it on the pillow. At three o'clock in the morning, I phoned Buhler: "We're going to Toronto."

Mike Buhler: Danny was washing dishes at the Continental. Being the bright young spark that he was, he decided to rob the restaurant. I didn't know anything about it. He called me the next morning. You'd think I would've been smarter.

Danny Thomas: Mike took his mother's truck, and we stayed at the Old Fort out on the highway with a pocketful of money. The next morning we were going to drive to Toronto. But we quickly realized that was a stupid plan, drove back to town, headed for the airport, and jumped on a plane.

Mike Buhler: We're in the air and Danny said, "I left a note for Mom."
I was like, "Really? Are you kidding me?"

We had a few hours before we landed, and I was freaking out in my seat. I knew we were going to get caught. The plane landed, and the flight attendant announced, "Mike Buhler and Danny Thomas, please wait at the gate."

We stepped off the plane and the cops were waiting for us.

Danny Thomas: Mom went to the restaurant early that morning and found out the place had been broken into, called Louis, and Louis said, "I just found a note from Danny. He's moved to Toronto. He'll call us when he gets there."

Just as this conversation was happening, Mike Buhler's father called our house looking for him. "Well, there's a note here saying Danny's gone to Toronto. I wonder if Mike is with him?"

Someone put two and two together and called the cops.

What made it worse was that we got stuck in Toronto for a few days before the cops from St. John's could come and get us. Both of us were underage; they couldn't put us in a holding cell. So they took someone's office and tossed a couple of mattresses on the floor. We spent two days in Mississauga at the regional police station. Coincidentally, a year later, my father lived right across the street from the station.

Mike Buhler: They sent two RNC [Royal Newfoundland Constabulary] officers to bring us home. One of them ended up being a [...] friend to me down the road when I needed help with some other things.

Danny Thomas: We got on the plane to come home, and there was a whole bunch of the theatre crowd there: Phil Dinn and Mercedes Barry, Margaret-Anne McCarthy, and Greg Thomey. As usual, in their half-drunken shit-disturber fashion, they decided it would be a good idea to get pissy with the cops. I said, "No, this is totally fair. We should be in handcuffs." That seemed to settle them down.

Mike Buhler: All our friends were waiting for us at the St. John's airport. The police just walked us through the lot of them and out to the squad car. Danny and I waved and yelled "Yahoo!" We went straight from the cop car to the lockup.

Danny Thomas: The following September, Mom [...] said, "I'm going to Mexico." And then she left.

Louis Thomas: I don't know if she was going through some mid-life crisis or soul searching. In hindsight, we should have been really worried about her. Anything could have happened. She could have gotten killed. But Mom was such a survivor that we didn't really think about it. Obviously, we were so caught up in ourselves that we probably didn't pay enough attention.

Danny Thomas: She grabbed her knapsack and hitchhiked across Mexico. We never heard from her for months.

Thom Thorne: Robbie had gone to Mexico and left the three boys in the house alone. When we pipped off school, we all went to Fleming Street. Louis was in charge. Every day that house was full of people from morning to night. You'd get dropped off for school at nine o'clock and walk down to Fleming Street. At some point, you'd head home or just sleep there and go to school the next day. It was basically an open house.

Danny Thomas: I was still attempting to go to school every day, mainly just to get the fuck out of the house. It was mayhem in there all the time. I built a bedroom in the closet under the stairs so I'd have some privacy. It still wasn't very private. Nothing in our house had a door except for that closet.

Danny Thomas: Mom called us the second week of December from a truck stop out on Kenmount Road. She said, "Does anyone have money for a cab?" She was gone from September to December.

Louis Thomas: The clock was ticking to when we had to get the place completely cleaned up. I just remember Mom walking in through the door with the last little sweep of the broom into the dustpan. With the exception of the inside of the house being painted red, from her perspective, we didn't burn the place down. It was still pretty much the way she'd left it.

Lil Thomas: We were being pretty delinquent about school. Mom said, "I can't keep you here anymore. You got to go." I kind of got booted out of the house. I bummed around St. John's for the summer, and I did some couch-surfing. My dad lived in Nova Scotia. I thought, *What the hell am I doing? I got to get my shit together*. I left for Nova Scotia to do my Grade 10 because I had flunked out in St. John's. I just wasn't going to school. The academic thing was not for me. But I was really homesick. I was dating Eileen Lush at the time, and we were trying to kind of keep a relationship going. It was really challenging, especially at fifteen. I hitchhiked back to St. John's in the wintertime, with my guitar and my amp on the side of the highway. When I got back, I started working at Mary Jane's. I went back to Newfoundland after I screwed up in high school for the second time and started working in a restaurant and moved out on my own.

Rhonda Pelley: I was up to the hospital to see Robbie when she was really sick. She said she regretted a lot about the way she was back then. She got a divorce from Reg, she was single for the first time in her life, and she wasn't that old, either. She was younger than I am now when all that stuff was going on.

Louise Moyes *(dancer)*: I lived with Robbie on and off for a long time. I spoke at her memorial service, and I think I said that the boys and the band equipment moved out and the yoga mats moved in. We were teaching yoga in the living room. Let me tell you, this was not Nova Yoga. An Israeli couple had joined the neighbourhood who were way out there. They were drinking their own pee, and we were doing yoga with them.

I'd known Robbie since I was four. When she was still with Reg, they were friends with Mom and Dad through the theatre community, and they would come over to our house. But Robbie was a very different Robbie then. She seemed more prim. This was the early '70s. I have a vague memory of her in a pin skirt and high-heel shoes. But sometimes I wonder if that is a reconstructed memory. It could have been an illusion. Robbie was always a free spirit, a beautiful free spirit. But she was a substitute mother for me. Not a substitute, because I had a mother, but another mother.

Becky Moyes *(activist)*: Robbie was a mother to everybody, and then she morphed into a friend.

THE GANG OF FOUR
PEACE-A-CHORD PART 1

Gene Long *(activist/politician)*: In the early '80s, the Newfoundland and Labrador Arts Council was trying to build capacity and profile. [...] I'd been away and came back, and this position at the Arts Council was there, and it was sort of tailor-made for someone who was coming home and needing to find work. We did that for six or eight months, and then the funding ran out. My girlfriend was working at NIFCO [Newfoundland Independent Filmmakers Co-operative], and I was working at the Arts Council. She then got a job offer in her hometown of Winnipeg to coordinate a music festival. I went there with her because the Arts Council job, which had kept us in rum and Coke for six months, was over, and it wasn't clear what was going to happen next.

I was out in Winnipeg and didn't like the cold. Someone told me that there was a job opening at OXFAM back in St. John's. I applied from Winnipeg, where I was doing some volunteer and project work, but I was mostly hanging around the house, not sure that I wanted to stay there. I did the interview over the phone and got the job.

The position was for Development Educator. My responsibilities included running a school-based education program that would support OXFAM's fundraising. But it also promoted awareness through the school system, with the support and cooperation of the school boards and the various local principals and teachers around the province. They would agree to have an OXFAM speaker come in for an afternoon and show a film to a couple of high school social-studies classes and maybe give a talk. We might also have a fundraising event in the cafeteria.

I was able to get the job with OXFAM because I had been politically active in Vancouver. A peace movement emerged in the early '80s in response to the increasing tension in the Cold War and the nuclear arms race. The

American and NATO decision to station massive amounts of cruise and Pershing missiles in Western Europe and the Canadian government's agreement to host the testing of cruise missiles in Alberta meant that Vancouver was home base for the peace movement.

During this time, their annual peace march grew to [...] fifteen thousand people, which was seen to be a great big success. Then in the spring of 1982, the march went to something like a hundred thousand people.

Within weeks, there was this sequence of three major demonstrations. One was a student demonstration against fee increases and cutbacks, and the second was the peace movement. The third was a very large demonstration in solidarity with the Sandinistas' Nicaraguan revolution, and against the American intervention in El Salvador and Guatemala [...].

I was well positioned to do an interview for a job at OXFAM. If the fit was okay with them, I was ready to come back and commit myself.

Gene Long: I grew up in St. John's—I'm a townie. My parents were from very small communities, Conception Bay and Bonavista Bay. I was born in Gander, but I played hockey for Gonzaga. I had local St. John's credentials, which OXFAM didn't necessarily have.

I can actually date when I started at OXFAM. It was the first week of October 1983. The reason why I remember is because within a couple of weeks of me starting there, this major international story broke, the Ethiopian famine in the horn of Africa.

We were entering the era of "Tears Are Not Enough," by Northern Lights. This was the beginning of rock stars raising money for causes they believed in. The first half of the '80s became [...] synonymous with this explosion of social consciousness in the music industry. When I think of those people, I think of Bob Geldof and the massive success of Live Aid. The famine crisis in Ethiopia went on through the winter, and my work as a development educator kind of took off. Travelling the province talking about the famine in Ethiopia, I didn't have to spend a lot of time reaching out to young people. In fact, we were trying to keep up with the incoming requests for speakers and people wanting to do fundraising. Newfoundlanders, like the folks in the north, are famous for their proportional generosity. A lot of that came through the door of our modest little operation on Duckworth Street.

The other campaign that OXFAM was already leading on internationally was anti-apartheid and the campaign to get Nelson Mandela out of jail. That was another big issue that artists were lending their voices and music to. Little Steven created Artists United Against Apartheid and produced this video that was promoting a very specific issue, the boycotting of Sun City, a giant entertainment complex that was a big draw for performers going to South Africa. Sun City was somewhere between Johannesburg and Cape Town, in a sort of remote area in the so-called "coloured territory."

Little Steven organized this boycott campaign, wrote a song called "(Ain't Gonna Play) Sun City," and got a bunch of musicians together to perform it. I had the video, took it to high schools, and jacked it up. I remember playing it over and over in high school history and social studies classes. I think the video included a documentary of about a half-hour, but it also had the four-minute song in there, too. Videos were just beginning to take off. That's kind of the musical context.

Sheilagh O'Leary: Peace-A-Chord did kind of grow out of the back room of OXFAM. Gene Long was one of the people who [...] introduced us to OXFAM. He worked there when the NDP movement was starting to take hold. There were a few people who were kind of connected to both OXFAM and the NDP. I wasn't even interested in politics. But we were shit disturbers, and we wanted to get involved in issues.

Dana Warren: I spent my second year of Grade 10 thinking the world was going to blow up. I failed the first time because my father died and the schools went on strike. High school was mostly a disaster. I was convinced that it was the end. There was Reaganomics. There was the Cold War. There was this standoff feeling. I actually quit high school as a protest against the establishment two days into my final exams, me and about seven or eight of us. I had this one high school teacher, Jim Moore, who kicked my ass. He said, "Are you really this stupid? Why are you doing this?"

Rhonda Pelley: Looking back, that seems like a turning point in our lives. Someone ended up in the dumpster and found copies of the exams. We had them, and we were passing them around studying them. Somehow, [our teacher] Derrick Moore got wind of it. He was dividing and conquering us. I don't think he ever got a name, but we handed over the exams. Not a lot of people wrote those exams. [...]

We all had jobs at the Continental Café. We all had great aspirations. At school, we didn't feel like we were being treated with respect. They didn't take us seriously at all. Dana and I quit. I think Danny quit. Sean Doran quit. Jack Lanphear quit. There was a whole bunch of us.

Jennifer Dick: Derrick Moore knew something was up and called us into the office. I just remember, before they separated us, Barry said, "Don't say a word."

They pressured us really hard for names. I said, "Look, if you want to punish somebody, you can punish me, but I'm not telling you anything. I'm not giving you names; I'm not squealing."

In the end, our grades were penalized. I knew that I was doing really well in a bunch of subjects and that I wasn't going to fail. It was one of those moments where you got to decide what kind of person you are. I remember thinking, *That was the right thing to do.*

Danny Thomas: Our teachers didn't understand us at all and nor did they want to. They just didn't understand we weren't part of the 85 per cent that listened to their garble all day and regurgitated it back to them. We saw through the racism and the sexism going on in St. John's. Five or six fourteen-year-old teenagers had had enough. We saw the hypocrisy that was going on. [...] And that angered us. [...] Doug Warren had his head shop, the Escape Hatch, which sold skin magazines. It obviously gave him a pretty bad reputation with the Catholics. The crazy ones would go from protesting Planned Parenthood and stop off at the Escape Hatch on the way home and throw a few eggs at his place for good measure.

The Catholic Church in Newfoundland had their finger on every pulse. They could change any rule and any law. They could make any cop show up anywhere. In the meantime, half the kids coming out of Brother Rice Junior High were beaten senseless. They were so hypocritical about all the stuff that they were saying. We're talking about Newfoundland in the early '80s. It was a different ballgame. Non-Catholic things weren't good.

Dana Warren: I was basically rebelling against my mother and that household and that life. I mean, I moved out when I was sixteen, probably more out of the pain in my heart than anything else. Looking back, it took a long time to figure that out. I rejected a life, for sure, and what was going on, but I always felt I would break that legacy of poverty. I felt that as a young child. That wasn't going to be my life; it was going to be different for me.

When I read the word "injustice" at OXFAM, I knew what it meant. I knew what poverty meant. I knew what it meant if it was happening in Africa, or if it was happening in St. John's. I related to what was going on. I grew up [in] downtown St. John's. I grew up in a family that had nothing and lived in the neighbourhood that nobody wanted to live in. I was absolutely fully aware of being poor. I think that was far more pronounced when I was young than it is in today's world. Poverty was a big "P" on your forehead.

    I used to babysit for Kay Anonsen when I was thirteen. Kay was part of the theatre scene. She was hanging out with people like Mary Walsh and Rick Boland. Mary and Kay were the best of friends. They were writing plays and doing that kind of work. That was sort of happening right under my nose. I remember that point in my life as being the most curious. Up to then, I was just this kid who was stuck. That to me was the first inkling of an opportunity for a different life. Kay had this amazing collection of records, too. She had the Beatles. She had Pink Floyd. She had all the things that made me think and question. OXFAM's slogan was "Think Globally, Act Locally." I grabbed onto that as a process.

Jennifer Dick: At that point in time, Newfoundland was pretty depressed economically. There wasn't a whole lot of hope. There weren't jobs. Even if you had money, you folded up the tinfoil and put it back in the drawer. That sort of stuff was ingrained in our collective psyche.

Sheilagh O'Leary: I met Dana at a party at [a government member's house]. [The Member of the House of Assembly] was a real freak show of a person. These were high and wild times, I'm telling you. He used to hang out at the gay bar. That's how I knew him, and he had a party at his house on Gower Street. Dana was a couple of years younger than me. Dana was loaded drunk, and someone was hitting on her. I swooped in and rescued her, and then that was it. We became fast friends.

    I can't imagine how it transpired after that, but we got to know each other. We loved music. We wanted to have lots of fun. We were also in the climate of the Cold War. It made for pushing for social justice issues. It was all so straightforward then. We had some real issues that we wanted to deal with. Now it's all so grey. It's hard for today's young people to have something to grab onto.

Gene Long: Jennifer had a very fond connection with Walter Davis. He was retired, but I was never really quite clear on his professional credentials. He was quite a character who was a classic case of a gadfly, someone who is a bit of a troublemaker and who likes to stir the pot. Whenever there was a meeting on an issue of public interest, you could count on Walter to be there. If there wasn't a microphone, he'd make sure that his voice was heard from the floor. Walter was an example of the intergenerational dynamic that occurred when I was in Vancouver. What happens when you have a bona fide social movement emerging, it means that you have a critical mass of the population that represents a substantial and visible manifestation. It's a reflection of the convergence of protest politics and left-wing progressive traditions.

Walter was a Christian activist. The progressive Christian communities contributed immensely to social causes. The Latin American movements were infused with liberation theology as a very explicit and deliberate feature of social revolution. That reverberated around the world where progressive Christians were an essential element in building peace movements. In St. John's, Walter Davis was one person who embodied that. He had that community of like-minded folks who were quite a bit older than the rest of us. Many of them were retired. They were active in the United Church especially. There were some Anglicans. There was the Roman Catholic Office of Social Action. That's where I first met Lorraine Michael. I locate Walter within that tradition. The thing about Walter that was different from a lot of those folks who might have been a bit wary of radical impulses like rock and roll: he had a very clear commitment to working with young people.

Jennifer Dick: Walter Davis was a very important figure in mobilizing local youth towards activism. Walter did things like start the milk campaign from his driveway. The milk thing is everywhere now, and it's national, but it started in Walter's driveway. He wanted kids to drink milk. He did things like go to Sri Lanka and chain himself to the bed of a leper to raise awareness that the disease was curable. He travelled around on boats and dropped off medicine and vaccines to coastal communities.

Somehow, Walter found me. He called me up and said, "I want to meet you." He had a dinner party and [invited me]. Walter really believed anything was possible, and he constantly demonstrated that by his actions and by his accomplishments. He always thought of the bigger picture.

Dana Warren: The crowd around Walter created Ploughshares Youth, which we [became a part of]. I don't know if I was necessarily politically inclined and then got involved, or if I got involved and then became politically inclined.

Gene Long: Ploughshares was the name of the main St. John's peace organization. Ploughshares, as a brand, was connected to Project Ploughshares, an organization on the mainland. It was really an ecumenical Christian organizing vehicle for peace purposes. It's based on an admonition from Isaiah 2:4: "And they shall beat their swords into ploughshares."

Rick Mercer *(actor/writer)*: I don't know if it was my idea or not, but Prince of Wales Collegiate's Ploughshares Youth group decided to change the name. I was certainly on the side of changing the name. There was this other Ploughshares group whose members were literally like seventy or something. Our little group had nothing to do with Ploughshares. We just shared the name.

We decided to change the name, and I got called to the principal's office. Somehow, Walter Davis found out, and he showed up at PWC. He was an elderly man at that point. He was so upset, and he asked to see me. The principal was about to have me hauled out of class when he realized the guy was really angry. And then Walter sat down and wrote this letter to me. He said [changing the name] would besmirch everything that Ploughshares had achieved. I didn't know where this was coming from. You don't think of any consequences like that.

There was a second letter that said he had decided to forgive me, and in fact, he was going to add me to the list of people he was going to pray for.

When Dana and Sheilagh were involved in Ploughshares Youth, I'm sure Walter was a real mentor to those young women. But he was never a mentor to me. I just knew him as the guy who wrote editorial letters in the *Evening Telegram*.

Jennifer Dick: Walter knew that there were hearings coming up for the CRTC [Canadian Radio-Television and Telecommunications Commission], and he wanted us to speak because they were trying to pass one of those silly bills that they like to pass every now and again to try and rein in the CBC. Instead of studying for my exams, I wrote a script for Dana, Tina, and Sheilagh. We all went to the hearing in our berets and sat down in front, demanded to be heard, got up, and kind of spoke our piece. It was a chance for Ploughshares Youth to make an appearance.

Tina Thoden *(activist)*: On our own soil, there was low-level flying in Labrador. Then there was the Berlin Wall and the nuclear arms race. We were learning about the injustices of apartheid. Those are the three issues that kind of instantly come to mind that we rallied behind.

Barry Newhook: The Cold War was ever-present in our lives. There was that sense of impending doom. I was talking to my kids and laughing and joking about that stuff. I said, "When Mom and Dad were teenagers, we knew the world was going to blow up." We didn't think it might. The nuclear clock was on 11:59. It was just a question of when. That was sort of hanging over everybody's head.

Jennifer Dick: We lobbied City Hall to declare St. John's a nuclear weapons–free zone. When it was passed in council, there was a crucial bit of information that we didn't know about. I don't think Mayor Murphy knew either. He said, "A nuclear weapons–free zone in St. John's sounds like a great idea." We were kind of following the model that was happening in other Canadian cities. Unbeknownst to us, Ottawa had already approved NATO nuclear submarines fuelling up in the harbour in the wee hours of the night.

Kent Noseworthy (showgoer/activist): We were being followed around by people with cameras asking us questions and harassing the girls. Tina Thoden's mother actually approached them and told them to get lost. The scuttlebutt was that it was CSIS [Canadian Security Intelligence Service]. We had to stop meeting at OXFAM because, apparently, they found bugs in there. But I don't know if there's any truth to that.

Jennifer Dick: Sitting in the Duckworth Lunch, a friend of mine pointed out that I was being tailed. How he knew that I don't know. But it was true. CSIS was following me around because we had declared St. John's a nuclear weapons–free zone. Ottawa must've thought we had connections with Russia or something foolish like that. I was pulled aside one time trying to cross the border into America and was threatened. This border agent took out all the stuff from my purse and showed me how he could peg me as a problem and have me arrested. I was really frightened. I thought, *Lesson learned*.

Rhonda Pelley: We felt pretty damn cool because we thought we were real outlaws.

Dana Warren: Tim Angel was a little older than us. Somehow Tim touched down in OXFAM. Nineteen eighty-five was International Youth Year, and Tim was going to the World Festival of Youth and Students in Moscow.

Gene Long: I have fond memories of that summer trip. Until now, I had forgotten all about Tim Angel. Canada had a delegation of about 120 people—however many people could fit on a chartered flight. There were twenty-six thousand delegates to the 12th World Festival of Youth and Students. The opening and closing ceremonies were in Lenin Stadium in Moscow, which held like a hundred and twenty thousand people, with a speech from Mikhail Gorbachev.

I went to that festival with some friends from my Toronto student politics days. I didn't like to make a big deal about it at the time because it was a festival sponsored by and supported by Eastern Bloc countries and communist liberation movements in the Third World. Within the leftist tradition there is a Communist Party dynamic that can be very unsettling and a source of great confusion and uncertainty for people who don't know the history or understand it. Red-baiting has always been a thing.

Dana Warren: Because the UN had declared 1985 "International Youth Year," we decided that we would have a peace festival. Music was the universal language. We thought it was important for us to do something that spoke to everybody. We could organize it. We could have a couple of bands play somewhere. We really didn't have any intentions. We thought it would be a great thing to do, and we could also have Ploughshares and OXFAM come and speak. We were having that conversation as part of our youth group meetings.

Gene Long: It was important to recognize what was happening in St. John's with this smallish committee of young people; they were reaching out and getting connected to the world. MTV and music videos were emerging, but it was also the era of pursuing politics and fighting the machine through rock and roll.

I met Dana and Rhonda at one of OXFAM's high school events. I was trying to do some community organizing, and what I found in St. John's was that the response was very strong to all of these intersecting movements.

Dana Warren: OXFAM was very interested in whatever it was that we wanted to do. We were their summer job. Gene was probably hired to engage the community and young people, especially in the movement surrounding International Youth Year. It was a very different time than today. We live in a neo-liberal culture. Do non-governmental organizations even exist anymore?

Danny Thomas: Initially, it was my idea to have a peace festival. I sort of floated the idea as part of our peace group. We were talking about how to create social change, and I said, "How do we get the most people in one place?" I'd been to dozens of marches, and it's just us there. How do we get hundreds of people involved?

Tina Thoden: There was a lot of music activity prior to Peace-A-Chord because we had to raise money to pay for the whole thing. We had to rent band equipment. Musicians helped, because a couple of them worked at Eastern Audio. I have to say, knowing virtually nothing about running a music festival, we threw ourselves into it and learned the hard way.

Dana Warren: Gene motivated us to think about what it would look like and what it would cost. OXFAM encouraged us to apply for grants. I think we got five hundred dollars from OXFAM, and we raised the rest.

Tina Thoden: We would be on the phone all day asking people for donations. All we had to offer was a thank you on the back of the newsletter or space for an advertisement. I thought Dana was awesome. I always say that people who had paper routes as kids are usually really successful later on in life. Dana was one of them. I learned a lot from her; she was bold. She was like, "The worst anyone can say is no."

I thought, *That's valuable*. I shared that with the other volunteers.

We were just making it up as we went along. When you're young, you pretty much live with blinders on unless you're really interested in watching the news. At that time, I don't know that we were. Of course, we loved the bands, and we loved the music, but we were moved by these social justice issues and getting the word out.

Dana Warren: Gene was totally getting off on what we were doing and the fact that we had the energy to do it. We would meet after school [and on weekends] in the back room of OXFAM. I spent more than one all-nighter putting together the programs and photocopying them. We were suddenly a little proud of ourselves.

Gene Long: That's the basic principle of community organizing—enabling the emergence of people's voices.

Jennifer Dick: We had some rather heated meetings. I remember Jon Whalen chasing me around the table because he was going to kill me. We got pretty close to throwing punches at one another. I can't even remember what it was we were fighting about. I think it was the name, Ploughshares Youth, because it came from the Bible. Jon was apoplectic about that. It's just a metaphor. It's bigger than religion. Me, I just kind of liked the whole concept. The whole religion thing is inescapable in Newfoundland. I don't want to be outside of it.

Dana Warren: Leadership from OXFAM was very soft. Where is the festival going to be held? Who is the entertainment? What are people going to eat? What does a full day of programming look like? Do we need permits from the city? All of that prompting was going on.

Jennifer Dick: In the end, the girls took over. Of course, that's what happens: the women organize, and the men do the work. There was the Thomas brothers. Danny and Louis are natural producers. They know how to put a show together. We could rely on them to coordinate all of the bands.

Tina Thoden: The first Peace-A-Chord was six hours long. It was from noon to six in Bannerman Park on a Sunday in the middle of August. The city supplied a small stage. My memory of it was everything ran smoothly. Everyone had a job, and we had lots of volunteers. I think we made buttons. We made a poster. I was the graphics person and artist of the group. We had a handwritten program. On the bottom, we thanked our mothers for supplying the chili.

Kent Noseworthy: You have all these G8 protests, guys in gas masks torching police cars. The protest becomes the story, and the issues are just lost in the mayhem. One thing I was always impressed with—the first few festivals weren't strictly about the bands. It was about coming down with the kids and having a hot dog, getting your face painted, and hearing about all these important social issues. The peace festival was effective in that way.

Jennifer Dick: It crossed boundaries. People from different areas of town showed up at a time when there was still a lot of segregation between the Catholics and the Protestants. There was still that kind of mentality.

Dana Warren: OXFAM, Ploughshares, Ploughshares Youth, the native community, and the Women's Centre were all represented at Peace-A-Chord.

Tina Thoden: You're throwing together a bunch of different people, and you are getting some who may not be interested in the movement. The festival might have had two hundred attendees. We always did a head count. Maybe the first year was preaching to the converted.

Dana Warren: The first Peace-A-Chord immediately prompted the second Peace-A-Chord. It felt to me like everybody started forming a band just so they could play the festival. There was an incredible momentum in the community. We were organizing musical events outside of Peace-A-Chord to raise money. We would take over bars. We would have all-ages shows. We would do things at the LSPU Hall. We would do things at the CLB [Church Lads' Brigade] on Harvey Road. We were holding events that would fund whatever we were doing in the summer.

Gene Long: I didn't know very much about Labrador or anything about the Innu people, but I soon began to learn a lot. Peter [Armitage] and I created a group called the North Atlantic Peace Organization, and sort of replicated the NATO logo, which was flying everywhere in the world.

Tina Thoden: I never spent time in Labrador. When you have someone who has been under a low-level flight describe it to you, it makes it very real. You realize, There's not a whole lot of people defending you. This is something our country is doing and our province is letting happen.

We protested apartheid and low-level flying and the acceptance of nuclear weapons in our lives. We weren't afraid to make a big sign and have a group of thirty-five people stand in front of the Confederation Building.

Sheilagh O'Leary: Peace-A-Chord had already been set for that summer when Barry and I came back from Toronto. We both moved to Toronto together for a little while. I had a couple of short stints there, but I always knew I wanted to stick around St. John's. I came back, and I moved into a house on Prescott Street which doesn't even exist anymore. That's when Barry moved in with me. Our crowds kinds of fused together. The next year, we were in the Peace-A-Chord fold, and that's when I became one of the principal organizers.

Gene Long: I used to call that group of young women—Sheilagh, Tina, Dana, and Rhonda—"The Gang of Four." The Gang of Four was a reference to a group of reformers in the Chinese Communist Party Central Committee. Those young women were a gang of four in their own right.

Dana Warren: Once Peace-A-Chord got established, we always also had an international element. OXFAM would bring in a band from abroad. Amauta came from Central America. Amandla came from South Africa.

Gene Long: For the second Peace-A-Chord, the headliner was Amandla. It translates to "people's power." They were the official cultural troupe of the African National Congress. The ANC was led by Oliver Tambo, who was exiled in London, and Nelson Mandela, who was imprisoned. They were the co-presidents. Amandla was exciting and powerful. As I remember, there was about fifteen or twenty of them. They did gumboot dancing, which was sort of an alternative to traditional drumming, something the apartheid government had banned.

I don't remember how we booked Amandla. That was one of the things that would have kept the girls busy. OXFAM was there to make sure they had housing. Bill Hynd [Outreach Officer for the Atlantic Region] was coordinating the housing piece. I think I was doing a lot of the logistics around programming.

Bill did most of the administrative stuff. For the Amandla tour to St. John's—nobody will probably have the real story on that—it would have cost more than we would have been able to raise. I think they played a second concert, and we did a big fundraiser to try and generate the cost. I think we put them up for two nights at one of the MUN student residences. OXFAM Canada would have been subsidizing the bill.

Jennifer Dick: I drove some of the people from Amandla. There I was in all my whiteness, driving my grandmother's Grand Prix with the sunroof down, sitting next to a man who had been exiled from his home and whose family had been imprisoned and killed and who had seen terrible things.

Tina Thoden: There's power in knowledge. We figured if more teenagers knew [about the issues we were promoting], they might talk about it with their parents. There was and is apathy. People think they can't do anything, so why do anything at all? We had a bit of a mob mentality.

Gene Long: From the very beginning, we had this challenge with working with the city to get the right kind of permit for Bannerman Park that would not be misunderstood by the police. We had to deal with the city on the one hand and the police on the other to make sure that we were covering all of our bases and wouldn't get shut down. There was one Peace-A-Chord— it might have been the second—where we had that problem of noise complaints in the evening. The police wanted to turn off the mics.

Dana Warren: The city didn't want to give us a special events permit. I'm sure it was OXFAM and the older adults in our lives who helped us fight that.

Jon Whalen had gotten arrested onstage; there were noise complaints. But we shut down as per the rules and regulations of the noise bylaw. We were discriminated against for being young and political. The city wanted us to put up fences, but we never charged admission. We always wanted to keep the festival free and accessible to the public. In the end, I think we cut back the time that the bands could play.

It's hard to stop something like Peace-A-Chord when some of our friends who helped out came from well-to-do families. It was no longer just our clique. There was a real divide between those little dirtbag punk rockers who couldn't give two fucks about the noise bylaw and kids like Jody Richardson and Ralph Pastore, whose bands had nothing to do with punk rock.

Sheilagh O'Leary: Jon Whalen was a shit disturber. He was leading the charge and cursing out the cops into the mic. He was smoking joints onstage. Jon was always in your face, but we were all like that to an extent. I remember saying, "Listen, there are narcs out there. There are all kinds of cops in plainclothes out at the back. Just be aware if you're having a draw." The police kept a big hairy eyeball on us for years. Peace-A-Chord was a threat to the powers that be.

I always eluded police; I never got arrested. I always had an angel on my shoulder. I was mouthy, but I was never disrespectful.

We were at an age where we wanted to take on the establishment. I'm still trying to do that. I still have that fire in my belly, and it's the same fire that I had from those days. You mature, and you get older. I got three kids, and I got lots of responsibilities. I have lots of ups and downs in my life. But life is about taking risks and going for it. I don't want to be that person who looks back with regret.

Dana Warren: The festival grew every year, and it didn't change for a long time. It held pretty tightly to the theme of promoting peace and justice in our community. I think the organizing committee became more and more marginalized by the authorities. Youth for Social Justice took over Peace-A-Chord, and it was a strong festival for a long time. What eventually destroyed them was alcohol and the suspicions from adults that they were doing something wrong. By that time, the festival was further removed from OXFAM.

THE FLEMING STREET MASSACRE

Gene Long: There was a great story in the *Globe and Mail* today: "Ontario Judge Rules Toronto Police Entered Home Illegally" (April 14, 2015). It went something like, "The Supreme Court finds police officer was wrong to believe he had a right to stay in the residence while investigating a noise complaint." I read this and nearly spit out my morning coffee. That's precisely the issue that Robbie Thomas's court case was about. A lot of what happened is now a blur, but the important thing is that the case was settled at the Supreme Court after the provincial prosecutor lost two or three lower court decisions. In the end, the Supreme Court of Canada made a very clear ruling that the police had entered Robbie's home illegally.

Robbie Thomas *(mother/businessperson, deceased. From* Provincial Court Proceedings, February 25, 1987*)*: Charlie [Tomlinson] wanted a place to have his birthday party, and he asked me if he could have it at my house. We arranged food and all this sort of stuff, but he did the inviting of people. I had been a bit concerned for two or three days previously because it was Charlie's birthday party. It wasn't me giving a party in Charles's honour. I think he had invited, I don't know, sixty to seventy people, or something like this, but I felt that there was a possibility that if each person who was invited hauled along three or four friends, that we'd end up with far too many people than the house could reasonably hold. I was a bit nervous about it.

Charlie Tomlinson: The party was during the 1986 Victoria Day weekend. It was chaotic, drunk, and full of young people. It was a summer of parties to come. It was the summer of love for that group. I was in my early thirties, and I was doing acid and mushrooms. Maybe I was trying to live the past over again. There was a sense of camaraderie. Were there nights of staying up and going to shows and seeing bands and walking home at five in the morning and feeling like kings of St. John's? Yes. It was a great summer.

Dana Warren: Charlie kind of hung around with a bunch of us: Barry Newhook, Jennifer Dick, Sean Doran. Charlie was having this adult party for his birthday. He was turning thirty-one.

Rhonda Pelley: Who was at that party? Charlie was there, of course. Janis Spence, Mercedes Barry, Graham Howcroft, Robbie. Then there was our bunch: Tim Angel and Duncan Cowan, Dana and Sheilagh. The regular people.

Charlie Tomlinson: I have this clear image, for some reason, of walking past the War Memorial where the young punks hung out. I remember saying, "I'm having a party. Do you want to come?" I didn't even know who some of them were. In those days, I would talk to people. My lot came, the thespian types: Bryan Hennessey and Mary-Lynn Bernard, Cathy and Andy Jones. I have snapshots of memories. I was just starting to get the taste for wine. My parents used to live on Riverview Avenue. I remember going from my parents' house, where I had supper, took my bottle of wine, and went to Robbie's for my birthday.

Louis Thomas: Some of Mom's core friends were up in her room just sort of sitting around chatting. People were rocking on the downstairs floor. The place was a full house party from the front door to the top floor. That's where I got arrested. I basically got pulled down over the stairs and out the door.

Noel S. Goodridge *(Provincial Court Judge, from* Supreme Court of Newfoundland, Court of Appeal, June 5, 1991): During the course of the evening of May 23rd and early morning of May 24th, a large number of people passed through the home of Mrs. Thomas. At the time of the alleged offences, there were various estimates of the number of people in the house, none of them less than 40. Loudspeakers had been affixed to the outside of the house, and music that was being played inside the house was broadcast outside the house into the neighbourhood. Several complaints were received by the police, who subsequently visited the premises. The exterior loudspeakers were disconnected and removed, but the noise emanating from the house continued into the night.

Lil Thomas: The walls in the house were paper-thin. I can't believe there weren't more noise complaints. There certainly were complaints, and the police came around every now and again, but nothing ever got too nasty. I would say that the Fleming Street Massacre was probably a culmination of a lot of different complaints against the place.

Danny Thomas: We'd have parties, and we'd have Figgy Duff's old touring PA stuck up on the roof. In all fairness, the neighbours probably didn't have to make noise complaints. I'm sure the cops could hear the racket up at Fort Townsend. I mean, we were not nice when it came to noise. The neighbours would come over and tell us to shut up, and we'd tell them to fuck off. As soon as they'd leave, we'd start up again. We were rehearsing bands in the house. Stolen Bones rehearsed in there. I jammed in there with Tough Justice. Don't get me wrong. Everything about the Fleming Street Massacre was completely wrong. But we definitely poked the bear a few times.

Lois Brown: Right before everything happened, Connie Hynes left the party, and she phoned and said, "There's a bunch of cop cars and paddy wagons parked tail to nose around the corner. Be careful because something is about to happen."

Charlie Tomlinson: The story goes that there were thirteen police cars on duty that night. Twelve of them were on Fleming Street, and one was in Mount Pearl getting bricks thrown through the front windshield.

Danny Thomas: The police were lined up waiting to come in to raid the place, not to knock for a noise complaint.

Dana Warren: When the police came to the door, most of us were downstairs, dancing our asses off to "Sun City" by Artists United Against Apartheid.

Jon Whalen: Andy and Charlie were the ones who let the cops into the house. Partly the reason why everything the cops did from that moment on was illegal was that they weren't invited into the house by the owner. That's the key to the whole debacle.

Noel S. Goodridge *(Supreme Court of Newfoundland, Court of Appeal, June 5, 1991)*: The issues in the case are (1) whether police officers were unlawfully on the premises of the respondent at the time of the offences hereinafter referred to, and, if not, (2) whether they were acting in the course of their duty. The charges against the respondent related mainly to interfering with the police in the course of their duty.

Tina Thoden: The cops arrived with their backs up. It wasn't a hostile environment they were arriving to, and they were welcomed in. Grown-ups answered the door.

Charlie Tomlinson: I went to the back door; I heard that there were policemen. Because it was my birthday party, I went there feeling somehow responsible. Letting them in was probably the mistake we made. It was a [rabbit-warren] little house. They were taken up the stairs to Robbie's bedroom on the top floor. They're navigating their way through this tiny house crammed with drunk people. They're taken to the top set of small stairs, along a little hallway, up another flight of stairs to a room where Robbie, Mary-Lynn, and Graham were with Mary-Lynn and Andy's baby.

Robbie Thomas *(from* Provincial Court Proceedings, February 25, 1987*)*: We were sitting on the [bedroom] floor, and we were talking. Mary-Lynn and I were the first two people that went up there, because I hadn't seen the baby for a while. The next thing was that Andy came back up the stairs with two police officers and entered the room.

Charlie Tomlinson: I think the police knew instantly that they had just gotten mixed up with a litigious group of people who were sticky about their rights and privileges, as opposed to just a house party with a bunch of drunk university students.

Dana Warren: In the beginning, there were just a couple of police officers. I was a really nosey person. I'm still a really nosey person. As soon as they went upstairs—I didn't know what the hell was going on—I followed them. There were two officers up in the room. They were talking to Robbie, and she was saying, "You have no right to be in my house. Get out of my house!"

Robbie Thomas *(from* Provincial Court Proceedings, February 25, 1987*)*: Officer Power said, "Who is the owner of the house?"

I stood up and said, "I am."

He said, "What's your name?"

I said, "Roberta Thomas."

Then he said something about arrest. That word "arrest"—I just focused right in on that word. Then I got really upset, and I started telling him to please get out of my bedroom, and he didn't. Then other people were saying stuff like, "Have you got a warrant?"

At this point, I don't know if he had hold of me or if I had hold of him, but I think somehow we definitely had hold of each other, and I was going on saying, "Get out of my bedroom! Get out of my bedroom!" I was just saying it over and over and over again because I was very upset at them being in there. I think I was beginning to scream.

Noel S. Goodridge (from Supreme Court of Newfoundland, Court of Appeal, June 5, 1991): Constable Power, the senior officer, directed a few questions towards Mrs. Thomas and received some answers. At some point, Mrs. Thomas ordered the two policemen out of her bedroom. At some point, too, both Mr. Howcroft and Mrs. Thomas became physically involved with the police officers. The evidence is in conflict as to the order in which things happened. According to the statement of facts submitted by the Crown, Mrs. Thomas told the police to leave after a short verbal exchange. The altercation then occurred.

Charlie Tomlinson: I remember Andy saying, "Calm down. Let's be reasonable here. Let's go downstairs and sort this thing out." Up goes the racket, and the policeman must have felt he was in some kind of danger. At that point, people realized just how many police cars were surrounding the house because the boys came in to get their colleagues. The police were doing what they were trained to do, I guess. They got to get their guys out. In the process, they got a lot of lip from a crowd of people who thought the police were fundamentally bad people.

Louis Thomas: I could hear something going on, and I ran upstairs. I shouldn't say the police were physical with my mother. I mean, they were physical with each other. I witnessed all that. I don't remember everything, but I went up and pulled the cop off Mom, and then the cop put the billy knocker at my throat and pinned me down over the desk. Then they put the handcuffs on me. I had a bad wrist, and I somehow must've convinced them I couldn't put my hands behind my back. So they put the handcuffs on the front, and then I just lost it and put my hands together and started swinging. I got punched in the face; I got my tooth knocked out. That's the point where they brought me downstairs.

Danny Thomas: I was on the second floor in my room necking with a girl. All of a sudden, I heard a big pile of thumping upstairs. I knew the baby was up there. When I went up, a six-foot-four police officer was flinging my mother across the room. At the time, I had three big heavy metal rings on my right hand. I clocked the guy. I was no bigger than 115 pounds, and this guy was huge. I mean, he threw my mother across the room. I plowed him and ran as fast as I could.

Dana Warren: Then the house seemed to be flooded with cops. That whole kerfuffle was happening on the top floor. Robbie's screaming, "Leave my son alone! Leave my son alone!" The police arrested Robbie, put the cuffs on her, and then they left her.

Robbie Thomas (from Provincial Court Proceedings, February 25, 1987): I'm not absolutely sure who actually put handcuffs on my wrists, but I think that was after I got knocked over. I got up and sort of went into the melee again, and I obviously got handcuffed then.

Charlie Tomlinson (from Provincial Court Proceedings, February 25, 1987): Gerard ["Flip"] Janes was having a cigarette. The policeman said, "What is that you're smoking?"
   Gerard, imitating a dog, went, "Woof, woof."

Andy Jones (actor, from Provincial Court Proceedings, February 25, 1987): He had barked at them. I told them right at that moment that Flip had the [physical] condition and not to grab hold of him.

Charlie Tomlinson: He was picked up, thrown along the corridor, thrown down the stairs, and then thrown outside. I got very angry. We just had a benefit for Gerard at the Ship Inn to raise money because he had a bad back. What they did to him was just gratuitous and totally unnecessary. I leaned over the rail and asked the policeman his name. That got me a lazy kind of slap in the face. I leaned over, asked him his name, and that got me another smack. He was the last policeman to leave the upstairs. It was like the end of the line. He was the cleanup man or whatever.

Jennifer Dick: The police were bringing a group of people downstairs. The policemen weren't in the best possible shape. I thought, If we could just knock them over, I could pull Robbie out. Tim Angel helped me. I said, "We're just going to knock everybody over, and you grab Robbie."

We had Robbie in the bathroom, and I left to try and find a hacksaw for the handcuffs. I guess I was kind of aware that it was illegal to take somebody's handcuffs off, but it really didn't matter. I couldn't stand the thought of Robbie in handcuffs. It was too much for me. She was somebody I loved.

I wasn't able to get back to the bathroom because I kind of got caught up in the melee. I'm not sure how, but I found myself outside. Mike Buhler played rugby. There was a policeman coming to arrest me, and Mike picked me up, threw me over his shoulder, and ran. I remember seeing the policeman getting smaller and smaller in the distance. I thought, *Thank you, Mike.* What a great thing to do. We waited around the corner for the paddy wagons to leave. Mike really saved my bacon.

Robbie Thomas (*from* Provincial Court Proceedings, February 25, 1987): I sat down on the side of the tub, and I stayed there. I think I suddenly realized what was going on. I was sort of just sitting there with my head in my hands feeling upset.

Danny Thomas: From the bathroom window the street looked like one of those huge biker brawls you see in the movies. Dana and Tina were getting beat up in the parking lot. Our friend Brian Gregory had a cast on his leg. They were beating him up, too. There was a bunch of cops who just put their hands up in the air. They were like, "I got nothing to do with this."

I jumped out the bathroom window, onto the roof and then the ground, grabbed Brian, and then we both got pummelled.

Kent Noseworthy: I pulled up on my motorcycle, and it was mayhem. People were running and screaming. Dana Warren was down on the lawn, and she was handcuffed and screaming. You knew Jon Whalen was around because you could hear him above everyone else. He was pounding on the back door of the paddy wagon, and me and Sean Doran went over and let everyone out. Jon had nothing on his feet. He was handcuffed, running down the street barefoot.

I wasn't in the house when the police started busting heads. I was out getting chicken.

Louis Thomas: A lot of people just ran. Obviously, when you're sixteen or seventeen, if you're at a party and cops show up, you run.

Barry Newhook: Jon took off down over the hill, and the cop had to stop because he was all out of breath. Jon yelled back, "Thank God for Ches's [fish and chips]!"

Tina Thoden: This huge cop had Dana, one of my best buddies. He had her by the arms, and she was screaming, "You're hurting me!" He was putting her into the police van. I went to her defence and jumped on the cop's back.

He went, "You—obstruction!"

The next thing I know, I'm in the police van with everyone else.

Dana Warren: I was in love with this boy. I remember the cops putting him on his knees and handcuffing him. They were just so verbally mean and abusive. It was like, "You're fucking under us now." They were so very authoritarian and frightening.

Rhonda Pelley: I was screaming at one young cop, "Do you know that they're beating people?" He looked bewildered, almost scared. It was as if he was in the dark about what was going on.

Charlie Tomlinson (*from* Provincial Court Proceedings, February 25, 1987): I was arrested for asking a policeman his name. I remember going up to him, not advancing, maybe taking a step. He was bareheaded. As I recall, he was cut. He was tense. He was excitable, and he was angry. "What is your name, officer?" Nothing. He stopped, and we made eye contact. He advanced towards me, and I can't remember if it was a word or a gesture he gave me by which I understand that if I said this again he was going to arrest me. I thought, *Shag it.* "What is your name?" He handed me to another officer who opened the door. I got in the car. There was no resisting going on. But that was what I was charged with.

Jon Whalen: In the end, twelve people got arrested and hauled off. It all started over a noise complaint.

Noel S. Goodridge (*from* Supreme Court of Newfoundland, Court of Appeal, June 5, 1991): The charges against the respondent arise out of these events and may be summarized as follows: 1. obstructing Constable GW Power in the course of his duty; 2. providing Constable Power with false information; 3. assaulting Constable Power in the course of his duty; 4. assaulting Constable RG Rumbolt in the course of his duty; 5. assaulting Constable IJ Layden in the course of his duty; 6. damaging handcuffs, property of the Government of Newfoundland and Labrador.

Lil Thomas: I was living on Gower Street, and I actually left [the party] before the police showed up. I was having a bit of a spat with my girlfriend. I headed back down to Gower Street, and I got a phone call about an hour later: "Your whole family is in jail."

Robbie Thomas (*from* Provincial Court Proceedings, February 25, 1987): I was probably in the bathroom about ten minutes. When I came out, everybody had gone. I don't mean everybody had gone, but there were no police officers in the house, as far as I could see. A lot of people had cleared out downstairs. I think all the police in the cars and the people who had been arrested had all left. Mary-Lynn was talking about going down to the police station and finding out about Andy, and she said to me, "Robbie, do you want to go down?"

I was humming and hawing, and I had the handcuffs on. I guess I decided it was idiotic to go down to the police station with a set of handcuffs on. I was sitting down on the chesterfield, and there was a young guy who said, "I've got something. I'll try and get them off." I guess he had tools out in his truck. He had a hacksaw, and he had a pair of vice-grips. Someone must have taken the handcuffs for a souvenir, because I didn't see them after.

Danny Thomas: When we went to the lockup, myself and Sean Doran ended up in a cell together. That seemed to be the story of our lives. Just to be an asshole, I said, "Get me out of here. I'm not old enough to be in here." All I wanted was get in front of the cop who had instigated everything.

I sat in the lobby of the lockup downtown. He came in, and I started right in on him going, "You know, you're a fucking psychopath. How did that punch in the face that I gave you feel?" I was only a little dirt bag, and he was this big brutal cop. He was literally twice the weight of me. I wanted him to punch me in the face in front of the guards. Because then there was no way around it. I pushed him, and I pushed him. But he wouldn't go.

Tina Thoden: I had my mother's wedding ring on. My parents were divorced. At the lockup, the police were getting us to hand over all of our personal belongings, and I remember taking the ring off my finger and putting it on my toe. It was this little moment of rebellion. Not that jumping on a cop's back wasn't a moment of rebellion, but it wasn't something I thought about doing beforehand.

Robbie Thomas (*from* Provincial Court Proceedings, February 25, 1987): Later that same night, somebody was looking out the window and said the police were back. There was a knock at the door, and I said, "It's okay. I'll go and answer it."

I opened the front door and there were two officers on the top step and probably one or maybe two further down. I said, "What can I do for you?"

These hands came through the door, and somebody said, "This is the bitch that we want."

Lois was there in the front porch saying, "You can't arrest this woman. You've got both her sons."

Their reply was, "Well, we might as well make it a match set."

Lois was following me down to the wagon, and then she got arrested. One of the officers said something like, "I suppose you are one of those peace people, too, are you?"

By this time I was in the paddy wagon, the police van, and the officer said to me, "Get in there, you whore."

Dana Warren: I was crying in my cell thinking, *What the fuck is my mother going to say?* I was hurt, and I was freaking out. I was a child who had been arrested. They offered us bologna for breakfast, and I said, "But I'm a vegetarian!"

Lois Brown: I'd never been in the lockup before. On the other side of the hallway were Charlie and Gene Long. Robbie and I were in the women's side, and Dana and Tina Thoden were with us. Robbie was like, "I really don't like it here. I don't even have my jail clothes on." I remember her saying that a million times: "I'm dressed for a party, not for a jail."

Charlie Tomlinson: Was it a great travesty? Maybe. Was anybody killed? No. Did we sing "Happy Birthday, Dear Charlie" in the St. John's lockup? Oh, yeah.

Lois Brown: Danny demanded to be taken to juvenile detention just up from Pleasantville. When we went to get him the next day, Tim Angel said, "Tell Danny his brother Tim is here."

Danny's like, "I don't have a brother Tim." He decided he was staying because he was watching TV. He was relaxing and couldn't be bothered.

Danny Thomas: I think you had to be eighteen to be in the lockup. When everyone got let out the next day, they were like, "Where the fuck is Danny?" They couldn't find me. They didn't know where I was. I went to juvie, but you can't get out from there until Tuesday because you got to go to Family Court first. Tim Angel came in saying he was my brother. I was the only person in there. I had already charmed all the guards. I was sat there watching TV in an armchair, and I had a bit to eat. I wasn't even in a cell.

I was like, "This is great, man: free food, nice armchair. They got all the channels." I was perfectly happy. I didn't have to clean up after the party.

Charlie Tomlinson: The next day, there was this kind of post-mortem of the event on Robbie's patio with everybody quite hungover.

Lois Brown: Robbie said, "The worst thing about the situation is that this is all people will talk about for the next six months, and it's going to be so boring."

I was teaching [at Prince of Wales Collegiate], and I had to phone my principal and tell him that I had been put in jail. I had to phone my dad and tell him, and that was hard. I remember him saying, "You must've done something wrong."

I said, "Hold on, Dad. Who do you trust? Me, your daughter, who you've known all your life, or the police, who you don't know at all? I'm telling you I didn't do anything."

There was a long pause, and he said, "I believe you." I guess that was enough for him.

Our argument was that we wouldn't have resisted if the police weren't trying to arrest us for no good reason. You can't just enter someone's home and arrest people for nothing.

Sheilagh O'Leary: It was an obvious attempt [by the police] to put the kibosh on a wild and woolly community of people. I think that's what the whole thing was about—making a statement.

Louis Thomas: It felt like the police were sort of teed up. They were positioned that night to deal with the situation once and for all. Maybe they thought there was something else going on.

Gene Long: Whether there was a sustained harassment outside of that one event, I don't know. I can't really comment on that. I would take it at face value, whatever those guys have to say about their own personal experiences as young people being harassed by police. I wouldn't be at all surprised they were identified and profiled in some way as the kids who ran the peace festival. But I don't think it was a very sophisticated campaign. I think it was more like asshole police officers pissing off kids who were doing their own thing in the community. But what else is new?

Dana Warren: That party was a huge event because the adults in the game said, "No, what you've done is not acceptable." They fought the charges. Jon's father, Norm, was the lawyer.

Norm Whalen (*lawyer, from* A Panel Discussion of R. v. Thomas: A Thirty-Year Reunion of the Fleming Street Massacre): For me, this happened thirty years ago, when my son, Jon, got me out of bed at five o'clock in the morning to tell me he had just come from a party at Fleming Street. Sometime after that, I was retained by Robbie Thomas and a group of others. Gene Long was represented by Jack Harris. One young gentleman pleaded guilty before he knew what was happening. It's unfortunate. Flip Janes was definitely not guilty. Beyond that, he was innocent. That's not something all of us can say.

Andy Jones (*from* A Panel Discussion of R. v. Thomas: A Thirty-Year Reunion of the Fleming Street Massacre): It's a perfect example of how the police are asked to do so much sometimes. It's the front lines of democracy. I don't know how much training they had. At that moment, you [would] have to say, "It doesn't matter that I'm being humiliated. The law is not being humiliated. It'll look bad if I got to back off." Man, that's a hard thing for a human being to do in a situation like that.

Dana Warren: All through that process, we wanted to raise money to help pay the lawyers. That's how the Fleming Street Massacre Blues Band got started.

Jon Whalen: As the singer, I got arrested at Peace-A-Chord for talking about police brutality in Montreal. That's where I had been living. A cop shot a Black kid from my neighbourhood right between the fucking eyes in the police station parking lot. That cop had a racist history against other

Black folks. He had turned up in the news only a few months earlier for beating a Black paraplegic Concordia professor into a coma and got a reprimand. But none of that was allowed to figure into his trial.

I was talking about this stuff in between songs at Peace-A-Chord. The police charged me with creating a disturbance for shouting and swearing in public.

Dana Warren: Jon's father really came down hard on us. He said, "Don't be so stupid. You guys are smarter than this. We're in the middle of a court case."

Jon Whalen: The case became the test for something known as "castle law." When can the police enter your home, and when do they have to leave? The two policemen were brought into the house by Andy and Charlie—not Robbie, the homeowner.

Charlie Tomlinson: The policemen had been brought in by "agents of the homeowner." But once Robbie told the police to leave, it's very clear in law that they had to go.

Norm Whalen (from A Panel Discussion of R. v. Thomas: A Thirty-Year Reunion of the Fleming Street Massacre): In this situation, the police were asked to deal with a noise complaint. Under the noise bylaw, they have a duty to try and do something, but they effectively have no real authority other than to ask you to turn down the music or to issue you a summons.

When you review the [court] transcript you'll find that there are, in fact, three incidents. The first one was at 12:52 [a.m.] when Constable Marrie and Constable Whalen went to the house. At 1:57 [a.m.], Constables Power and Rumbolt went to the house. And, at 1:25 [a.m.], a large number of police officers and cars descended on the property.

Two gentlemen invited them in. They say, "We want to see the owner." And they're taken to the owner. When they get to Robbie Thomas's bedroom on the top floor, she's there with a few friends and a baby. As [the police] start to say what they're there for they're asked to leave. But at one point [during his testimony], Constable Power indicates that he's getting information. I asked him [at trial], "What information? You know who owns the house."

He said, "Well, we needed to get her date of birth." Obviously, that wasn't required information for anything.

Eventually, as the people were going down the stairs they fell. I also remember when Andy Jones was giving evidence. He was like the peacekeeper. [...] He tried to calm [the situation] down. [...] Having given his evidence, he was being cross-examined by John Byrne, who did the original trial [...]. But there's an omission in the transcript. As Andy was going down [the stairs], the group fell. At some point, he was hit on the head by something hard. During cross examination, Mr. Byrne said, "You didn't really see who hit you. It could have been anyone."

Andy was quiet for a while. And then the humour [in him] came out. "Yes, it could have been anybody. It could have been a dear friend who hit me on the head with a stick."

Jon Whalen: We beat the charges in Provincial Court. Then it went to the court of appeal, and then it went to the Supreme Court of Newfoundland, and then it went to the Supreme Court of Newfoundland Court of Appeal. Then, finally, it went to the Supreme Court of Canada. Each time the judgments got more and more condemnatory of the police action and reiterated the sanctity of the law that protected everyone in the house.

Charlie Tomlinson: I do appear in court, and I put off a performance. I thought I'd give a show. You could see the court wasn't used to a constant parade of loquacious and eloquent speakers, one after the other, for a matter of some kind of public drunkenness. The police's side of the story was that a bunch of yahoo young people, hippie-dippy people, threatened one of their guys, and they went in to get him. At some level, that's all it really was. But I got my moment in court. The Crown attorney said something, and I used the word "hectoring." He asked, "Do you mean 'heckling'?"

"No, sir. I mean 'hector.'" What a ponce. The judge looked at me and nodded.

Norm Whalen (from Panel Discussion of R. v. Thomas: A Thirty-Year Reunion of the Fleming Street Massacre): All four judges, from Provincial Court to the trial division to the Court of Appeal to the Supreme Court of Canada, were unanimous. The officers had no right to be [in the house] to issue a summons under the noise bylaw. And it was the skillful writing of Chief Justice Goodridge of our Court of Appeal that was adopted completely. I've practised law for forty years. Since then, I've been doing another part of the law where I read judgements as an arbitrator. [Judge Goodridge's] decision comes up repeatedly as sound, solid, and well-reasoned. And there's probably no better example of that than when this decision went to the Supreme Court of Canada. Here's what [Chief Justice Lemire] said: "We agree with the Newfoundland Court of Appeal that, even if the police were authorized to go into the respondent's house, that authority was revoked by the respondent, thereby making the subsequent arrest unlawful. Accordingly, the appeal is dismissed."

Gene Long: When I won the provincial by-election in St. John's East [in 1986] and went into the House of Assembly, that kind of changed everything for me. That was December 9. I get the dates mixed up with John Lennon's death. He died on December 8, I think. The day after the election, a reporter from NTV called me and asked if I would come down to my campaign office for an interview. Evelyn Riggs had coffee on and was beginning to clean up. The NTV reporter wanted to know how it felt the first day of my new career.

He had me on tape in the campaign office at eleven o'clock in the morning. I was quite hungover. We were talking about community organizing, and then he said, "Mr. Long, I'd like to ask you about these outstanding charges for assaulting a police officer and resisting arrest. We understand you were involved in this occasion of a group of people at a party being arrested a year and a half ago."

I served as an MHA [Member of the House of Assembly] for more than three years, and that story kept coming back at regular six-month intervals. The Fleming Street Massacre became associated with my name because I was a member of the group who spent the night in jail. It seemed to me that most people believed the delays on bringing the proceeding forward were used as an opportunity to slander me on a regular basis by associating me with Peace-A-Chord militants and police-fighting rock and rollers.

Dana Warren: At this point, there was an incredible momentum in the community, a resistance to the right-wing attitudes we felt surrounded by. We were organizing musical events outside of the Peace-A-Chord. We would take over bars. We would have all-ages shows. We would do things at the LSPU Hall. Music sort of became the avenue for discussion. We always had a speaker. Peter Armitage would talk about what was happening in Labrador with low-level flying. The Women's Centre was on Military Road. Lisa Ziegler was the executive director, and she would come and talk about what was happening to women in poverty. We always had an international element to Peace-A-Chord. OXFAM would bring in a band from abroad, like the African National Congress cultural group Amandla. So the stories of apartheid came to us. When you're at OXFAM talking to people about what apartheid really meant and then meeting someone who was not allowed to visit his country or his family for twenty years, who knew brutality because they have the scars on their body to prove it. Police brutality, real brutality, became so much more real to us. They'd had experiences we couldn't even imagine.

When we got arrested, it was still injustice and oppression. When you get a bunch of teenagers together who feel oppressed, watch out. That whole period of our lives was about pushing authority.

Sheilagh O'Leary: Strength comes through adversity. That event made the community stronger and made us want to fight even harder.

Noel S. Goodridge (*from* Supreme Court of Newfoundland, Court of Appeal, June 5, 1991): Whatever their powers may have been, the police officers had a duty to do something about the noise which was being generated from 15 Fleming Street that night. It is one thing to describe the duties of police officers; it is another thing to describe their powers. The issue is one of alleged trespass. The courts have consistently protected the ancient principle of law that a man's home is his castle. "The house of everyone is to him as his castle and fortress." Those comments set the stage. The traditional demand was "Open in the name of the King." Mrs. Thomas in her evidence said that her instruction to the police was to get out of her bedroom. Nevertheless, no doubt Mr. Tomlinson and Mr. Jones acted in good faith when they invited the police officers in and the officers likewise acted in good faith in entering. Even if this gave them implied authority for them to enter, the situation changed when Mrs. Thomas told them to leave. The Crown must rely only upon the unrevoked invitation. There was none. The police officers were trespassers.

Jon Whalen: It seemed strange that the police would fight us so hard when it became clear that they'd overstepped their boundaries. I guess it became a line drawn in the sand. What's their authority, and what's our individual liberty? They were willing to fight that one all the way. That was a very important message to come out of that episode.

EVERYTHING IS POSSIBLE
OR, HAVE SOME GUTS AND QUIT SCHOOL

Lois Brown: I was teaching [high school literature and drama] just before a law was passed in the House of Assembly which made you much more aware of how you're acting around students. I was really pally with my students. After that, I became a little more careful, and then I stopped teaching just as that law was coming into effect. You know, I was really lucky. Teaching at Prince of Wales Collegiate [PWC] was one of the most special and fantastic times of my life.

I had a degree in drama [from the University of Alberta] and an education degree. Then I came back to Newfoundland. My dad was a teacher, and he was into curriculum instruction. It was something I always understood and was fascinated by. Once I had my degree, the school board was putting an emphasis on extracurricular activities. I applied for a job at PWC. The principal, Clyde Flight, had a bunch of students who he felt really needed someone to connect with. He decided he was going to employ several younger specialized teachers.

Clark Hancock: Have you ever seen the photo of us from *The Twenty Minute Psychiatric Workout*? There's me, Barry Newhook, Don Ellis, Rick Mercer, Andrew Younghusband, Ashley Billard, Ken Tizzard, and Eli Baker. And that's just the people who I can remember.

Lois Brown: Tina Riche took the photo.

Sean Panting: There's an argument to be made that without Lois Brown, there's a whole bunch of [successful] people who wouldn't be where they are today.

Rick Mercer: As an educator, Lois certainly would have had the largest impact on my life. It was because of her that I got involved in the entertainment business. She's a tremendous [performance] artist and theatre director. [...] She's a great poet and writer. She's been a mentor to a lot of people.

We were fortunate to go to school in the very brief period when Lois decided to get a straight gig. She applied for that job and never thought that she would get it. PWC didn't have a theatre program or a music program of any consequence. Clyde Flight, the principal, wanted it, and he made some bold choices. He hired Lois to run the theatre program. Lois is fairly eccentric now, but in those days she was a bit wild. She wasn't wild in any disrespectful way. She was just on a different plane than the career teachers.

Lois Brown: I always picked the students who I thought were interesting and talented. Ashley Billard was in all my classes. He had a few things going on that caused the principal to be concerned about him. "Let's put him with someone who is relaxed." He decided that I was that person.

Rick Mercer: Ashley was in Grade 10, and the rest of us were in Grade 11. He went out to the smoking area and saw me and Don Ellis. I was wearing a Ramones shirt, and Don was wearing a Clash shirt. Ashley said, "I guess you're the guys I'm supposed to hang out with."

Barry Newhook: I was the last of the Grade 11s. I didn't really have any interest in school. I sort of whiled away my time in Grade 10. I was always on the pip. I had pains in my stomach and couldn't go to school. I'd leave the house and wait outside at the Merrymeeting Road bus stop, knowing that by nine o'clock my parents were gone to work. Then I would head back home. In the process, I missed over half the year.

Jennifer Dick had left school and wanted to go back and finish Grade 12 at Booth Memorial High School. I'd been out [of school] for two years at that point. I was maybe seventeen. She said, "Why don't you come and do that with me?"

I thought, *I'll do that until the mid-terms in January. I'll sort of half-apply myself.* Booth is where I met Clark Hancock. He was this young kid with a mohawk hanging around outside the school. At the time, we were still scrambling for an identity. Clark and I became good friends.

Lois Brown: Clark was a scary kind of guy, and then he changed into an open kind of guy. I always liked Clark. He was a very compelling person. You felt like you had better keep your eye on him. He could compel you to come and pay attention to him.

Clark Hancock: The first day of Booth, I got hauled into the office because the principal used to be the principal of MacDonald Drive Junior High, George Hickman. George Hickman hated me. Admittedly, I was probably the worst student that he ever had. Myself and Paul Crant both had mohawks. George Hickman sat us down: "I don't want any funny business out of either one of you. The first time you mess up you're out of here." It was a kind of shot across the bow. I was just after getting out of the boys' home.

Ken Tizzard *(musician)*: Clark was robbing car stereos.

Clark Hancock: Because [of] all that history between me and George Hickman, I ended up transferring to Prince of Wales. I spoke to Clyde Flight with Mike Buhler and Ken Tizzard. Mike had a mohawk, but he was treated with respect. Clyde Flight had no problem taking me in on the word of a couple of students.

Lois Brown: Clyde supported me through really good times and bad times. If you hire somebody like me, you get this passionate person who wants to do all this stuff and achieve all these goals. There were areas where I wasn't able to maybe relate to every single type of parent. Andrew and Geoff Younghusband told me that their dad, who didn't normally come to parent-teacher meetings, showed up because he thought I was really weird. I remember him kind of looking at me in a very curious way, like he was assessing me. He went home and said, "I didn't find her very weird at all."

Dealing with someone who was a little disgruntled was just part of the job. It wasn't about always trying to be perfect. It was more about recognizing that you can't be perfect and dealing with areas where you fail a little bit. When Clyde saw my dad, he would always be very laudatory about my teaching. I really respected Clyde. His impulses might be conservative, but he would go beyond his personal sensibilities for the students that he didn't understand.

Steve Hussey *(musician)*: I hated Portugal Cove. I had really long hair, I was chubby, and I had earrings. That was totally gay in the '80s, even though

I'm not gay. But that didn't matter, of course. I got gay-bashed more than once. Portugal Cove was a rough place to grow up.

My family had a subsistence farm. My dad drove a forklift for the Newfoundland Liquor Corporation on Kenmount Road. My mom was legally blind. We had nothing. We raised chickens, pigs, and sheep. That's why I'm a life-long vegetarian. I can't kill my little buddies. I got bused in to PWC, and every year I would go to summer school just to get out of Portugal Cove.

Lois Brown: Steve Hussey was a totally unique person from the rest. He had a certain kind of sweetness. He probably doesn't remember this, but he refused to open his book. Then he wouldn't bring the book. One day, I flew off the handle. Andrew Younghusband was in the class, too. He said, "I don't know why you let him get away with that for the whole year."

I said to Steve, "I don't know why you come here. Why don't you have some guts and quit school? Why are you wasting all this time? You won't even open your book? Either open the book and commit to being here or quit school. Who cares if it's illegal and you can't quit school? Quit school!" The whole thing turned out to be this big, long speech. Maybe he remembers it. Maybe he doesn't.

After this one incident at school, Steve was really protective of me. I had to supervise a dance. I never wanted to go to the dances, but it was my turn to supervise. Somebody was kind of giving me a hard time at the door. Steve just came along and basically asked if I wanted him to deal with it. I have a real soft spot for Steve. When you talk to him now, he's almost formal in how he interacts with people. I don't know him well enough anymore, but I know that underneath all of that there's a heart of putty.

Lois Brown: The '70s was a time when Newfoundlanders didn't think we measured up to everybody else. I remember Greg Malone [CODCO cast member] recently telling this story. Greg said that during the late '70s, everybody at MUN used to have fake British accents to kind of make up for our collective inferiority complex. Then there was a kind of Newfoundland cultural renaissance with CODCO and the Mummers Troupe. There was Figgy Duff making world-class music. There [were] painters like Gerry Squires doing the *Stations of the Cross*. Edythe Goodridge opened up Bond Street to allow CODCO to rehearse there. There was the Fogo Island Project. Just as this renaissance came around, sort of in the middle of the semester, people dropped their fake British accents and started talking like Newfoundlanders again.

Suddenly, there was this sense that what we have here is precious.

Sean Panting: Lois was a really good example of someone who was part of the existing community but wasn't trying to shut us out. There was a little bit of friction at the time, especially through the LSPU Hall. There were people who had worked really hard in the '70s when there was no path, when they built something out of absolutely nothing. Rightfully, I guess, they were kind of protective of that. When my generation came along, it was like, "Thanks for kicking the door open. I'll be competing with you for money, jobs, and audiences now."

We had a different way of doing things. They were more like, "Let's drink a bottle of Old Sam's, punch each other in the face, not have a director, and come up with a show in eight hours." They had the Irish poet–drunken-artist thing that I certainly found pretty tiresome. It's sounds like I'm hacking on them, but I'm not. It's just the way it was done, and we wanted a different way.

Andrew Younghusband *(actor)*: There was a table at the Ship Inn every night: Janice Spence, Mike Wade, Frank Barry, Phil Dinn, Mercedes Barry, Bill Barry, and Flip Janes. There was always the odds of them turning on someone in the bar or turning on themselves. It was rare for them to throw a punch. Punches didn't happen. But they'd fucking eviscerate you with words.

Geoff Younghusband *(musician/promoter)*: There used to be a set of swords, like ornamental swords, on the wall. Mike Wade got banned by pulling one down off the wall and challenging somebody over something. It was a big argument over art inevitably.

Sean Panting: The other example was Andy Jones. When I was a kid, I always promised myself that I going to be Andy Jones. I wasn't going to be Mike Wade.

Ken Tizzard: I know Charlie Tomlinson always believed in getting kids involved in theatre. But it wasn't always a polite place to be. I was at some party, and Lois brought me into a room and introduced me to Mike Wade. Mike was stuffing his face with food. He turned around, looked to me and said, "Why don't you die in the gutter, you fucking cunt?"

Lois Brown: Early on [my theatre arts class] produced *Paperwork* [1984] and toured it to Ottawa. The next year, I decided to open for auditions and create a collectively written play.

Andrew Younghusband: "We're going to write a play ourselves." That's what Lois said. Back then, people were still talking about "collective theatre" as a movement. Paul Thompson was the guy who founded the National Theatre School in Montreal. He had done *Farm Show* [1972], where the actors wrote the script. Writing your own stuff has been the basis for sketch comedy since forever. But full-on collective writing is tied to Paul Thompson.

Rick Mercer: Collective theatre is a process that I've come to loathe. But Lois believed in the collective. Of course, there is a great tradition in Newfoundland of collective theatre. I'm thinking about the Mummers Troupe and a lot of the RCA [Resource Centre for the Arts] stuff. There's the early Mary Walsh stuff. That was all collectively written. Some of the bigger shows were, too: *Makin' Time with the Yanks* [1986], *High Steel* [1984], and all that stuff.

Lois Brown: I don't know if I'm part of the legend or if this is even the truth. I think I was one of the first people who wasn't a cleanup director. I was a real director. I just didn't come in to clean up the mess. Janis Spence spent a lot of her professional life doing that.

Andrew Younghusband: Lois didn't want to do Chekhov. She didn't want to do Shakespeare. She wanted to create something from scratch.

Rick Mercer: I hung out with the theatre company doing backstage stuff. Most of them were in Grade 12, and I was in Grade 10. They were an interesting group, but they didn't have much to do with me. They were doing *commedia dell'arte*, which I thought was ridiculous. I mean, my joke now is that I ended up in the high school theatre company because there was no such thing as a gay-straight alliance.

Lois Brown: I met Rick because he published a zine with his poems in it. I thought, *This guy is really good*. He kind of identified me as somebody who was different. He kind of followed me around, and I got him to stage-manage something. I was like, "You're the worst stage manager in the world. I can't even direct when you're around because you're always telling jokes." People were trying to act, and I was listening to him.

I said to Rick, "You have to write something and get up on the stage." I kind of persuaded him to do that. He would have eventually become a writer or a journalist. That's kind of where he was headed.

Geoff Younghusband: I met Rick when I was a camp counsellor, and he was the assistant counsellor. Every week, we always had the best campfire sketches. You would name your tent when you first went to camp. The groups in his tents had names like "The Existentialists" and "Karma Tent." It was stuff that fifteen-year-old camp counsellors thought was smart but probably didn't understand. It took a week just to teach the kids [...] how to say "existentialist."

When my family came back from Australia, there was this hubbub about Rick's fanzine. Terry Burt was in my homeroom, and he took me to my first all-ages show. Rick was there; Rick was sort of well known. He was a charismatic guy around school. He had sort of big, curly hair. He always wore a jean jacket with the collar flipped up, and he drove a motorcycle with a Beer Not Bombs sticker on it. *Who is this charismatic, funky dude from Middle Cove with the zine that gave out the principal's home phone number and then managed to survive the office talking-to?*

Lois Brown: Clyde said, "No teachers would buy something like that." He was really angry. Not angry, I guess, but he was frustrated. But I already knew that at least half the staff had purchased the zine.

Rick Mercer: Me and Terry Burt were at Peace-A-Chord, and we picked up *Wabana Riot*. Terry was into fanzines. He would order them from places like New York, Los Angeles, and San Francisco. We were like, "If we were allowed to run the school newspaper, we'd do one like a zine."

A week before school started, we were bored, and we went into Terry's father's office. He ran a small structural engineering firm, and we took over the photocopy room and started writing. That [1986] was the year the teachers went on strike. We had an editorial in there supporting them. We had a big spread on condom use.

Back in those days, there was no literature being passed out about sexual health. It's outrageous when you think about it being the beginning of the

AIDS epidemic. And there was always a teenager pregnancy epidemic. We had created this condom character [to talk about those things]. The kicker was that we published the principal's home phone number. He was furious when he found out about it. He was furious about so much of the paper. But he didn't notice his number until he was yelling at us in the principal's office. He looked through the pages and saw his number and lost it. I think it read, "Any questions or comments about the paper, please direct them to Principal Clyde Flight."

Andrew Younghusband: In Grade 11, me and Rick formed a political party. We called ourselves "The NEUROTIC Party"—The Newly Elevated Unorthodox Rising of the Insane Class. His entire speech while trying to get elected school president was that he would get the Ramones to play the school dance.

Lois Brown: Rick wasn't even in school. He went on tour with Beni Malone instead.

Andrew Younghusband: Rick did a kid's show for three weeks or a month up in Labrador. He was living downtown, doing professional theatre, and supposedly going to high school. I had the same job a year or two later. So did Christine Taylor. Sheilagh O'Leary was our driver and stage help, and she ran a robot that had dryer-duct arms called "Octobot." Beni would spit kerosene over a flame to create this big fireball. I used London Dock instead. I blew flaming rum all over Octobot. Suddenly, its arms were burning and dripping gooey hot plastic. The kids thought that it was great.

Lois Brown: Rick was like the politician who loved going door to door, sitting around, and talking with people. He's still like that today. If he wasn't, he wouldn't have had his show [*The Rick Mercer Report*] and be doing what he's doing. You can see he's truly enjoying himself when he's playing with a girl's lacrosse team or something.

Andrew Younghusband: We wrote a play, *The Twenty Minute Psychiatric Workout*. Everybody else did the expected and safe thing. Here we were writing our own play with a rock and roll band and probably having a little bit too much fun.

Lois Brown: Donna and Rick were talk-show hosts taking phone calls and giving really funny advice. They were called "Dr. Feltgood" and "Dr. Feelgood." One caller asked, "Dr. Feltgood, do you think I should have an abortion?"

Donna's like, "Only if you're pregnant."

On the night of the show, Rick ad libbed: "Oh, those Holy Heart girls." It was kind of shocking.

Donna was in love with Andrew, and he was an international terrorist. Rick, however, was also in love with Donna. They were chasing each other through a bar, and WAFUT is playing.

Andrew Younghusband: We made a seriously entertaining show, and it created some controversy because the guitar player in WAFUT was Barry Newhook. Barry didn't go to Prince of Wales Collegiate. I'm pretty sure he was like three years older than me. Clark sang and played guitar. Clark didn't go to PWC, either. He had dropped out.

Clark Hancock: Me and Ken Tizzard were trying to get a name together for our first show up at the old pool hall on the corner of Duckworth and [Cochrane], the Brass Rack. We were driving around in Don Ellis's car. It was really steamy inside because there was like six of us jammed in there. Ken saw a truck across the intersection and said, "What a fucking ugly truck." Then he wrote W-A-F-U-T on the window with his finger. The next day, someone asked me for the name of the band. We still hadn't decided, and I went with WAFUT.

Ken Tizzard: That's just one of the stories. Everybody has a different memory of how the band got its name.

Lois Brown: That drama club won the provincial drama festival in Gander. Donna Pinhorn had never acted before, but she was super fantastic.

I couldn't go to Gander because I was in a play. I persuaded my colleague Elizabeth Mouland to go instead. She said, "I will never do you that favour again."

The next year, when I went to a meeting of the school drama clubs, the administrators were like, "We have some new rules. One of the rules is that everyone must be attending school, and they must be from your school."

I was like, "That's a rotten rule."

Andrew Younghusband: The provincial drama festival in Gander was a life-changing moment for me. That's when me and Rick Mercer sort of got joined at the hip.

Rick Mercer: We wrote a sketch called *Coffee with Chuck*. Lois said, "You guys are doing comedy, but you can't put it off in school because you're swearing and doing all this crazy stuff." She said, "You have to go to the LSPU Hall." Myself and Andrew and Ashley Billard and Christine Taylor formed this comedy troupe [Corey and Wade's Playhouse] and started doing shows.

Lois Brown: I never thought of them as amateurs or professionals. I just thought of them as people. Sixteen is such an exciting age, whereas nineteen and twenty is a whole other thing. When people start university, they become a lot more self-aware, and they're putting a lot more limitations on themselves. They're in a different headspace. Sixteen to eighteen is when you're discovering that a lot of people lie to you, and you're the only person who knows the truth. You're so wound up with ideas. It's really exciting to be around that age group. It's a time when, as a teacher, you can say something and actually change people. Everything is possible.

Sean Panting: Lois convinced us that there was no distinction between professionals and amateurs. "If you're prepared to book the [LSPU] Hall and do a show, well, that makes you a professional. Don't let anyone tell you that you are substandard."

Ken Tizzard: This melding of two worlds happened, and it was two worlds of two very strong-minded and opinionated groups of people. I was sixteen or seventeen, hanging out with people who were forty and doing theatre. The support and the confidence that it created in all of us, I think, led a lot of us to where we are today. I still credit Lois with so much of my life. It's not like I can attribute any one thing to her. I mean, yes, she let me smoke cigarettes during class as long as I stood out by the door. Yes, she invited me to parties where there was drugs and alcohol involved, but she gave me confidence in who I was and what I was doing and allowed me to explore. She was part of the glue that brought everyone together.

Andrew Younghusband: We booked time at MUN Extension on Duckworth Street. It was literally like a dollar an hour, or something. Just before we went in there, a nude model was posing, and just before that they were using the back corner as a darkroom. All the local artists were using that space. Here we were, four teenagers, and CODCO was rehearsing in the next room.

We would rent the rehearsal rooms at MUN Extension and see if we could work something out. Sometimes it was just straight-up stream of consciousness. Sometimes there was an idea. Most of my ideas were just rip-offs of something I'd seen on TV.

Where did the company name come from? Shelly Cornick's father had a cabin in Brigus, and Wade and Corey were locals who sold hash that was squeezed together between two quarters. It was fifteen dollars a gram, but you'd get fifty cents back.

The LSPU Hall called us and said, "We need a name to write something down on the calendar. You can change it later. It doesn't have to stick." Corey and Wade's Playhouse was written in as the place holder. We never got around to changing it.

Rick Mercer: We wrote *Hardly a Sensible Evening* and performed it at the LSPU Hall. They said, "We'll split the box office with you eighty-twenty."

I said, "Well, that's no good. How about fifty-fifty?"

"No, we get twenty, and you keep eighty."

To this day that's the best offer I've ever had in show business.

Sean Panting: Rick comes up to me and goes, "Can you write a song for tonight?" Rick's idea was that he wanted to open with him sitting around his living room. I would sing "Don't Mind Me, I'm on LSD," and the room would come to life.

Rick Mercer: We started doing late-night shows, and we kind of became a hit around town. We played bars, and sometimes there would be a band. The Wonderful Grand Band was the model. Trinity was going to be our first real test. If that worked out, we would do a Newfoundland tour and play church halls everywhere we went. We budgeted for three hundred people. We were going to rock the joint. Twenty people came out, and we lost our shirts.

Andrew Younghusband: Rick, as the ideas man, wasn't always correct.

Rick Mercer: I would've considered myself the producer, but Andrew certainly took over that role, especially the finances. It's interesting because both Andrew and I are now producers in television. I was more talk, and Andrew was more action.

Andrew Younghusband: We started off by trying to be like the Blues Brothers, going around town in the car with bullhorns: "Big show tonight!"

Sean Panting: We put off *Snow on a Hot Sunny Day in Summer* out at the parish hall in Trinity. It was a disastrous trip. There are a lot of differing accounts of what happened. But the heartbreaking thing about Corey and Wade's Playhouse was that when I stopped doing the shows and went to play in bands, I realized that they were a lot funnier without me. I thought, *Maybe I'm just supposed to be the musician.*

Andrew Younghusband: I remember being really excited, and then being really embarrassed. Some backstage people came with us, too.

Rick Mercer: I saw a production of *A Christmas Carol* at the LSPU Hall. A boy came out onstage. Years later, I found out that it was Geoff Seymour. He was a theatre technician around town for the longest time.

Geoff Seymour *(theatre technician/showgoer)*: The year I graduated high school, which would have been '87, I trucked off to Stephenville for the drama festival, came back to town, and Rick Mercer said they had a show booked in Trinity: "Do you want to stage-manage?"

Andrew Younghusband: It was a whole bunch of townies thinking Trinity would find us interesting. We only convinced a few people to come. I don't even think we took their money.

Sean Panting: This was pre–Donna Butt. This was pre–New Founde Lande Trinity Pageant. There was no culture of going to the theatre. I got electrocuted by a pot light and slept in a rolled-up carpet. It was a pretty wild and woolly bonding experience. There was one guy, Beaver, who I met years later. I wondered if I'd made him up. Beaver rode up on a BMX bike. He stole his grandmother's wheelchair, and we were sending people down over the hill in the dead of night. I even drank moonshine.

Andrew Younghusband: A couple of the boys from Trinity decided it was time for the townies to get the fuck out. I recall there was some fancy footwork done so that we didn't get run out on a rail.

Geoff Younghusband: It's 99 per cent of any band's first tour. We're huge at home, and we're going to hit the road. Then twenty people show up at some five-hundred-capacity room. You start second-guessing everything, every line in every song. I'm sure that in the theatre world it feels the same way when you're delivering a punchline and there's no one there to laugh.

Andrew Younghusband: We had a business account with Corey and Wade's Playhouse. We'd budget $50 for props. Lora Longerich, Tina Riche, and Shelley Cornick made posters and signs. We always said, "Fifty bucks is just not enough. If we had seventy, this show would be perfect." It's a lesson I carry with me to this day. If somebody has a $1 million budget they're like, "If only I had $1.2 million, I'd actually make this right." There's something in human nature that wants 20 per cent more than what you got. And that was true back then. For costumes, you went upstairs from Eastern Edge. The Hall had this huge costume and set storage bank up there. In the '90s, with the collapse of public funding, that was one of the first things that the LSPU Hall cut.

Geoff Younghusband: The Arts and Culture Centre absorbed the whole costume bank, and I would assume the sets just got trashed.

Rick Mercer: I wrote a play partially based on my cousin, Paul Wade, because he grew up in Bishop's Falls and would only play the Beatles. He had this band, him and Wayne Hynes, who were unbelievable together. We created a tremendous set made of wood from Robin Hood Bay, the dump. Everything was begged, borrowed, and stolen. Geoff Seymour was our stage manager. There was a sketch where someone got beaten with a bouquet of flowers—just a cheap bouquet of flowers. Every night Geoff would come in with a new bouquet of flowers. It was only years later that we found out that he would pick them up from the graveyard.

Immediately our shows looked like Sheila's Brush productions because Sheila's Brush had the backdrop, which was this big Newfoundland quilt. Tommy [Sexton] and Greg [Malone] gave us wigs. There was this storage space that the LSPU Hall and the Resource Centre for the Arts had. We basically had carte blanche access to whatever junk was in there. To us, it was a treasure trove.

Andrew Younghusband: Nineteen eighty-eight was my last year of high school. By then, we were performing in bars all the time. We got into

Bounders. I could go down after school and put my school bag behind the bar. We spent a lot of money on a Halloween show with an actual coffin. I think we put Ashley in there. I was a bit freaked out by the coffin. Maybe some things aren't supposed to be funny. Maybe we should just leave coffins to dead people.

At the end of the night, we were wrapping out, and everybody was lugging gear, and I probably had three or four rum and Cokes in me. I thought to myself, *I'm going to get inside the coffin, and I'm going to stay in the coffin so long that people will wonder where I'd gone.* All of a sudden, I'll pop out. The next thing I know I was having that dream where everything is a little bit claustrophobic. Then I woke up. It was pitch black; I couldn't see a damn thing. I was like, *What the hell's going on? Okay, I'm in the coffin. And dead.* It was one of those does-not-compute kinds of moments. Everybody was gone; the bar was empty. I think it was like four or five in the morning. I ran down to Gulliver's and grabbed a taxi home.

It was a school night. The folks used to say, "If you want to do theatre, you got to keep your grades up and not miss school—ever. It can't get in the way of other stuff."

We always had university boarders staying at our house. I got home, but I had no money and couldn't pay for the cab. I tiptoed up the stairs with the cab parked outside and the meter going and tried to wake up John, the university boarder. "I just need you to give me five dollars. I'll explain later."

I went out and paid the cab, came back in, and the old man was standing at the top of the stairs, backlit like a horror movie. "So, you finally came home. I don't need to know about this now. You can tell me about it tomorrow."

We have a pretty honest family. The next morning, I said, "Funny enough, I decided to lie in the coffin, and I passed out."

Dad was unimpressed, but the hammer didn't come down. I got home and made it to school the next day. I asked him years later what he actually thought had happened. He said, "What do you mean? I thought you actually fell asleep in the coffin."

Rick Mercer: A couple of colleagues at work have kids either just finishing university or kind of struggling to get their kids into university. They asked me have I ever gone to university. I never went to university, but I could have. Paul Thompson was running the National Theatre School, and he flew down to Newfoundland and had a meeting with us where he basically said that Corey and Wade's Playhouse was the new voice of Newfoundland

Theatre. He wanted us to come to the National Theatre School. That was a problem because I wasn't even a high school graduate. He said that as the guy who ran the National Theatre School, he could make anything happen.

Andrew Younghusband: Andy Jones had some history with Paul Thompson. He started hyping us. Whatever was said to him, I have no idea. Having never seen Corey and Wade's Playhouse, Paul organized a meeting with us at the Ship. He went and bought a pitcher of Guinness, and he talked about how important the National Theatre School was to the country and to anybody who went there. "Based upon what I heard, you are all welcome to attend National Theatre School." There would be no audition, no process. If we had agreed, we would have been a quarter of the entire graduating class.

If you go to the National Theatre School, you have to be completely dedicated. No side projects. No other performances. Extracurricular activities would get you tossed. Rick said, "No way. We're not doing that. We're doing too good performing and working. We'll get our education onstage in front of an audience."

Rick Mercer: We probably said, "[We're not interested.] We're creating artwork about Newfoundland for Newfoundlanders."

I told this story recently. I hadn't even thought of it in twenty-five years, and the people I was telling it to were appalled: "What did your mom say?"

"I don't think I ever mentioned it to her."

Andrew Younghusband: One of the other things that can't be overlooked is that downtown was for poor people. Artists are poor people. Nobody in that scene was making thirty grand a year. You lived near the theatre. You lived near each other. You would be tripping over each other. Ed Riche pointed out something to me. He said, "At that time, everybody was on unemployment insurance." You could squeak out ten or twelve weeks of employment by doing a play, by getting a part in a movie, and then you'd have forty weeks to go hang out at the Ship and argue about art.

The fact that unemployment insurance was so accessible was necessary if you were in the arts community, because you weren't making any money. "Who needs two stamps? I hear you need two stamps. Do you want two weeks of work? Do you want to do something in this play? We'll get you your stamps." The community looked out for itself.

Rick Mercer: Some of this stuff falls into Newfoundland stereotypes, but this was at a time when the government's entire employment strategy was hiring people for enough weeks over the summer to go on UI for the winter. Everyone was doing it. It was a brief shining period that allowed people to be constantly writing and creating.

Andrew Younghusband: Ultimately, we each started doing different stuff. There was a moment when we officially said, "This is done." For our official breakup—we had like two hundred bucks in the bank account—we blew it all at Casa Grande on Duckworth Street. It was our swan song. We drank green margaritas and ate fajitas until we flattened the bank account.

Rick Mercer: The idea was we would wait until everyone was out of high school—I was a year older—and then we would go up to Toronto and do some shows and become a big hit. That was kind of the plan, but it didn't really work out that way. The only time we ever played on the mainland was a few years later, when I was doing my one-man show *Show Me the Button: I'll Push It (Or, Charles Lynch Must Die)* in Ottawa at the National Arts Centre. Corey and Wade's Playhouse came in and did a greatest-hits package.

Andrew Younghusband: We thought we'd go up there and kill. I remember it as a disappointing experience. We weren't Monty Python. Rick's one-man play, now that's Monty Python. I went to Toronto and watched him do it there night after night. You knew that Rick was going to break away because he was just better than anyone else. There wasn't a hope in hell that I could pull off anything that good.

Rick Mercer: Everyone kind of had different interests. Christine Taylor did a one-woman show *Man on the Moon, Woman on the Pill*, which was a Corey and Wade Production. It was a big hit, and she toured the hell out of it. She relocated to British Columbia for the longest time. She's an amazing performance artist and a great comedian. Andrew had other performing interests, too.

Andrew Younghusband: Like anybody in an arts career, one thing leads to another. Corey and Wade was the foundation. It's the beginning of a great story. Without that, who knows where I would be. I probably would have gone to university and done something different. It was the serendipity of meeting Lois, meeting Rick, starting to write, and being involved with Corey and Wade. Still to this day, there's lessons from that time that I took with me. Stuff like after a big joke, you got to leave the four-second pause so people can actually have time to laugh. It was the first steps in a long journey.

Lois Brown: Rick really wanted to continue on with Corey and Wade's Playhouse. But the rest of the crew were a year younger, and he was waiting for them to graduate. But when they graduated, they took jobs with Rising Tide. He was a little devastated. He kind of had to branch out on his own, and the group kind of fell apart.

Rick Mercer: Gerald Lunz was working with CODCO as the associate producer of their TV show, and he was dragging around Cathy Jones's *Wedding in Texas* [1987]. I was hired to work backstage by Cathy, which was a dream job. Gerald was the producer, and he wanted to fire me because I was awful. Cathy hired me because she thought I was funny, and she hired Sebastian Spence because she thought he was dreamy.

I'll never forget the night *Wedding in Texas* finally closed. It was such a huge hit that they were taking it to Toronto. No one could get tickets. I had teachers at school offering me fifty bucks for a ticket to see Cathy Jones downtown. That night Cathy was going to the Ship and there was supposed to be this big party. We loaded up the cube van in a snowstorm until like two o'clock in the morning. I thought, *I should be at the Ship. I should be the one who just did the comedy show that everyone came to see. Someone else should load the frigging truck!*

Gerald was the mainlander who was down here working with CODCO. Some people thought he was a Canada Council spy, like the Canada Council actually had people down here spying on the Newfoundland arts community. Gerald was seen with some suspicion. The National Arts Centre was under the impression there were all sorts of Newfoundlanders doing one-man shows. They asked Gerald to produce one because they were going to do a run of solo-based performances at the Atelier, a small sixty- to eighty-seat theatre in Ottawa. It was under the auspices of the National Arts Centre of Canada, which sounds very fancy, but it was just a garage that smelled like oil. There was some money, and there was probably five or six weeks' work involved.

All Gerald really knew about me was that I never shut up. I was always shooting my mouth off, and I was in a real blind rage about the Meech Lake

Accord and Newfoundland's place in Confederation. I was becoming a bit of a separatist. Gerald said, "Do you want to go to Ottawa and do a show? You don't shut up about this Meech Lake stuff."

I'd never really been onstage alone for more than two or three minutes. I mean, I always had my people with me—my troupe. I don't know what prompted me to say that I would do it, because it was a really big step. This was the mainland, which was very intimidating. But I was kind of driven by rage.

It was a different time. From a political point of view, I don't necessarily think that the Meech Lake Accord was a bad deal. It was a lot of people trying their best. The real anger, in Newfoundland, was because [Premier] Clyde Wells had these serious problems with Meech Lake. Whether you liked him or not, you knew that he was a smart guy. He was a constitutional lawyer, and it was a constitutional issue.

It was kind of like a sneak peek at when former premier Danny Williams took the Canadian flag down [at Confederation Building]. In hindsight, we're perhaps all a little embarrassed by how much we supported Danny. He wouldn't stand for the fact that we were being treated like second-class citizens. That's what Meech Lake had to do with. It had nothing to do with the agreement itself. Every province had to sign off on it, and nobody would tolerate Newfoundland screwing it up. We knew that Quebec or Ontario or British Columbia, for instance, wouldn't get that same treatment. We were quick to hurt, and we were angry. We felt like the rest of Canada was looking down their nose at us. We were like the red-headed stepchild of Confederation.

I don't think that attitude exists now. We have become something like a cool destination. My generation was at the end of the people who got asked, "Where are you from?"

"Newfoundland."

"Oh, I'm so sorry."

We created *Show Me the Button: I'll Push It (Or, Charles Lynch Must Die)*, and it was a bona fide hit at the National Arts Centre. Gerald took these ads out in the *Evening Telegram*: "Congratulations Rick Mercer on his tremendous success." One was Peter Gzowski: "Newfoundland's fastest-rising comedian." Gzowski interviewed me because Alison Gzowski, his daughter, was a friend of mine.

Then we came home, and we ran the play at the LSPU Hall. I remember there was some consternation. Opening night, Gerald put big lights out in front of the Hall, something no one had ever done before. People were incensed. I was rolling into town like I was the Rolling Stones or something.

Gerald even booked a holdover. No one had ever heard of such a thing. He had blocked off the time and wasn't going to tell anyone. In Newfoundland, a show was never held over. Gerald was fixing the sins of CODCO. He had just dragged Cathy Jones around and couldn't figure out why there wasn't a built-in holdover for *Wedding in Texas*. Then he brought in extra seats. People were aghast.

Gerald said, "Twenty bucks a ticket says we can."

The show was me ranting and screaming. There was a Newfoundland national fervour on the go that we kind of harnessed. Eventually, we moved it to the Arts and Culture Centre and toured the island. Gerald said, "Now we're going uptown!"

YOUTH CRUSADERS
SCHIZOID PART 1

Rod Wills *(musician)*: I was born with a hole in my heart and couldn't get involved in sports. My parents said, "What do you want to do?" I was interested in music, so they bought me a drum kit. I was just too sick to do anything else. The drums were a set of Stewarts from the Woolworth's on Water Street, special-ordered from a catalogue.

I attended MacDonald Drive Elementary. Everybody was in the choir. Then there was the ukulele band, and I was the drummer. We played the Kiwanis Music Festival. Don Cook was the musical director at MUN. We played the Arts and Culture Centre, and he was doing demonstrations. After everybody had played, he said, "Rod, come up here." I got behind the kit, and he gave instructions about different rhythmic patterns. He was playing the piano, and I was playing the drums.

When I got home, he contacted my parents and said, "There's this drum instructor here from Toronto. He'd like your son to come to Memorial University to do an audition."

Don Wherry was a drum instructor at the Toronto Symphony Orchestra, but he decided to stay in St. John's and become a teacher. He picked eight students, and I was one of them. I went to MUN at age thirteen and took music theory under his supervision. He told my parents that he saw something in me. He said that I was "rhythmically inclined" and that I had a "natural ability." But I wasn't very disciplined. I was more interested in John Bonham. He'd give me Buddy Rich and Jimmy Cobb records, the Headhunters, and different jazz albums. Benny Goodman and Gene Krupa—that kind of stuff. But I had no time for it. He said, "Rod, you've got to learn this stuff."

"Yes, but check this out, Mr. Wherry."

YOUTH CRUSADERS

I'd play a paradiddle around the whole kit, and he'd ask, "Who taught you that?"

"I taught myself."

He'd say, "You're learning stuff more advanced than what I'm trying to teach you, but you're missing the basic elements."

Then he put me on CBC with the Wonderful Grand Band. The show was *Step to Stardom*. I played "Moby Dick" by Led Zeppelin.

Going to the doctors, they said, "What he's doing is the best thing for him. He's building up the heart muscles." My parents were fully into it. My dad built me a music room downstairs with a stage and lights. Any records I wanted, they would buy them. Looking back, it was an absolutely incredible childhood.

Johnny Fisher: Rod was phenomenal. He was left-handed, and he would do things like start the show off on his right-hand side. Then, in the middle of a song, he'd lift the high hats without missing a beat and switch them over to the left. I guess he was ambidextrous. As our scene went, he was a superstar. He was doing cheesy stuff like lighting his drumsticks on fire and twirling them. He did things we could only dream of. Rod was a consummate showman.

Bob Armstrong: [He] should have ruled the world. The Def Leppard guy that lost his arm had electronic assistance. I always thought Rod wouldn't need that.

Rod Wills: I met Bob Armstrong through MacDonald Drive Junior High. Then we kind of drifted apart, and I went to England. I came back and Bob was in my brother's driveway. They lived next door. I told him I bought a bunch of new albums: Venom, Onslaught, Slayer. He said, "Have you ever heard the Accüsed?" He was into *Maximumrocknroll* and a lot of those bands that were starting to change their sound: D.R.I., Corrosion of Conformity, the Accüsed. Their first few albums were punk, and then their later albums were more metal.

Bob was in a band, Public Enemy, with Tony Meaney and John Pastore. "We're playing the Grad House."

I went to the show and everybody accepted me, even though I was this nerdy suburban kid with flannel pants. It was my first punk show ever. Bob said, "Do you still have your drums?"

We jammed in my basement. It was weird because my drumming style was completely different than anything Bob was used to. Public Enemy were doing straight kick-snare, kick-snare beats, and I was all over the map. Bob would lend me records like Minor Threat and the Dead Kennedys. It was pure all-out aggression. It was all about speed and not much else. Later on that totally changed.

Bob Armstrong: We were getting into the punk and metal crossover thing that started to happen in the mid-'80s.

Chris Jerrett: They were taking a couple of metal guys and a couple of punk guys and putting them together and bringing a metal sound to the punk scene. That was a big changing point. It brought a lot more people out to the shows.

Don Ellis: You know what really happened? In the mid-'80s, when a lot of bands got into metal, shows started to get violent. That kind of happened everywhere. The first couple years of the hardcore scene, people didn't drink because they were mostly teenagers. It was just this great group of friends.

I was always a bit of a metalhead. I liked the Accüsed. I liked D.R.I.'s *Crossover* record. I liked Slayer's *Reign in Blood*. When *Reign in Blood* came out, nobody could believe it. Here was a metal band completely wiping the hardcore bands' asses. But part of that scene was also about getting drunk and beating people up. When I moved to Toronto in 1987, this kind of disintegration was starting to happen. I went to see the Exploited, and it was just a drunk throw-up fest. There was vomit everywhere. Vomit, vomit, vomit. People were passing out loaded. It was senseless violence—fist fights and all that stuff. Maybe that was always there, but I just didn't see it in our nice little multi-genre alternative scene back in St. John's.

Phil Winters *(musician)*: Knocking around the neighbourhood led me to Rod Wills. We'd hang around in his basement, listening to Black Sabbath and making prank phone calls. Just bullshit teenage stuff: drinking jungle juice and beating the streets. We were suburban kids. Through Rod Wills, I met Bob Armstrong and Chris Jerrett. I wasn't part of the punk scene, and I really didn't know what their connection was. I was just some guy that Rod knew. I started listening to hardcore, and they started listening to speed metal. We were sort of feeding each other music. But I didn't really play then, either. I kind of picked up the guitar at maybe sixteen. I could sort of play in a rudimentary sense.

Bob Armstrong: Phil had a mullet. He didn't have a clue about punk rock. We had to school him quite a bit. He showed up with his guitar up around his chest, and he left with it down by his knees.

Phil Winters: At that time, in high school, there were divides between the various cliques. The metal guys didn't mix with the punks. I guess there were preconceived notions there, but they were quickly dispelled.

Rod Wills: Public Enemy was breaking up. We met at John Pastore's and messed around. It's funny because I got the first tape. Don and Ken Tizzard were in the back room talking. They didn't realize that the tape machine happened to be in the same room and that they were being recorded. They're like, "What do you think of these guys?"

"I don't know. It's different." It wasn't what they were used to. "Listen to that drummer." Over the years, I brought this up to Don a couple of times. He laughed.

John Pastore: In the winter, after we left the games arcade, everybody converged on Atlantic Place and ordered a coffee, which I think cost something like forty-five cents. It was one of those afternoons when Chris said that he wanted to call the band "Schizoid." Chris never could spell very well, and he asked me to write it out on a piece of paper.

Someone said, "I think it's 'Psychoid.'"

Someone else said, "I think he means 'Schizoid.'"

If it had been left up to just me and Chris, the band may very well have been called Psychoid.

Phil Winters: Barry Newhook's shed on Vinnicombe Street was where the actual loudness first happened. Schizoid officially formed on New Year's Eve 1985. The shed had a wood stove, but it hadn't been on. It was very fucking cold; you could see your breath.

Rod Wills: Phil was just learning guitar solos. Bob was more open-strumming. Chris was a total maniac screaming his head off. Danny Thomas was on bass, and he was also in Tough Justice. This might surprise you. When we first started, I remember the songs being really slow.

Bob Armstrong: We didn't intend to be a speed-metal band. We just wanted to plug in and play and see what would happen.

Rod Wills: Bob had the song "Schizoid," which eventually became "Possessed." We would play that over and over again. We did a countdown from ten to zero, there was this big blast of noise, and then we screamed, "Schizoid!"

Kent Noseworthy: I stayed with my grandparents for a while, and Barry Newhook lived two doors down from them. The boys would practise in one of those eight-by-eight sheds in Barry's backyard. It's funny because it was this quiet suburban neighbourhood, and there was Eugene Vaters Pentecostal School right across the street.

Phil Winters: There were drums and a couple of amps [in the shed]. It wasn't Rod's basement, but it was a space.

Barry Newhook: We'd have that place cooking. The stove pipes would be glowing red hot. The drums were back by the stove, and drummers were always complaining about the heat. It was pure hell to be up against that thing.

Clark Hancock: It was so frigging loud inside of that shed. I was outside of the shed in a snowbank in the middle of winter with my guitar and a microphone stand hurling away. I got this weird feeling that someone was watching me. I turned around and there were all these school kids stood up by the fence.

Phil Winters: Bob wrote the music; Chris wrote the lyrics. Certainly, they brought a few ready-made tunes. One of them they played in Public Enemy: "Youth Crusaders." Bob was sort of the band leader. He was the man on the phone. He was the go-getter and the doer. I was just following along.

Chris Jerrett: "Perpetrator" kind of set the tone of the band. I started writing lyrics like "Gun in Hand." Bob wrote "Possessed," and then there was "Black Night."

You might have seen me in pictures with a golf club onstage. I used to bring all kinds of props to the shows. Right from the start, the idea of the band was that we were kind of poking fun of the whole metal scene. We were trying to be ironic.

Bob Armstrong: The first show was at the 301 Club on March 15, 1985. Apparently, there was a blizzard that night. I remember doing an interview

YOUTH CRUSADERS

with Pat Janes for his show on CHMR. We had high hopes. I've often talked to Rod about all the times trudging through snow to play shows and all-night parties.

Phil Winters: The lineup was Tough Justice, WAFUT, and Schizoid. There was a surprising amount of people there considering the weather. I guess, because it's just up from downtown, a lot of people walked to the venue. Most of us were underage. But there was beer; there was drinking. We were in the basement playing, and the bar was upstairs. It was small, it was dark, and there was a blizzard outside. Was it a good time? Let's just say the show went over fairly well.

Chris Jerrett: For about a year, the 301 Club was a strong, reliable venue. The place is still there on [Hamilton Avenue]. It's called the Laurier Lounge. I think I was walking by there one time and looked in. Me and Bob might have called and talked to the owner. At first, they were kind of standoffish. But it was a dead space. The 301 Club was the bar on the top floor. Maxine's was on the bottom floor. I guess it was something that they couldn't get off the ground. It wasn't like they were filling the top floor, and they had to put this thing on the bottom floor. Back then, George Street existed, but it wasn't where everybody congregated. There were pubs and bars all over town. That's something that's really changed.

Phil Winters: It's been called the New Laurier Club since about 1990. It's not too fucking new anymore.

John Nolan *(musician)*: There was always skeets and skanks upstairs drinking—the locals. Just try to imagine a punk rock show going on downstairs, and there's the locals drinking and puking and fighting upstairs.

Rod Wills: The manager and bartender were friendly right from the beginning. We were free to do whatever we wanted. They might come down and check on us, but that was about it. We always played in the far corner. I think there was a bar in the back, but it was never open. It was just one big open space with tables and chairs. They might've had bingo down there. I don't know.

Phil Winters: We don't have a recording of the first show. We got the second, third, fourth, fifth—that sort of thing. Some of that stuff came off the board. There were other tapes that were just a ghetto blaster behind the drums recording through a condenser microphone.

Don Ellis: Every show, I was the guy who brought everything. Eventually, I started doing sound as well. For our first show, there was feedback all night. The guy doing sound will remain nameless. To this day, he's one of my dearest friends. When we brought the PA back to Eastern Audio, I complained about the incompetent sound guy that they sent down. Years later, he became the best sound guy that ever come out of Newfoundland. But our show was also his first gig.

Phil Winters: The scene was not large. It was three or four bands: the Riot, Dog Meat BBQ, Schizoid, WAFUT, Tough Justice, and the Asthmatics, who was Johnny Fisher and Llewellyn Thomas. There were a few others outside of our immediate circle but that's about it.

Natalie Spracklin: With the scene up on [Hamilton Avenue], those shows were pretty much packed to the gills. A lot of kids, a lot of noise, and a lot of sweat. It was a very masculine energy. There weren't any chicks playing punk rock back then.

Geoff Seymour: But there was a fair contingent of girls: Joanne Lee, Martina White, Kelly Squires, Lori Brophy, Carolanne Ryan, and Lori White.

Natalie Spracklin: We weren't always 100 per cent punk. There were a lot of people in our scene who really didn't hang a sign on their backs and identify as any one particular thing. If you want an example, just look at the whole Ploughshares Youth peace festival. The St. John's scene from that time was punks and hippies. I think that would be an accurate portrayal.

Bob Armstrong: We were used to redneck preppies beating the crap out of us if we stepped on their Pumas. We would get chased from parties. Clark Hancock was good with the girls. He always knew where there was a party. We'd be there five minutes, and we'd get chased down the road. Someone would have a car; we'd dive in and take off. I still say today that the chances of a fight in an average bar establishment are way higher than a punk rock venue.

Geoff Younghusband: My dad is an academic guy in genetics. We moved to St. John's when I was nine because he was chasing degrees, and then he got a faculty job at Memorial University. We went to Australia on sabbatical when I was fifteen. That's when I discovered punk rock. A guy in school played me Dead Kennedys' *Fresh Fruit for Rotting Vegetables*. We were in the library with four of us plugged into the headphone jack of a tape recorder, listening. I thought metal was angry, but this was angry *and* funny.

I came back to Newfoundland to start Grade 11. The first day of school, I sat down with Ken Tizzard. At that time, he played in WAFUT. He's since gone on to play in the Watchmen and Thornley. He's a nationally recognized musician. I swapped him a beret for a mixed tape that included the Stretch Marks, the Exploited, and the *Let Them Eat Jellybeans!* compilation. Ken wore that beret for years. A few weeks later, he sold me a copy of *Wabana Riot*. I went to my first local all-ages punk show when a band from BC called the Resistance were supposed to play. It was Schizoid's second show ever. The Resistance never showed up.

Chris Jerrett: To do something like putting off your own show now would be such a monumental task. Back then it all seemed so easy. If there was a setback, it didn't matter. There was never any kind of real pressure. It would always come together. I'd say that it was our energy and not being bogged down with other things. I never finished high school. Most of these guys we're talking about didn't finish high school. After Grade 10, we barely went. We were too focused on music.

Phil Winters: We played at the 301 Club for probably a year. What were the gigs? March 15, May 2, May 18, September 20, and October 21. We played maybe six or seven times that first year, and then I think the 301 Club changed management. They didn't want the crusty punks hanging around anymore.

Bob Armstrong: How did we get SNFU? Once again, digging out some numbers and finding their manager. Two shows were planned. One of the two got cut. That must have been when Maxine [manager of the 301 Club and Maxine's] left, because it was some other dude that cancelled the show on us, the guys who ran the 301 Club.

Geoff Younghusband: SNFU was supposed to play an all-ages show and then a bar show. The main thing to remember is that there was a weekend of shows planned. We showed up to go to the first all-ages show, but the 301 Club had changed hands that week, and it was rebranded. The new owners wouldn't let the all-ages show happen because they'd installed a bar down there, whereas before there was no drink service. That was the end of the 301 Club.

Rod Wills: We should have gotten a written contract.

Arthur Haynes: The Newfoundland and Labrador Liquor Board and the Newfoundland Constabulary shut down those shows because you couldn't just close down a bar, host an underage event, and say you wouldn't sell booze.

Bob Armstrong: SNFU were sound-checking when we found out. I had to walk up and tell them.

John Pastore: I just read *SNFU: What No One Else Wanted to Say*. The Newfoundland thing was mentioned. The band was having a bad run of shows leading up to that point, and then they got to Newfoundland.

Geoff Younghusband: There was a mad frenzy trying to find a venue. The next day, a place was lined up on Solomon's Lane down the steps from the Ship. The ground floor happened to be a gay bar. SNFU played on the top floor in a vacant office space.

Phil Winters: It was just an undeveloped room. All the gear was rented from Wallace Hammond.

Geoff Younghusband: The PA was dragged up over the stairs, and the speakers just missed the ceiling by a foot. The band squeezed in with maybe a couple dozen people, and the rest of us wedged into the hallway and sort of peered in and watched them play.

Bob Armstrong: SNFU asked us if they could go on early because they knew the show would be shut down. They had way more experience with that stuff than we did. Sure enough, they got up and played five or six songs and were promptly shut down.

Geoff Younghusband: It was an all-ages show, but you had to go through the bar to get there. The bar was aware of what was going on, but we couldn't just linger around outside waiting for the doors to open. We all hung out around Atlantic Place, and two or three of us went down at a time and crossed the street. There was a little crowd of kids on the opposite side of Water Street, and we all slipped up the stairs.

Bob Armstrong: I can't remember if the cops were on the way or the owner got nervous. There were too many people. It was not really the right situation because it was a small space, and underage kids were cutting straight through the bar.

Geoff Younghusband: SNFU had hockey flags hung over the windows. It was so hot in there that the windows were wide open. I just remember Brent [Belke] and Muck [Marc Belke] playing guitar in front of the windows with these hockey banners behind them and fog rolling in while they played. With the cold air meeting the hot, it was like a smoke machine. Chi Pig was doing his whole infamous jumping off the kick drum. He'd have to keep his head down so he wouldn't smash it off the ceiling. The organizers didn't make SNFU's guarantee, and I heard that there was anger there for quite a while.

In the long run, there was some shows that Schizoid played at the Battery Hotel which allowed people to get their money's worth. If you bought the two-night ticket, you got into the Battery show for free. People who paid for the Battery show…all that money went to SNFU.

SNFU was on the *If You Swear, You'll Catch No Fish* tour. That show was one of the great scene moments of my life. There was this great scramble and frenzy, yet the show happened, and it was spectacular.

Bob Armstrong: The band took whatever money that they could get. They drove across Newfoundland through a storm, after having been on the ferry for seventeen hours in rough seas, and then the show got cancelled. The band didn't blame any of us. It was a rough period for them, but it wasn't their roughest.

Don Ellis: Just about every band that came here in the '80s lost money. It was shocking. We were supposed to pay SNFU twelve hundred dollars, and we gave them seven hundred. That's all that we had. And we borrowed some of the money.

Phil Winters: I'm sure SNFU were touring to Halifax and Fredericton, but they still had to cross the island in the middle of winter […]. There might've been forty people at the show, including the bands, which was the scene.

Arthur Haynes: In my mind, if I look back on it, my father was probably responsible for the show being cancelled [...]. One of his best buddies was with CID [Criminal Investigation Division]. My dad would come to me with little pieces of information, telling me we were being watched, or whatever. There were rumours that CSIS had files on all of us. It seems so fucking ridiculous, but you're talking about the mid-'80s, when there were really no subversives. There were no freaks. If you were a freak in St. John's in the 1980s, you took a beating for it. Again, that was part of the reason why the scene meshed the way that it did: self-preservation. Is it possible the cops were taking pictures of us and keeping files on us? I think so. I think it's an absolute when there are only a couple dozen of us to keep an eye on. SNFU show posters were up all over downtown. Everybody knew Chi Pig was coming to Newfoundland. It was a big to-do, and they shut us down.

We all went to the Kent-and-Llew Society [on the west end of Duckworth Street]. It was our punk rock hangout. Sitting in the room with SNFU, combat boot to combat boot and mohawk to mohawk, they were just a bunch of wacky dudes. Chi Pig was a crazy man, but he was just a guy. We filled the apartment, got high, and threw things out the window.

RELENTLESS
THOMAS TRIO AND THE RED ALBINO PART 1

Jody Richardson *(musician)*: I was raised in Conception Bay South on Fowler's Road. Chamberlains [town in Conception Bay South] is a great place. Some amazing people have come out of there. But there's not a lot to do. It's not like you're living in Bay Roberts or you're living in Woody Point. There's no central location. It's just a collection of communities. You really have to make your own stuff. I was a kid who was into metal, and then I heard "Games without Frontiers," by Peter Gabriel, on the radio. That song just changed everything for me.

I wasn't in a musical family, but my mother's side of the family are all very creative. They're all poets and historians and filmmakers. We just didn't have that type of environment. But we were self-starting, and my parents always supported us. I was always singing. I was in glee club, and I kind of liked acting. But when I was really young, my brother, Chris, who is a fantastic documentary filmmaker, was the actor and the big character in the family. I got into singing and acting just to try and overshadow him. It was normal sibling-rivalry stuff.

This is so long before the internet and even cable television. We only got one channel. All of our news came from Detroit, which showed all of these horrible things. *Stacey's Country Jamboree* was something that used to come on at night. Another really interesting thing was OZFM. It was at that point the only FM station [in Newfoundland], and they would play raunchy humour, probably around six o'clock in the morning. We would get up early so that we could listen to foul stuff from Robin Williams, Lenny Bruce, and George Carlin. You'd hear *Friends of Mr. Cairo*, that crazy Jon and Vangelis album. We were out there in Conception Bay South, but we had a radio station that would play all these things that educated us.

MUN had a television station. They would send out a catalogue of all the films that they had available. You would call in and request a certain movie the week before. Obviously, CBC was always fuzzy, and you could never get reception on the dial. MUN would have this catalogue, and we would request stuff like *Nosferatu*. For all I know, this guy could have been Mack Furlong. I just remember thinking of him as the quintessential long-haired and bearded university-type hippie. I was born in 1966, so this would have been the late '70s.

Those were all big influences that showed us that there were other things. Maybe that laid the seeds of creativity.

But I was into metal, living in Chamberlains, and the school dress code was denim. The hockey team was the student council. One time on Halloween, they dressed up as the KKK and surrounded the one Pakistani guy in the school. I remember thinking, *This seems strange*. There wasn't even a school assembly. You know what I mean? When something like that happens, it's like, "This is a learning environment, and we're going to have a lesson here." But not at Queen Elizabeth. It wasn't a really progressive environment.

Two years ago, Queen Elizabeth was ranked the 127th high school in Newfoundland. I was like, "There's more than 127 high schools in Newfoundland?" The schooling at Queen Elizabeth was more about just getting us through.

I had an English teacher who was a younger guy, and he sort of cultivated my interest in theatre. He was the English teacher who ran the drama club and played in bands. He was the perfect thing we needed. I got involved in the drama club, I was playing music, and then I started listening to Peter Gabriel, Kate Bush, and the Talking Heads. I was that kind of geek. Mostly it was just the theatricality of the music. I was completely shaped by that stuff for a long while. It had something going on outside of the music. It had a presentation that I found fascinating. Between the three of them, you can look back and see how relevant they were.

Then, in Grade 10—high school only went to Grade 11—we started to hear these horrible rumours of a Grade 12. Sure enough, it happened. But I didn't pass Grade 12. Then I came into St. John's and attended Booth for my second try. I liked Grade 12 so much that I did it twice.

Once I got to Booth, it was completely different. Just small things. Somebody else actually had on Converse sneakers. I used to wear my mom's clothes. It's not like now. If you want to look cool, you watch this video, you go to this store, you buy these things, and then you have your uniform. At that time, I was wearing my mom's blazer in the basketball team's picture for the yearbook. All of the team were in their uniform, and I was standing there with this David Bowie haircut and my mom's blazer on.

I immediately got into theatre with the Elysian Theatre Company and acted in their production of *Curse of the Starving Class*. Once I was in a more creative environment, everything moved forward. It was like I had walked into the end of the Blind Melon video: *Oh, everybody is a bee*. I started meeting people really fast. That's when we put the Dervishes together, myself and Nick Rockel, and things started to congeal. All of a sudden, it was like going to Universal Studios. It's what I'd been waiting for.

Thom Thorne was in my class. So was Dave Guy. Dave was the best-looking guy I'd ever seen in my life. He had long blond hair, and he played an actual Gibson.

Thom Thorne: The first day Jody Richardson got transferred from CBS to Booth, the only empty seat in the class was right next to me. We've been friends ever since. Lil, Louis, and Danny went to Booth. Jon Whalen went to Booth. Bob Armstrong and John Pastore went to Booth. We all went to Booth—everybody. I introduced Jody to the Thomases. That's how that connection started.

Jody Richardson: I eventually graduated Grade 12 with a 50 in math. My teachers honestly thought, *There are calculators in the world. He's not going to use this stuff. There's no point*. I had the exact same number of "absents" as I had "presents" that year on my report card. I'm so proud of that. It was a true Zen balance.

The Dervishes was me and Nick and Susan Jackson. She learned to play on a fretless bass. She was of that ilk. But she played guitar in the Dervishes. Nick was so much smarter than me. We were in a creative writing class together, and we had to write a couple of poems and a play for the end of the semester. It was unbelievable, the brain on Nick. I was really attracted to working with him. We just started putting tunes together at his place with Sue.

The Dervishes was silly new-wave stuff. We did a variety show at school and played three songs, and they were incredibly embarrassing. I have a picture of us playing at the Legion in Pleasantville. I had the drive to put something together once I had the right people. Bruce Cooper, who was also in the Dervishes, now works for the government. Most everybody is in actual jobs except for me.

Music will get you laid. It's a simple equation. When I was out in Chamberlains, after my band, Rebel, played the school variety show, the same guys who were giving me a hassle came up and said, "That was pretty good, fag." They couldn't give the whole compliment. But then I got some attention from the ladies. That made total sense: be in a band. The people that hate you won't hate you as much. That's a direct application. You can't deny that to a kid.

The Dervishes was putting together music and playing shows, and then I went to Montreal and attended the National Theatre School of Canada. I think they let me in because they needed somebody from Newfoundland. I went because my marks weren't good enough for MUN. While I was in theatre school, there was a band competition back in St. John's. The winner would open up for Paul Young at Memorial Stadium. "Every Time You Go Away." Remember that one? It was a big hit on the radio.

My father was a car salesman, and he owned a bunch of Burger Kings. He's an amazing man, my dad. He rigged the competition so that my band would win. I found this out years later. He was doing a ridiculous amount of advertising with OZFM. He called them up, and the fix was in. But the Dervishes were actually pretty good, and we were original.

Nick initially was writing the lyrics, although I was the singer. But his stuff was so good that I would lose his lyrics all the time and bring my own. The lyrics could have been brilliant, but I just didn't allow it at that point because I was young and stupid. Years later, I thought, *God, I wish I still had those things*. I was writing original stuff even when I was in Chamberlains. I had that bug. But they were terrible. It was more like, *This is how a song should sound*. It wasn't about what I was thinking and feeling. It was more posing. But a lot of us do that. We imitate, assimilate, and then create.

When we won the competition, I was away at theatre school; I came home, and the band was at the airport with a banner: "Welcome home!" It was a really sweet thing. There were like two or three other people who joined the Dervishes for that gig. We did all originals except for a cover of "Walking on Sunshine," which Nick sang.

I was seventeen. Maybe eighteen.

We had a home crowd. We were the ones who supposedly won this prestigious competition.

It made me a horrible person. I became impossible to talk to.

That concert gave us enough of a profile to do the ill-fated tour of Newfoundland. Eastern Audio came on board as a sort of sponsor. The night before we were scheduled to leave, all of our gear got stolen from the station wagon. Because I'm an idiot, I packed everything up and left it in the car. We didn't cancel the tour; we decided to leave anyway.

We bought replacement gear from Davis Music. We never even decided on the stuff. We just said, "We need a guitar. We need a bass. We need a bass amp. We need drums." It was ridiculous. Davis Music fronted us the instruments, and we had to pay it all back after. They charged us an absolute fortune.

The tour was horrible—unbelievable. Our first gig was in Corner Brook. After that night—we were supposed to be there for a week—the bar manager said, "You got to learn some songs, or this is over." We put on the radio, and we listened to the first twelve songs that were on the Top 40. We tried to learn them in a day and continue on.

We went from playing Memorial Stadium in front of two thousand people to Plum Point, where everybody hated us. We were taken down a notch very quickly. We were at the Blue Mountain Lodge, about twenty minutes outside of St. Anthony. There was the club itself, and out back there were a couple of rooms where we stayed. Our room had a hole in the wall that went outside. There were two mattresses on the floor for us to sleep on.

The first night we were finally starting to learn these Top 40 songs. But nobody was dancing, and we couldn't figure out why. Somebody came up and said, "You got to turn the lights down. They're too bright." As soon as we turned down the lights, the dance floor was packed. I think that was the only good night of the entire tour.

The manager was always in screaming matches with his woman. Then he started beating her. We had to kick in his door to stop him. Then we had this big tussle in the hallway. He tried to throw us out, which was a day early, and he wasn't going to a pay us, so I stole his chainsaw and put it in the back of the station wagon. Then somebody stole it from us.

We went to Blanc-Sablon, and we went to Labrador. The only thing they do there is drink and beat up bands. We were perfect to beat up. We weren't a tough punk band. We had the wrong type of uniform. Here I was with my David Bowie haircut, and they're like, "I'm going to kick the fucking shit out you." With the French men, their bar would close, and they'd drive down the road to Newfoundland. Because of the new time zone, we closed later. They would come in at the end of the night, ready to scrap. This one time, it all went down. The French men were rushing the stage. We had this great guy doing lights and sound for us, Juan O'Quinn. He's a criminal lawyer now out in British Columbia. Juan took the lighting board, threw it on the ground, and screamed. Everyone turned and went, "He just threw the lighting board to the ground. That cost thousands of dollars. What the fuck are we going to do?" He used the fact that the lighting board was really expensive to completely dissolve the situation. It was brilliantly done.

It was one thing after another. The band essentially broke up while we were on tour. It was the worst. I was like, *Why am I doing this? I just want to go home.* We were all at each other.

Springdale, Gander, and Clarenville were really intense. It was just brutal. We didn't make a dime; we were so hungry. That was my first introduction to the road. I came back home and slept for like a week. The Dervishes played the Strand at one point, and that was hilarious because it was the same sort of thing as the tour. The music that we played made no sense to anybody. The crowd was like, "Just play some John Cougar Mellencamp."

After the Dervishes, I was in a band called the Dirt Buffaloes. That was more of a fun cover band to help us get laid. Sue moved on to bass. The great Bob Sutherby was on guitar. Nick wasn't around anymore; it was a different lineup. And then we started playing clubs. That's when I hooked up with the Thomas boys.

* * *

Lil Thomas: Mostly, I was a dreamer. I guess I would have been eleven or twelve when I started playing guitar. Louis started playing drums around the same time. We literally went out and bought his first drum kit and just started jamming away and making noise together. The three of us all kind of took to music fairly readily.

The first band I had was Stolen Bones with Louis, Brian Kenny, and Brian Gregory. We did some school dances, anywhere a bunch of youngsters could find a place to play. This would have been well before the bar scene.

Louis Thomas: When I was fourteen or fifteen, I was already working in the Village, [then] a sandwich shop at the bottom of Prescott Street, and then I worked at the Sundance. It was just to have some spending money and to be relatively independent. I figured out quickly that if I wanted a pair of Levi's, I wasn't getting them unless I had my own money.

Eventually, me and Dad ended up on Hamilton Avenue. That's when I got a stereo and a drum kit. I was by no means playing then. I remember Dad trying to teach me some guitar, and I just wasn't getting it. Maybe I was frustrated with his teaching methods. I went to see an April Wine show at the stadium, and Jerry Mercer was playing drums. He had a big set of Sonor up there on the stage, and I was like, *Okay, that's what I want to do. I want to get a set of those.* I think I saw some Sonor drums for sale in the paper and went out and bought them. They were probably three hundred or four hundred bucks. I had them set up in my room on Hamilton Avenue, and then I remember them being in the closet under the stairs.

None of us brothers really got into music until Fleming Street. That's when I remember the three of us started playing. That's when we met Brian Gregory and put together Stolen Bones.

Stolen Bones wrote some original stuff and made an album. Wallace Hammond recorded it [Vikki-Beat, 1986]. It was a cassette, obviously. Brian would have written the lyrics, and Lil would have written most of the music. There was a song called "What's Da Dirt?" There was this woman who used to cook at Mom's restaurant [the Continental Café], and that was something she used to say to the kids. There was a song that the Trio reworked called "What It Is." But that wasn't on the cassette.

Brian lived on Hayward Avenue with his brother, Beni. We sort of met them on one of our mushroom or acid walks over by the nunnery on Military Road. Brian was always singing Journey covers. So we sort of asked him to come down and jam with us.

David Guy *(musician)*: It's the same thing with every teenage band. You know a riff, you play that for an hour, and everybody just jams along. There's no chorus, no bridge. It's only later that it developed into writing skills.

I had a band called No Fixed Address. That was one of my Booth High School bands. We used to play at the Grad House and private parties at the Lion's Club with Stolen Bones.

Stolen Bones played covers, but Lil had a bunch of original riffs. That was sort of the genesis of [the Thomas brothers] writing their own material. We rehearsed together for a while at the Cochrane Street Hotel. Louis actually played a couple of shows at the bar downstairs, the Alcock and Brown. I can't remember who the guitar and bass players were. They accompanied this African guy who danced on broken glass.

The Cochrane was no longer a working hotel. All the rooms were empty. That's how we were able to get in there. I think Louis had some kind of quid pro quo deal playing the bar in exchange for rental space. The bar was on the first floor, and the upstairs was abandoned. Our room actually had its own bathroom. But a lot of the rooms didn't. It may have been used as a boarding house at some point. Hotels in the old days were like that. You'd basically have cots in rooms with a master bath off the main hallway. We had to clean the room out of old chairs and scraps of wood to make it usable. It was painted that sort of weird hospital green, and it was freezing cold. I don't remember for sure what the situation was for power, but we may have had to run extension cords up the stairs. At one point, someone got in the bathroom to play because the bedroom was so small.

The Cochrane Hotel had been around for a long time. It gets a mention in Wayne Johnston's book *The Colony of Unrequited Dreams*. The Joey Smallwood character was living there. I believe Leo Tolstoy and Leon Trotsky stayed there.

We stopped rehearsing there because the place burned to the ground.

Lil Thomas: I remember going down there and seeing a burning heap of rubble. I remember the feeling in the pit of my stomach. I had a guitar that I made when I was in Nova Scotia. Fortunately, I took it home a couple of nights before. Usually, we just left everything down there. I was really thankful that it didn't burn because I had built it with my father. We lost the PA system. I think Louis's original Sonor drums were gone. I had an old Roland CUBE-60 amplifier. I remember finding a little tiny piece of the chassis in the middle of the rubble. The amp had basically melted. There's a ride cymbal we have at the recording studio [Sonic Temple, Halifax, Nova Scotia] that survived the fire. Other than that, we pretty much lost everything.

Some stuff was recovered through insurance money. There was a clause in our home insurance called "Effects Temporarily Away from Home," or something. We said, "The stuff usually stays at the house, but we were using it at another location." There was some money that came in as a result of the insurance claim. It was enough to put towards another guitar amp.

Someone may have mentioned a homeless person staying at the hotel that may have passed out with a lit cigarette, but I don't recall anything definitive.

David Guy: I was at school and Danny came and got me. It was the same day as the annual science fair. I actually got permission to leave school. Jim Moore, my homeroom teacher, was very sympathetic: "Don't worry about it. Go take care of what you got to do. But you have to be back this evening for the science fair." We spent the afternoon standing on the side of Cochrane Street. We could see the unpainted plywood of the PA speaker hanging precariously out of the side of the building on the third floor. The Cochrane was in smouldering ruins, and the machines were pulling it all down. The building was completely gutted. I remember seeing the missing wall, our gear, and then seeing the stuff fall into the pile of rubble.

Later that night, myself and Louis went down to investigate a little deeper into what had happened. In hindsight, it seems kind of ridiculous. We just sort of walked right into the rubble and poked around. I'm assuming the fire was electrical. That place was held together with gaffer tape.

I can't remember what time of year it must've been, but it was cold. Where the fire department sprayed everything down with water, right in the middle was this massive block of ice. When we chipped some of the ice away, we discovered that underneath this monolith was the beer cooler full of beer. We got in touch with Tim Angel. We loaded up the back of his truck with beer, stopped and got a platter from the Tan Tan Take Out on Gower Street, went back to my house, and had Chinese food and Cochrane Street cold beer. We filled the back of the truck with beer and started dropping them off to our friends.

Lil Thomas: Danny had been drumming in punk bands and playing bass guitar. Myself and Louis had done a lot of jamming together. It was kind of like, "Why don't the three of us get together?" We did something down at the LSPU Hall for the Greg Thomey play *Six Guns Headed for Tulsa*. That was the first time the three of us ever performed together onstage. But none of us sang. I don't think the Thomas Trio existed for any length of time without Jody.

Louis Thomas: In the script and on the promo, we were called the Hot Young Band. I'm sure this is all complete bullshit, but I remember Greg Thomey saying, "We thought you guys were going to suck, but you're actually really great." My recollection is that the play was sketch comedy, and we were like the Paul Shaffer Band. We did a weekend: Thursday, Friday, and Saturday.

Lil Thomas: The next band I was involved with was Part-Time Reggae.

Thom Thorne: We did Stiff Little Fingers, the Clash. We did the Specials and the English Beat. We did the Violent Femmes. We did Camper Van Beethoven and R.E.M.

I ended up being the singer because I couldn't play an instrument. I wasn't even that great a singer, but I wrote most of the original material. I would bring in a bare-bones song, and the boys would work their magic around it.

Louis went off to Toronto to attend Trebas [Institute] music school. That's when Jim Fidler took over on drums. Louis never played drums with Part-Time Reggae after that. It wasn't until he moved back from Toronto that the boys got the first incarnation of the Thomas Trio on the go. That's when Jim Fidler went on to form Pressure Drop.

Lil Thomas: Part-Time Reggae got a fair bit of exposure down at Bounders. Jack, the owner, was [...] older than us. He was a bit of an odd bird, too. I popped in for a beer or maybe just out of curiosity, and he had this room available upstairs.

Thom Thorne: Lil Thomas was working at Mary Jane's, next to Bounders. Jack, who had just bought the place, was there renovating and came into Mary Jane's to get a sandwich and a coffee, and Lil served him. They started talking. Lil asked, "What are you doing over there? I got a band."

Jack was like, "Do you guys want to play this weekend?"

Lil called us up: "We got a gig."

Dog Meat BBQ opened. That was the start of the Bounders scene.

Danny Thomas: I was still playing with Tough Justice and Schizoid, and someone basically said, "Why don't three of you guys play Peace-A-Chord as the Thomas Trio?" But we had one problem: none of us could sing. We decided to get a bunch of different singers. We had Brian Gregory and Jody. I think Dana [Warren] sang a couple of songs. Maybe Paddy Madden. We just put the band together for the purpose of playing Peace-A-Chord. I think it was called the Thomas Trio and Friends. When Jody performed with us, it was quite obvious to everybody that something interesting was going on there.

We then got asked to do a lunchtime concert on the stage outside of the LSPU Hall. We approached Jody: "Are you interested? We'll learn a bunch of songs and do it."

Jody was kind of band-less, and we were kind of singer-less. He was still doing some stuff with the Dirt Buffaloes, but [the band was] only home during the summer months. I think a couple of them didn't come back that year. The Dirt Buffaloes kind of flipped a few members around, and it wasn't as fantastic anymore.

We did that LSPU Hall gig, and that's when Jody was named "the Red Albino." In the middle of the summer, the three of us brothers were pretty brown, and I'm sure we were wearing almost no clothes. At the time, you were lucky to get a pair of shorts on us. Jody, on the other hand, can't be in the sun at all. He's pale, and that's where the name came from. The dark Thomas Trio brothers had a red-haired albino singer.

Jody Richardson: Peace-A-Chord was incredibly instrumental for building the scene. It was a very necessary tool to check out what everybody else was doing. I was involved with helping out Tina [Thoden]. Danny was the perpetual roadie who would run the stage. Louis did sound. I knew [the Thomas brothers] as really strong characters. I was always downtown. I lived on Forest Road, and then I lived on Rawlins Cross. All the Fleming Street stuff was just around the corner.

The Dirt Buffaloes were playing Club Max, and the Thomas boys were kicked back on the other side of the room. After the gig, I was sitting and drinking with them. That was kind of the hatching of the band. They respected me because I was relentless.

WORLD DOMINATION
SCHIZOID PART 2

Rod Wills: Our first demo was recorded in my basement with two mics hanging from the chandelier. Like everybody did back in the day, we sent out the tapes to different zines and independent record stores. Brian Taylor was the singer for Youth, Youth, Youth and worked at the Record Peddler in Toronto. He did a crossover show on CKLN-FM, a university radio station, and he liked what we sent him. People actually started calling in and requesting the songs. Brian produced Sacrifice, Slaughter, Razor, Dayglo Abortions, and Sudden Impact. The owner of the Record Peddler also ran Fringe Records. He put out all of those albums. Brian was interested in doing a record with us, but we never had the money to fly up to Toronto. We decided to hire Wallace instead.

Don's mother was fabulous. All the gear was at his place, and his mother and father opened their door to us. They were such nice people. Wallace was crammed into some little cubbyhole, and we were in Don's bedroom. We were so creative back then. I just wish that session could have been a bit more professional.

Phil Winters: Eight songs were recorded, and that became the *Datin' Satan* tape.

Don Ellis: Everything was recorded to cassette. Nobody had a four-track. There were no multi-tracks around. Nothing was easy. Wallace had this little board and a reel-to-reel. We finished the recording in less than a day. Mom fed us tea buns.

Chris Jerrett: We might've sold a few cassettes. One guy would buy it, and the next guy would tape it off. But that's the way we wanted it. We wanted our fan base to go home and listen to the music and share it with their buddies. That was a big turning point, people coming to the shows and knowing the songs. We didn't think of it as a business enterprise, like bands do today.

Rod Wills: Brian said, "This is not acceptable. We can't release it. The recording is not up to the label's standards. Let's do a full album. Can you come up to Toronto? I'll record it; I'll be your engineer."

Bob Armstrong: Toronto was the most logical place to be. We already had a lot of friends there who we had met through the fanzine. Brian Taylor from Diabolic Force Records played our tape on his radio show, *Aggressive Rock*. Some Toronto friends said, "This guy is going crazy over your band." We started corresponding with him directly.

We figured we'd make the move to Toronto, get our chops going, play some shows, and eventually do a proper recording session.

Don Ellis: As soon as we finished high school, we were gone. We got an apartment on Lansdowne Avenue and Bloor.

Phil Winters: Me and Don ended up sleeping in the living room. Bob had a bedroom, and maybe he shared it with Rod. Tina Riche was living there. So was Peter Martin. There was no shortage of Newfoundlanders in Toronto. Liz Pickard and Justin Hall were there together. So was Dave Sweetapple. We were all dirtbag punks, and Toronto was not nice to us.

Bob Armstrong: Our plan was world domination. It's the classic story. Rod and I had been there the year before, checking out bands and buying records. I wonder if that was the birth of Schizoid. We stayed at a place called Happy House. That's where Tony [Meaney] lived. It was a notorious punk rock hangout. I went downstairs, and the Accüsed were sitting in the basement. There was about two or three hundred people involved in putting off shows, and half of them lived at Happy House. We stayed there and ended up freezing our butts off. They made us clean the bathroom. In exchange, we got to sleep in the basement. We had no blankets. I had an overcoat, which I used to throw over me. Sometimes we would sleep in Tony's room because there was some actual heat in there.

John Pastore: I worked at a health food store two blocks from Happy House. The main venue was another block from there. I thought I was going to move to Los Angeles, believe it or not. I went out there to see Grady Schneider. He's long gone now, but he was part of the scene back then. His family moved to California around 1984. I was really into LA hardcore, but I didn't realize what a terrible place that city could be. I went out to visit him just before I moved to Toronto. State schools were still free in California. I was going to go out there, work for a year, and then go to university. But Grady was still in high school. I was like, *I don't know if I'm going to have the wherewithal to pull it together enough to move there when the only guy I know is still in high school.* And Los Angeles was a giant city. It took us like four hours to get across town to see a show.

On my way to Los Angeles, I flew through Toronto, which was where my brother was living. I had a couple of days' layover. Dave Sweetapple was there. Dave was like, "There's a room opened up at Happy House in the basement." I got back to Newfoundland and packed.

Rod Wills: Dave Sweetapple was kind of like our manager. We mostly let him take care of things. We thought it would be more professional. That's what Brian wanted, anyway. The band was given the scoop: "Diabolic Force will release the record. They'll pay for the cover, the printing, the distributing." But we had to come up with the money for the actual recording, which was a thousand dollars.

Bob Armstrong: We never had a dime.

Rod Wills: We were just lost. We had to get jobs. Being young, that was the furthest thing from our minds. All we wanted to do was go to shows and drink beer.

Phil Winters: It was not the glamorous situation we had imagined. I couldn't take the fucking heat. I used to blow-dry my hair after I got out of the shower. By the time I was finished I was sweating so much that I'd have to get another shower. So I just let my hair dry on its own, and that's why it's curly now, the Toronto heat.

Chris Jerrett: Brian Taylor respected our band, and he had Sudden Impact on the label. They were a lot like Schizoid. They were kind of like our parallel band from Toronto. We didn't have a clue about recording costs. It seemed like we were offered a fair deal. Whatever Brian sold, he'd recoup his pressing cost, and we'd own the recording. He'd split the profits with us thirty-seventy, or something like that. It was a verbal agreement. Back then, most indie label contracts were done with a handshake.

We're talking about five guys who landed in Toronto without one red cent. The recording never got done. We missed that opportunity.

Dave Sweetapple: I went up to Toronto to do hotel management and transferred into business. At the time, I was working for the Beer Store. So I always had money. Schizoid moved up and got an apartment in this really ugly neighbourhood, which is now kind of trendy.

Bob Armstrong: There would be scuffles out in the street in the middle of the night. It was the beginning of crack, and rent was cheap.

Dave Sweetapple: They would go down to the food bank and get packages of Kraft Dinner, eggs, and milk. It was kind of a desperate scene at their apartment. Chris was like, "I can't fucking handle this. I'm moving in with you." So Chris and his girlfriend both lived with me on Yonge Street. Phil got really depressed. He was dating someone, and they broke up. He just kept pining on about that. Rod kind of cracked up and locked himself in the bathroom. Don got really stressed out because he had never had a job before. He worked at a cheese factory.

Don Ellis: I saw a guy get stabbed outside the apartment. Like a lot of those kinds of neighbourhoods—Parkdale at that time was really seedy, too—you had to have your wits about you. I didn't mind our living situation. I didn't mind squalor.

Dave Sweetapple: There was a spot on Don's head that was as smooth as a baby's ass. Every last hair had fallen out. It was on the side of his head, so he couldn't cover it up.

Don Ellis: I went to the doctor and he said, "That's psychosomatic stress." I had to get the hell out of Toronto.

Dave Sweetapple: His mother used to call asking about him. "How is Don doing? I'm so worried about him. How is that hole in the side of his head?"

It was just like a comedy. Their excursion to Toronto was pretty short-lived. They moved up in July '87 and moved back home a few months later.

Bob Armstrong: We were on the brink of starvation. I don't know what it was with us, but no one wanted to work. I had a bunch of jobs for two days, got a paycheque, and spent it. It was forty degrees. I wasn't bothered by the heat because I was born in Ontario, but the rest of the guys were going crazy. You don't know humidity until you've experienced Toronto in July. Everybody was miserable. Don seemed to be doing fine. He seemed to have an endless supply of food and money.

Chris Jerrett: Don used to go down to the ATM and take out money his parents put in a bank account for him. The rest of us didn't know what we were going to eat the next day.

Don Ellis: I was working at an international cheese factory in an industrial wasteland. The shift started at five-thirty in the morning. In those days, bars closed at one. I'd be home for two o'clock, get like three hours sleep, and then go to work at the cheese factory. These little Italian guys ran the place. Nobody spoke English. The tables were like two and a half feet high, and here I am six foot six. I took cheese out of the brine and hung it up. My arms would be elbow deep in this vat of brine, bent over with no rubber gloves on. One day, my back completely seized. I called the boss. "I actually can't come in today. I'll send my buddy Phil." I never went back to the international cheese factory.

Chris Jerrett: I didn't work; I didn't get a job. I had enough money saved up so that I didn't have to work. At the time, me and my brother owned a skateboard shop in our garage, Bead Skates. I was the skater; it was a university project for him. He was pretty pissed off with me that I was leaving. In the end, the shop sold enough boards to cover the loan and make some profit.

Dave Sweetapple: Three nights before our first show, Bob was walking down the road with a couple of friends. Some rednecks drove by in a truck and starting screaming at them. Bob must've gave them the finger or told them to fuck off because the truck turned around, came back, and the guys inside got out with sticks. Bob had dyed his hair. He had piss-yellow hair and this massive black eye, playing shirtless. It was totally disgusting.

WORLD DOMINATION

Bob Armstrong: We were sort of wandering around Unionville, pool hopping in the rich neighbourhoods. We were climbing fences and swimming in backyard pools. There was this kid with us who was a lot smaller and younger than me. A bunch of guys drove by in a car, and a couple of them got out and started walking towards us. You know how it is. The smallest guy is the easiest target. One of them had a stick, and he was threatening to whack this kid. I managed to wrestle the stick out of the guy's hand. He said, "Let's make this fair. Throw down the stick." I'd never been into a fight before in my entire life. I put the stick on the ground, and the guy blindsided me. I had a bloodshot eye for about a year.

Don Ellis: I was having so much fun seeing so many great bands in Toronto that I kind of ignored the fact that Schizoid was actually not on solid ground.

Rod Wills: We were lost. Being young, getting jobs was the furthest thing from our minds. Tommy Dunphy was up there working as a roadie for Anvil. Me and Tommy were hanging out, and I was going to metal shows. I was thrilled to tour the studio in Mississauga and see what it's like at Rock 'n' Roll Heaven and the Gasworks. Tommy was going to New York, but I never had my papers. Plus, I was doing the Schizoid thing anyway. Then the band just fell apart.

Bob Armstrong: I don't know that there was a plan. We played a show at Ildiko's with Dioxine and SamFuckingHain. There was absolutely nobody there except for a few Newfoundland friends.

Chris Jerrett: There might've been ten people in attendance. No one knew about the show. There was no marketing and promotion.

Rod Wills: I was a kind of pen pal with Johnny Hart, who represented Voivod. I got talking to Michel Langevin. We were going to bring them to Toronto, and whatever profit was made would help pay for our record. Then Voivod signed to Maze Records and were getting ready to release *Dimension Hatross*. They couldn't do the show because they were under new management who wanted them to head out on the road for something like ten months straight. They said, "How would you like to open for us in New York at L'Amour? We're touring with Motörhead. If you can get the money together, you can come with us across the border." I ran into the kitchen and told the rest of the guys. They're kind of vague on it now. I think Bob remembers it. We were kids; we just wanted to party and have a good time. We didn't know how to handle the situation. Everybody just left Toronto.

Don Ellis: When Phil left, we were given a bit of a fait accompli. A big part of our sound was the crazy, whammy bar, dive-bomb soloing on a BC Rich Warlock—all that Slayer stuff. We just felt like we couldn't do it without him.

Rod Wills: I stayed in Toronto for a period of time. Bob called me and said Schizoid was asked to do some kind of skateboard show for Coca-Cola back in St. John's.

I remember going to El Mocambo to see Anthrax, and I happened to bump into Brian. Anthrax had just released *Among the Living*. We were in the lineup, and he said, "What's going on with Schizoid?" I told him the story. "I'll get you in any band in this city that's looking for a drummer. Don't go back to Newfoundland. Forget that band and stay here."

I explained how most everyone else in the band had gone home, and I told him the story about the skateboard show. Steve Milo [Sudden Impact bassist] was like, "No offence to Newfoundland or anything, man, but do you really think Coca-Cola would do a skateboard show there, when every summer they already put one off at the Canadian National Exhibition? Why would they do that? Is St. John's known to be a big skateboard town?"

"No, not really."

Brian said, "Stick around. If you really want to get in a band, let me know."

When I got back to the house, I called Bob. I guess it boiled down to the fact that I missed everyone. The next day, I went into the Record Peddler and said, "I'm heading home."

I came back to St. John's, walked off the plane, got in the car, and went to the Curling Club for the big skateboard show. I walked in, and the place was empty.

Bob said something like, "The show fell through."

I don't think there was ever was a skateboard show. I just think he wanted me back home.

Bob Armstrong: Me and Rod were record collectors, and we said, "We got to make this album happen." No one else really had any money to put towards a record. We got the seven hundred bucks together and did what everyone else used to do. We looked on the back of a Sudden Impact album, saw where it was pressed, and called up the record plant. That was from the same recording session that we did in Don's basement with Wallace

WORLD DOMINATION

Hammond. The pressing got screwed up, but it was an absolute dream come true. We sent them the reel-to-reel tape, and they put one song on there that wasn't supposed to be pressed. They put another song on there twice.

We looked at each other and said, "This is an accident, but it's like a miracle." Rod called up the plant and explained the situation. We took out maybe a hundred albums and sent the rest back. I guess they got destroyed. There's a bunch of those records floating around, which are ultra-rare.

Rod Wills: We were selling them at shows and throwing them out into the crowd. It didn't matter where they went.

Bob Armstrong: Our shows were fun. We jumped around and played heavy music. For a front man, Chris was one of the best I've ever seen. I'd often look over and he wouldn't even be on the stage. He'd be out running through the crowd getting people to scream into the mic. I remember he borrowed this black shirt with a white skull on it. Chris wore it one night over his head, singing through it while he stood on top of the speaker.

Chris started bringing a lot of props. I guess he got that from Chi Pig because Chi Pig always had a shovel. Chris used to bring a skateboard onstage. He lit one on fire once. He used to sing to a skull. It was crazy theatrical stuff.

Don Ellis: Rod was the question mark. *Is he going to drink forty-eight beers tonight and play everything at quadruple the speed that we rehearsed last night, or is he going to be spot on?* He was the great question mark. Some of us didn't drink at all. Phil never drank. Bob and Rod were drinkers. Me, I always wanted to be able to get through the show.

Dan Moore (*musician*): There was a Schizoid poster on the wall at Fred's [Records] for a show at the Star of the Sea Hall. All the hardcore crowd were there with shaved heads, thrashing around. I remember Chris Jerrett running around screaming, with his shirt off. We were only youngsters, and we were frightened to death.

Bob Armstrong: S.O.D.'s [Stormtroopers of Death's] first record had the song "Speak English or Die." That band took all kinds of crap for being racist. Phil and Rod loved the record because it was heavy. They didn't care about lyrics. There were constant arguments. I was taking a punk rock stance that it was a stupid record. They were always pushing us to do the songs. So Chris changed some of the lyrics and mumbled the rest. But the chorus was really strong: "Skate Vision or die." Chris owned a Vision skateboard. It was a good line because everyone who skated followed the band.

Phil Winters: We played at the retired citizens' club. We played at the Curling Club. We played at the 19th Hole. This is jumping around over a couple of years.

Bob Armstrong: We just seemed to have more people coming out. One of the turning points was the all-ages shows at the old-age home.

I remember walking into the place, and it was already packed to the gills. That was the first time I could say that I never knew anybody there. There were regulars in the crowd somewhere, but that was the first time [that] people were coming out who we didn't know.

It was exciting to create a scene from scratch and see it come to fruition. Going to bars with Duncan, Dave, and Craig, we would watch a band play to seven people. Then coming into a place where you're playing and there are a slew of kids that you didn't know was something else.

John Nolan: The seniors' centre was where The Rooms is today. It was cheap, and the guy managing the place didn't seem to mind. A couple of times he'd run up and shut us down: "No more music. No more music." It was like a place for seniors to play cards. I guess it would have been rented to bridal showers and stuff like that. Down in the basement was what we considered our green room. It had a fireplace and an amazing pool table donated by some English lord.

Rod Wills: The scene in St. John's changed because of Bounders. You'd go there and see everyone from every kind of crowd. People were going down because they heard Bounders was a bit of a freak show and a happening place.

Then there was the Battle of the Bands at the Corner Stone. Schizoid was asked to play. I don't know how that happened. I guess the organizers wanted to include every genre of music. That was a big deal for us because it was our first time using professional gear of any kind.

Don Ellis: The other day, my mother pulled out a shirt she happened to come across at the house with all the bands that played at *Star Search*. On the back of the shirt, there are three rows of band names. Something like sixty bands played *Star Search '89*.

Chris Jerrett: Schizoid got back together in December '89 to play the Battle of the Bands at the Corner Stone. That's when we covered Guns N' Roses, and I lit a skateboard on fire.

Rod Wills: We were called a "speed-metal Satan band." We used to meet people on the street and have arguments with them. It was just random people walking home from the bar. "Are you the guy in Schizoid? Are you a Satanist?"
"Yeah, I'm the guy in Schizoid."
"You're a devil worshipper, man."
  We got that stuff after the Corner Stone gig. That happened because we played for a different crowd. No one knew what to think of us.
  We came up with the idea to do something different. This is where the devil part enters into it. Tommy Dunphy designed an upside-down cross to put behind the drum riser. I thought it was great. The rest of the band weren't so sure. Don loved it. He thought it was funny. We were going to bring Chris out in a coffin. We went to the theatres and costume banks, but the caskets were too heavy.

Bob Armstrong: We had some sort of scary music blasting, and a bunch of guys carried Chris out on his back like he was dead and unceremoniously dumped him on the stage. People had never seen stuff like that, especially at the Corner Stone.

Rod Wills: We knew that there was no way that we would win. We're going to win, the speed-metal Satan band, and they'll send us across Canada? Impossible. Even though Slayer, Agnostic Front, and C.O.C. were popular, all that stuff was still underground.

Don Ellis: Wallace was always supportive of bands playing at the Corner Stone. But the Corner Stone was mostly a cover-band bar. We played *Star Search*, and Doug kind of liked us. We played great up against all these other bands because the showmanship was so spectacular. Chris was crazy; he was wild. He was diving off the PA system; he was diving off the monitors. We finally had a real PA system that could actually put us out there full blast. Rod had a full luxurious set of Canwoods, and he proceeded to beat the absolute living shit out of them.

If you got six hundred or seven hundred people at the Corner Stone, it was dynamite. Doug Warren offered us a gig, and he paid us fifteen hundred dollars. Wallace had nothing but good things to say about Doug. He said that he never had a cheque bounce. He said Doug was always reliable. If he asked for something to be done, Doug would do it. [...]

Schizoid got a decent crowd, but it was nothing spectacular. I think we played two nights, and Doug handed us the cheque. He never reneged, which I always respected. That was near the end of his tenure with the bar. I don't think it lasted much longer. It was sold to the bunch who put a dance club in there. We all lamented. We'll never get that bar back again.

Chris Jerrett: We finished fourth in that battle of the bands. The Thomas Trio won. Then the Thomas Trio went to Toronto and won the Canadian leg of the competition. All those dudes like Jody Richardson weren't into punk rock. [But] we were the ones who built the scene. We were the starting point for all the underground music. I don't think the Thomas Trio would have had such success if it wasn't for the punk rock days.

Rod Wills: Schizoid played a show with In Rage, an early Ward Pike band, at My Place on Water Street. They were a kind of blues-based hard rock. I vaguely knew Ward from Eugene Vaters. He's a Pentecostal guy. I think we met at the In Rage show and got to talking. Maybe a couple of weeks later, I happened to bump into him at Fred's Records. He was there buying a Yngwie Malmsteen album and invited me up to his house. Ward was this guitar wizard. We started writing songs. The amount of songs we had was unbelievable. The name we came up with was ridiculous: Dr. Spook's Rock and Roll Circus. Two of us did a demo and started passing it around. We sent it to Attic Records. They were interested and wanted to sign us. I still have the letter saying that they wanted more material. We got Joe Riche, who played in the Wake. They were a Strand band. We sent up the new stuff, but they weren't all that impressed. It was too commercial. Joe left and moved to Toronto.

We continued playing together as the Privateers. It was more about Ward's heritage of pirates or something. I don't really know. He got a guy from Mount Pearl, and the band became popular for some reason. We played the OZFM Dance Party. I had my hair cut, and I had a scarf around my neck. I thought, *Rod, you went from Dave Lombardo to Glass Tiger. What's going on here?*

Bob Armstrong: In 1989, I ended up going to Toronto for work. Back in St. John's, there were all kinds of bands coming up. Everybody was doing their own shows. I heard all kinds of stories that the scene was blowing up. It went from five or six guys to a couple dozen bands. I was working, and I was pretty sure that I was going to stay put. I guess you could say that's when the band ended. After the Toronto thing, we sort of got it together for a while, but I think we were all sort of drifting apart.

Rod Wills: Schizoid's final show was at the 1990 Peace-A-Chord. Bob was going to fly down. He phoned me. He said, "Rod, I got five hundred dollars. I can put five hundred dollars towards a new jeep, or I can do the Schizoid show."

"Bob, listen to me. Take the five hundred dollars and put it into your jeep. One of these days, maybe me and you will go for a ride."

Da Slyme at a MUN Radio beer bash. *Photo courtesy of Craig Squires.*

"The Gang of Four." Peace-A-Chord coordinators Sheilagh O'Leary, Jennifer Dick, Dana Warren and Rhonda Pelley. *Photo by Sheilagh O'Leary.*

Charlie Tomlinson at 15 Fleming Street. *Photo by Justin Hall.*

The Fleming Street Massacre Blues Band at Peace-A-Chord 1988. Jon Whalen, Barry Newhook, Sheilagh O'Leary, Colin Clarke, and Jim Fidler. *Photo by Paddy Barry.*

Lois Brown's Prince of Wales Collegiate Theatre Arts Class. *Featured in the photo:* Barry Newhook, Ashley Billard, Don Ellis, Eli Baker, Shelley Cornick, Rick Mercer, Andrew Younghusband, Paula Dyke, Clark Hancock, Lois Brown, Donna Pinhorn, Ken Tizzard, and Debbie Combs. *Missing from the photo:* Tina Riche, Gina Best, Teena Thorne, Lori Small. *Photo by Tina Riche.*

Sebastian Lippa. *Photo by Sheilagh O'Leary.*

Schizoid at Ildiko's Bar in Toronto. Phil Winters, Rod Wills, Bob Armstrong, Chris Jerrett, and Don Ellis. *Photo by Dave Sweetapple.*

Potbelly. Doug Jones, Tony Tucker, and Geoff Younghusband. *Photo by Katherine Pittman.*

Squat art gallery on Water Street. *Photo by Sheilagh O'Leary.*

Bung. Arthur Haynes, Justin Hall, Phil Winters, Barry Newhook and Jon Whalen. *Photo by Justin Hall.*

Mike Wade. *Photo by Sheilagh O'Leary.*

Fred Gamberg. *Photo by Geoff Younghusband.*

Fred Gamberg's Duckworth Street mural. *Photo by Tony Moore.*

Thomas Trio and the Red Albino reunion. Jody Richardson on George Street. *Photo by Ian Vardy.*

NO ONE GOES TO NEWFOUNDLAND BY ACCIDENT

Don Ellis: That September I stayed on in Toronto and had a couple of odd jobs. [...] Then I joined Godcore with Tony Meaney, who used to be Public Enemy's singer. I played some shows and lived at Happy House. I can't remember exactly how long I was there—about a year, maybe—but I do remember going to Newfoundland for Christmas and then heading back to Toronto that winter. I don't remember if I went straight to Montreal or not. John Pastore was living there, and he invited me to play with his new band that had formed from the ashes of Fair Warning. I loved Montreal. Toronto was a different city in those days. It definitely wasn't as kind and as happy a city as it is today. Now when you go to Toronto, it feels great. In the late '80s, Montreal was culturally diverse, friendly, and easygoing.

I always found that in Newfoundland—and that's what drew us all back, I think—you never felt alone. That's not how I really felt in Toronto. The city was overwhelmingly against that whole scene. It felt like you were always barking up the wrong tree. Toronto bands have always had a real hard time rising to the top in that city.

John Pastore: Montreal was insanely dirt cheap. I really wish I bought a house while I was living there. I could have bought a house as a nineteen-year-old, but I didn't want to pay any more than two hundred dollars a month for rent. For that, you could get a beautiful apartment in a Victorian mansion.

The mid-'80s wasn't too far after the whole FLQ [Front de libération du Québec] terrorism thing. All the businesses had moved to Toronto.

Montreal had no businesses, no jobs—nothing like that. But it had an amazing artistic scene. It had amazing food, beautiful architecture. It was the cheapest place imaginable.

Don Ellis: The Toronto freak scene that we were a part of was really subversive. And it was a struggle. The people who were in that scene were dirt poor. They were living in squalor. Toronto felt like an unfriendly and violent city.

Clark Hancock: I was done with Toronto in two weeks. There were buildings going up to the sky and people getting ground down to the dirt. I didn't want anything to do with it.

Don Ellis: Schizoid had disintegrated, and I was kind of off the hook. I came back for the summer and fell in love with Becky Moyes, and then left to go to Montreal because John wanted me to play in his new band.

John Pastore: You worked terrible part-time jobs because that's all you needed to get by. Nobody had any higher aspirations. You could be completely into music. Bob and Chris worked at a sandwich shop and lived in the apartment right above it. We'd come home from a show, open up the deli, grab some beers, and make ourselves sandwiches.

Chris Jerrett: I moved to Montreal in the fall of '88 and stayed there from August to December. That was a pretty influential time for me. I would go to Foufounes Electriques every weekend. That club is still on St. Catherine Street. All played. Government Issue played. Bob Mould played. The travelling bands were strong. The punk rock scene was strong. A lot of the Montreal bands had broken up, but there were still enough of them kicking around.

Don Ellis: At that time, it was just on the cusp of Nirvana. Living Colour was big. There was the Bad Brains influence, too. We were into Dag Nasty. That slightly metallic, slightly hardcore sound was popular. Bob was into the Descendants and Big Drill Car. That's what Rise kind of became. It was an emo-pop hardcore band. We were into that whole scene, when emo was actually emotional music.

John Pastore: I was friends with Sylvan LaCue from Fair Warning, which was a straight-up hardcore band. He was learning how to sing and wanted to do something where he wasn't just screaming. We started Rise with Fair Warning's drummer, but we didn't have a bass player or a second guitarist. When Bob and Don showed up, we had pickup bass players and second guitarists—nothing solid. Rise was definitely me and Sylvan, and then Don and Bob came on and were gone maybe a year later.

Don Ellis: You could be really weird and subversive in Montreal. You had your scene, and you had your people, and you could play your gigs for forever, and that was just fine. Everything was weird. The dance community was weird. The theatre scene was weird—everything. Rise rehearsed in this gigantic old brewery. There'd be string ensembles and Voivod and ethereal pop music. Godspeed You! Black Emperor is Montreal in a nutshell.

Metal is kind of an exclusive club. We were definitely feeling that in Toronto. I bought the Slaughter single. I bought the Sacrifice album. I just didn't like that stuff. But the metal bands in Montreal were incredible. I saw Voivod like ten times. They were a metal band, but they didn't have this cock rock, get loaded and beat people up mentality. They didn't have that stupid mullet metal thing that you found all over Toronto. Voivod were really interesting and really strange. The drummer, Michel Langevin, was the lyricist and an artist. They had these big theatrical shows where the guitar player would have four Marshall cabinets. The next week, they'd play in a small club. No problem. A week later they'd play a benefit for a women's shelter. No problem. They were that kind of excellent. They were heavy but really off the wall and down to earth and artistic. That was more my scene. There were all these weird bands that came out of Montreal—always weird and sarcastic and humorous. It just felt more like home, where we didn't take ourselves too seriously.

John Pastore: We recorded the *Joy* album with Bob and Don. After Don left, we never had anybody who compared to him.

Don Ellis: By the end of my time in Montreal, I was a bit depressed because nobody had a job. A lot of my friends from that time are still living the same lifestyle. The twenty-somethings and the thirty-somethings are working, and it's a vibrant city. My mid-forties friends are like, "I'm still holding onto the apartment because it's only one hundred and eighty-five dollars a month." They're collecting welfare. If you spend your whole twenties doing that, it's tough to get out of that cycle. Once the economy starts happening, you're not part of it. They're like, *I'm forty-five, and I've never really done* *anything with my life.* If you've been there long enough, it's still easy enough to coast along, but if you lose that apartment, or whatever, you're thrown headfirst into reality.

John Pastore: For over twenty years, I've lived off music exclusively, not from a band, but from a label and record-distribution company [Outer Battery Records]. I haven't had a non-music job as a source of income since the early '90s. I couldn't have had this sort of career in Newfoundland. The main problem with Newfoundland was the remoteness. I suppose that's what makes it interesting, the fact that for so many years, the island wasn't plugged into the wider world.

It used to be that nobody goes to Newfoundland by accident. St. John's is on the furthest eastern portion of an island that's stuck out in the middle of the Atlantic. But if it wasn't for that isolation, it wouldn't be the city that it is. It's an exciting place because it sat alone for almost five hundred years. It developed its own unique culture. That whole us-versus-them mentality has fashioned my whole life. I still don't have much to do with mainstream popular culture. My whole ethos was completely shaped in Newfoundland. No question about it.

IF I CAN'T DANCE, I DON'T WANT TO BE PART OF YOUR REVOLUTION

Bruce Gilbert *(activist)*: The story you're going to get from me is how Peace-A-Chord and Youth for Social Justice kind of ran in parallel for a period of about ten years.

I was born in Ontario to a Newfoundland father and a Toronto mother [but I grew up in Nova Scotia]. I ended up in Newfoundland because I got a job with Katimavik. It was Canada's national youth-service volunteer program. For nine months, Katimavik would take people from across Canada and put them in groups to live in three parts of the country. It was a kind of community-service program. The senator who started that [was] Jacques Hébert. He also started Canada World Youth. Those were the two youth programs of the '70s.

I worked in Newfoundland for Katimavik for five years, between 1981 and 1986, until Brian Mulroney finally shut it down.

I've been in Newfoundland ever since. Like a lot of us, I left for work. I went away to do a doctorate and worked for Canada World Youth in Africa. I spent a year in Namibia with OXFAM. I spent four months in Malawi and another four months in Indonesia with Canada World Youth. I spent six months in South Africa and Namibia doing AIDS education. But I always kept my stuff here. I've always lived in the downtown.

Then I was hired on by the Newfoundland and Labrador Human Rights Association, which was one of the founding partners of Youth for Social

Justice. I pitched to the executive director, Jerry Vink, an idea about a youth camp. He told me to go for it.

From my perspective, as a guy raised in rural Nova Scotia and not very radical, St. John's was a hotbed of activism. There's all these groups: the Peace Centre on Garrison Hill, Ploughshares and Ploughshares Youth and OXFAM and the Human Rights Association. OXFAM and the Peace Centre were kind of the meeting spaces. There was really edgy political theatre going on. There were protests. There was the whole anti–low-level-flying movement. There was the Roman Catholic Archdiocese Social Action Commission that was trying to change labour laws. There was an emerging environmental movement.

I [had] worked with some people at Dalhousie [University in Halifax] to develop a proposal that was submitted to the Secretary of State of Canada [now HRDC]. It was a proposal to bring groups of young people from twenty communities in Nova Scotia to learn about diversity, tolerance, and anti-racism. [They] said it was the best proposal that they'd seen in years. They told me to be patient and to hang on. We waited and waited and waited. In the meantime, I was in Halifax for a couple of months and got the Newfoundland job.

Eventually, the Secretary of State called and said, "We got some money for you." The proposal was called "Youth Celebrating Diversity." Without that funding, the project would have never happened. The innovation was getting young people to form groups in their communities.

I showed my boss the proposal and said, "Why don't we do it here?" OXFAM was doing all kinds of stuff with young people. They had Ploughshares Youth meetings in their office. Youth Acting Against Apartheid was just forming. They were doing all these participatory youth ads about getting young women to work in industry. It was the first time I had ever seen that.

My memory is that the proposal was dropped on the desk of OXFAM and the Peace Centre, and I said, "Let's do a camp." But Evelyn Riggs challenges me on that because, for her, there's a different reality. She was at OXFAM, and they were dealing with the National Youth Council of St. Vincent and the Grenadines in the Caribbean. They did youth study camps. Youth camps weren't a new idea. But Evelyn's memory is that we built on the stuff that they were already doing in the Caribbean.

Dana Warren: I went with Canada World Youth and lived for four months in Quebec and for four months in Brazil. Then I came back here to St. John's. I think I did a semester at MUN, and then I moved to Montreal to study French.

The other part of my life was that I got involved with Youth for Social Justice. I was a young person working with a number of adults on the instructional and organizational side. We used to do these amazing week-long camps where we'd bring youth together from all over the province. I think the largest camp was eighteen groups of five. We'd always bring in some international participants. There were some from Labrador. They were all between the ages of eleven and fifteen. They were political camps. You'd learn how to make a newspaper. We had a newscast every night. We even had a pirate radio station. We used to do radio broadcasts every morning, and then we put on plays at night. It was all about empowering kids to do community work. I might've been eighteen. I was just a kid myself.

Bruce Gilbert: The first Youth for Social Justice camp was in 1988.

Andrea Cooper *(activist/organizer)*: It was a group of teenagers with some support from adults. At one point, they had funding to hire a network coordinator, which was Becky Moyes.

Becky Moyes: Although I didn't realize how challenging it was at the time, we had a board of directors that was comprised of all teenagers. We were, as adults, the advisers. I was twenty-three; I was ancient. The teenagers would all come down [to the office] and tell me their high school troubles. I was as much a counsellor as I was an organizer.

It was a moment of magic, seeing this awakening of hearts and minds. The teenagers were looking for something to help them make sense of the world. The workshops were a way of being introduced to popular education. It was all about making that connection, cheesy as it was, between global and local.

"Think globally, act locally." That was OXFAM's slogan.

Bruce Gilbert: The key people were me, Alison Dyer, and Evelyn Riggs. Neil Tilley and Fred Campbell were at MUN Extension.

Behind each of us was a cadre. My executive director was fully behind it. Bill Hynd at OXFAM was fully behind it. That's the beauty of collaboration [...]: a bunch of threads came together and [we] managed to pull off something that the young people loved, and their energy and their interest kept it going for ten years.

Becky Moyes: The Network Coordinator provided support. There were lots of teams from St. John's. But then there were groups from all over the province: Holyrood, Clarenville, Gander, Stephenville, and St. Anthony. Inuit and Innu communities were involved. My role was to support them in their local activities and help provide the tools that they needed to give a workshop or information session. I was also responsible for networking with four other youth groups—two in Canada and two overseas.

We shared tools and resources. If one group developed a workshop, we'd share it and see how we could modify it. We had an educational toolkit that we produced collectively. We had exchanges at least once a year where all five groups would meet in one place and have a conference around social justice activism.

Lesley Thompson (*activist/organizer*): In terms of doing activist work, I'm a lifer. I think I probably saw a poster downtown, or I probably heard that there was some connection between Peace-A-Chord and Youth for Social Justice. My first Youth for Social Justice meeting was at the Peace Centre on Garrison Hill.

I have a memory of Becky, who is tremendously theatrical, basically lying on the sidewalk and squishing herself in through the downstairs window. That's how she made her grand entrance into the meeting.

Becky Moyes: Bruce applied for the funding for permanent staff. I first volunteered with Youth for Social Justice in 1990, when they had the provincial camp in Gros Morne. In 1993, there was no one to coordinate. Theresa MacKenzie had left, and I took on the summer position. It was timely because Health Canada had a Brighter Futures program, and OXFAM secured three years' worth of funding.

Andrea Cooper: I think my older sister, Stephanie, had friends involved with Youth for Social Justice. I was genuinely interested in the peace festival and volunteering in the summer instead of doing tennis lessons.

Karmella Perez (*activist/organizer*): Me and my friends from the neighbourhood went to the Avalon Mall to meet Chalk Circle. They had an autograph session at A&A Records. I would have been in Grade 9. We started talking to some girls in the lineup ahead of us, and we all went to see *Cry Freedom* together. That movie really affected us. Denzel Washington was in it. It was about South African apartheid and Steve Biko. One of the girls in the group called OXFAM because someone there had done a workshop at her school. She told them there was a bunch of thirteen- and fourteen-year-olds who were interested in politics.

We started going down to OXFAM on Saturdays. Once they put us in touch with Ploughshares Youth, we started hanging out at the Peace Centre. I think they were pretty enthusiastic about seeing kids coming in and wanting to know what was going on in the world. That's when my group of friends and I started Youth Acting Against Apartheid.

At the time, Bill Hynd and Linda Ross were at OXFAM. She's now at the Provincial Advisory Council on the Status of Women [2009–18]. The guy who did most of our workshops was Bruce Gilbert.

Bruce Gilbert: The first Youth for Social Justice camp was at the Brother Brennan Centre, just off Salmonier Line. There was a main room and a couple of cabins. We just took over everything. We had a darkroom in one of the bathrooms. We took a video suite out from MUN Extension and set it up in the kitchen. We pitched tents for drama performances.

Then we went to Killdevil Lodge in Lomond, all the way across the island. That provided much more versatility. Who were the teams? The Plum Point lads and lasses got together. The St. John's teams were the Youth Acting Against Apartheid and Peace-A-Chord. There was the Ploughshares Youth team. There was the Young Filipino Youth Council.

Karmella Perez: Camp took place in the summer during the first week of August. We would spend all year organizing. Once the funding came in for Peace-A-Chord, March, April, and May would be focused […] on the festival. Peace-A-Chord was always in early July, and then we'd have a month to get everything tied up before camp.

Each group had to sign up for different workshops, whether it was newsletter, radio, or television. There was an adult mentor, and there was a youth mentor. I ended up being the newsletter [*Sound and Vision*] youth mentor for pretty much the entire time I went to camp.

Obviously, you're taking people from different social backgrounds. There was a group from Shea Heights. There were groups from Labrador. There was a group from Belize and the Caribbean. There were a few times when there were people from different parts of Newfoundland who had never seen Black people before.

Bruce Gilbert: In 1990, there was maybe a hundred people at the camp. We didn't reinvent the wheel. We would have plenary in the morning.

"Yesterday was human rights day, and today is environment day." I led human rights day. It was basic participatory education. Each one of the adults led a content session. When it came to the afternoon, I was in charge of theatre. Fred Campbell was in charge of media.

Becky Moyes: Fred would drive out in his shitbox old Saab, hoping it wouldn't break down on the way with all his video gear in the back.

Bruce Gilbert: We were colourful and fun, and there were a lot of young people. I did my master's thesis on popular theatre. It was theatre put together by the common man that would mirror what was going on in society and which would maybe agitate people. There's the whole Augusto Boal *Theatre of the Oppressed* stuff. That's what I did for my afternoon sessions. Our job was to listen to what young people were concerned about and present some sketches about those issues.

Karmella Perez: We did news broadcasts. Each person got to learn how to use a video camera, and there was an anchor. We all had to write our own news show. We had a small radio transmitter. The one thing the adults told us was not to say where we were. One night, on the last radio show of the evening, someone mentioned our location. All of a sudden, there was dead silence in the camp. We thought we were going to get shut down. The next day a car turned up with this antenna on the roof, and everyone freaked out. Fred Gamberg took the transmitter, put it in his backpack, and disappeared into the woods.

Becky Moyes: Youth for Social Justice was definitely a training camp for social activists.

Bruce Gilbert: Some people around town called it "Young Commie Camp."

Becky Moyes: The purpose of the camps was to sort of give participants ten days of core training. YSJ was the great springboard to propel them into the next part of their lives.

I work for Canadian Heritage. My [current] boss was going to Nain to see the construction of a new cultural centre. He was going to stop over in Hopedale for a heritage conference. I [recently] found my friend Sean Lyall on social media. I thought, *I've got to ask him if he can get some traditional dress for my boss because he's going to this big feast. I wonder what Sean is doing now*. I searched him because I didn't want to seem completely ignorant when I asked what he's been up to. I found out that he had just been named the Minister of Culture for the Nunatsiavut Government. You could see that the YSJ camps were just another step to his activism and his leadership. There's so many [camp participants] who are now leaders in their communities.

Lesley [Thompson] is a perfect example of someone who is not compromising her values. By the time she was sixteen or seventeen, Lesley was organizing Peace-A-Chord and facilitating workshops. She learned facilitation and leadership skills that most kids in high school wouldn't have a clue about.

Louise Moyes: I'm stating the obvious, but teenagers have lots of ideas about how the world can change.

Lesley Thompson: Early on, two projects [that] stick out to me were the collaborations with OXFAM and the Fish, Food and Allied Workers. We were in the midst of the collapse of the cod fishery. We were thinking in terms of an environmental perspective, a sustainability perspective, an economic perspective and then, because of the relationship between Youth for Social Justice and OXFAM, the international perspective. I went to a meeting and there was talk of starting a fisheries forum in Petty Harbour that would invite people from other countries who had experienced overfishing and, of course, local fishermen.

It was like, "The fishery is collapsing and our economy is in the tank. We can't be alone. There has to be a sort of global narrative to all of this. There's like 30 per cent unemployment in the province. Something is definitely wrong."

Bruce Gilbert: I think YSJ waned because the young people were moving on. Every year you're starting with a new group and trying to get them mobilized. There was turnover; everybody changed roles. The Peace Centre shut down after the first couple of camps. Alison probably ran the Peace Centre on one of those Section 25 or Section 38 programs. A lot of us were working on government grants.

In 1991, MUN Extension shut down. We were all in there [the president's office]. I pushed Art May's door open with the video camera running: "Hello, Dr. May. We're here to see you." Behind me was a chain of people that went down the stairs, out the door, and around the building, including Greg Malone, Tommy Sexton, Cathy and Andy Jones, and Gerry Squires.

MUN Extension shutting down was a major problem for YSJ. There was Extension Arts, Bond Street, and Duckworth Street, and then there was Extension Field, the outreach offices around the bay. Art May was trying to kill the whole thing. But he didn't understand that Extension Arts was going well, it made money, and everyone was happy. I think in their attempt to kill Extension Field—the shit disturbers, the popular educators, the social activists—the government was leaning hard on the president.

In the paranoid ex–MUN Extension world, people said that they took MUN Extension out of rural Newfoundland at the worst possible time. The official narrative was that MUN Extension had outlived its usefulness. There's a reason why the protest against the closure lasted for months and months. To this day, people still talk about MUN Extension. MUN Extension's resources in YSJ disappeared. The Human Rights Association lost a lot of its funding. The Peace Centre shut down. Key people moved around. With a lack of resources, people ran out of gas.

Maybe it was time for YSJ to end. It liberated all those people to do other things.

We got to work together better to fix this world. While we're at it, we should have a good time. I think that's what Youth for Social Justice and Peace-A-Chord were all about. I often think of the Emma Goldman quote: "If I can't dance, I don't want to be part of your revolution."

Jody Richardson: When the Trio and [Fleming Street Massacre Blues Band] played, we used to say, "All the love and hate you need."

Geoff Seymour: One of the biggest influences on where the music went was D.O.A. and Jello Biafra's EP *Last Scream of the Missing Neighbours* [1989]. It changed the way Phil played guitar, and that led to the sound Bung developed. He was used to playing thrash metal. The way everything came together on their first album, the '80s riffage combined with three-chord punk rock opened up a lot of avenues for him.

Jody Richardson: Bung was about tearing it all to shreds. You could call them "punk," in terms of their ethic, but they had a real groove. They had a dark elemental sound like rolling waves.

Arthur Haynes: Schizoid, Tough Justice, and Malpractice, which turned into Tumblebug, played everything at breakneck speed. With Bung, it wasn't so self-indulgent.

Phil Winters: Bung's groove comes from Justin Hall's style of drumming.

Barry Newhook: Myself and Jennifer could be here and put on Dog Meat BBQ and think, *There's nothing studied about what Justin did.* Everything was organic. But it's a true compliment when I say that. Nothing he did was ever the same as before. The way he played a song was constantly evolving.

It's very hypnotic. A song starts one way, and Justin doesn't make any major changes, but he gradually starts adding things. I think it's subconscious. He doesn't even know that he's doing it.

Jody Richardson: Bung's recordings never matched their live performances. But that's so often the case. Those were some of the greatest gigs I've ever seen, let alone been part of. Jon was rake thin and really knew how to work a crowd.

It was Newfoundland rock that was more akin to Black Sabbath. St. John's used to be a rock town. What happened? Now everybody is playing ukuleles.

Natalie Noseworthy *(musician)*: I always looked up to Jon Whalen because he had such conviction. He could be a cult leader. In a way, he kind of was. He'd say, "I want to be free. I want to be free to ride my machine without being hassled by the Man."

Everyone was like, "Yeah, fuck the Man!"

Johnny Fisher: Bung crossed all genres. They had hippies in the band. They had punk rock guys in the band. They had a member from the original '70s movement. They had the metal-grunge crossover thing down. They were drawing from a wide spectrum of people. They had concise songs, but they could riff for forever. You could lose yourself in them; songs could be twenty minutes long.

Arthur Haynes: There's a demo which exists from before we did *Whole*. It's a five-song demo that we recorded with Don Ellis at 333 Duckworth Street. In my opinion, it's the best representation of what Bung sounded like. It's tear-your-face-off huge.

Geoff Seymour: I moved to Halifax to try and get in on some film work. During the Victoria Day weekend, I went to my cousin's house, and I put on the Bung demo tape. The whole room went silent and didn't say a word until it was over. Everybody was listening. Finally, someone got up at the end of "Nation" and said, "Did you say this is happening in St. John's?"

BLOWING SMOKE (UP YOUR ASS)

Marcel Levandier *(musician)*: Something happened in the early '90s with one trip to Halifax. After that, everything was about hype.

Geoff Younghusband: Certainly some of us had the Mudhoney record [*Superfuzz Bigmuff*], and some of us had copies of *Bleach*. We were listening to the Seattle scene before it completely exploded. I pulled out the Discord Records release list the other day. I think I have twenty-seven or twenty-eight of the first thirty Discord releases.

    The Sub Pop Singles Club was probably what introduced us to the whole Seattle scene. Sub Pop's marketing was spectacular, and we were all record collectors. Don Ellis, Woody Whelan, and Rennie Squires worked at Fred's throughout the years. They would order a ton of punk rock. I bought everything by Discord, I bought everything related to SST Records [Solid State Tuners], and I bought everything out of Seattle.

Barry Newhook: Punk rock and underground music wasn't so out there anymore. It was maybe closer to what people wanted to hear. It was what people read about and wanted to be a part of.

Geoff Younghusband: In those five years from 1990 to 1995, our bands went from having twenty and thirty people at all-ages shows to playing the Loft and putting four hundred people in there. We used to have line-ups at the LSPU Hall, hiring our friends as security to keep everything under control.

Doug Jones *(musician)*: I discovered Mudhoney in 1989. For me, that was the change. It had nothing to do with Nirvana. I watched the *Sonic Highways* episode on the Seattle scene last night. They got into the same sort of things that were happening here: the weather keeping people indoors, no one working because of the terrible economy.

Geoff Younghusband: In that whole era when Nirvana blew up, the press was talking about how there were scenes everywhere. Kids started looking for them, and we were there to cash in artistically. But nobody was putting money in their pockets. Every band I have ever played in took every cent that we made and turned it into records or promotion.

Jon Swyers *(musician)*: Punk and underground music was fuelled in many different places. It was the culmination of many things. St. John's being particularly destitute socio-economically made it more of a hotbed. I guess people were out of work and had nothing better to do.

Jon Whalen: What's that line from *The Commitments* movie? "It feels much better being an unemployed musician than an unemployed pipe fitter."

Jon Swyers: It didn't just happen in Newfoundland. It happened worldwide, but specifically in North America. There were lots of hotspots. Seattle broke the commercial market, and it led to all of these micro scenes happening. St. John's had a great one. Halifax had a great one. Moncton had a great one. If you go further down the East Coast, you'll find Chapel Hill and North Carolina. Chicago was huge with Touch and Go Records.

Doug Rowe *(musician)*: The first band that I played with? Undermine. That was in 1991. It was me and Paul Gruchy, Stirling Robertson, and Rennie Squires.

Paul Gruchy *(musician)*: We played our first show in 1991 at Bar None. Our first all-ages show was at the LSPU Hall.

Doug Rowe: We played three nights in a row at Bar None—Tuesday, Wednesday, and Thursday. We were still eighteen. I couldn't believe we were playing in an actual bar. That show was with Rubber Samuel, who were Doug Mason, Bob Dicks, Jason Lane, and Marcel Levandier. I don't know what happened to Undermine. Doug and Stirling went their own way and started Potbelly with Rennie and Geoff, and me and Paul went the other way with Bob and Doug Mason from Rubber Samuel to start Ditch.

Doug Jones: Ian Nightingale may have had Mudhoney's "Touch Me, I'm Sick" single. It had the same power as punk and hardcore, but it was chaotic and noisy. Undermine covered "Touch Me, I'm Sick." I think it was shortly after that when Undermine dissolved because Paul and Doug weren't convinced. But I was sold.

Potbelly started jamming in Stirling's basement. We brought Ren in on drums. Of course, we needed a bass player. Geoff would know this story better than I do. For some reason, I remember putting wanted ads around MUN.

Geoff came up with the name Potbelly. It was supposed to be a riff on Crooked Stovepipe—potbelly stove, crooked stovepipe. Geoff was part of the downtown scene. I'd see him around. I don't think I even knew that he played bass, but we had the same kind of idea about what we wanted to do. Stirling had great stage presence. He'd take his guitar off and throw it to the floor and haul it around and make lots of noise.

Geoff Younghusband: I'd seen Age of Majority, and they'd broken up. I heard Doug was jamming with Rennie Squires and Stirling Robertson.

Rennie Squires *(musician)*: Doug's girlfriend and my girlfriend were roommates.

Geoff Younghusband: I ran into Doug on the street and said, "I hear you need a bass player. I want to join a band." I came back from England, Danny Thomas was upgrading his gear, and I bought a bass from him. That's the one I still use to this day, a Daion with Yamaha pickups that Danny installed.

I didn't know how to play bass. I had a basic concept of how to hack my way through a song, but I don't think I ever played a full song until I joined Potbelly. We jammed in Stirling's basement; his dad would storm through and blast a few honks on the bagpipes, dance around, laugh, and go back upstairs.

Rennie Squires: Doug wasn't a great singer. He was a vocalist and the guy with the words. He was the only one who cared enough to write lyrics. Take it or leave it.

Geoff Younghusband: The first song I wrote for Potbelly was "Mudslide." I also wrote stuff that Doug sang. By the end, I probably wrote at least half of the *Glid* cassette [1993]. Mostly, my songs were about getting high and being punk. Doug always had a slightly more political thing going on. He wrote "Dirty Paw" about the Montreal massacre, which was the seven-inch that we put out with Grasshopper, a band from Toronto. Most of my songs were based around one riff and a few words that were very open ended.

Doug Jones: We started off by playing open mics at Bar None on Wednesday nights.

Jon Whalen: I took over the lease on Bar None. It had actually closed down for a while, and the original owners reopened a place across the street called the Fishing Admiral, which used to be a bar and restaurant. Bar None was kind of sitting empty. They vacated it in January, and I had it up and running again by June. I ran that for about a year and a half.

That was a bad time to open a bar. That was the year [1991] the GST [Goods and Services Tax] came in and [in 1992] the cod moratorium started. There were as many bankruptcies in Newfoundland that year as there had been in all of the province's history. I was one of them, basically. I couldn't make a go of it. People weren't spending money. A lot of the bands that could really draw a crowd, like Dead Reckoning and the Thomas Trio, had gone off to the mainland.

Natalie Spracklin: In this town, you couldn't be a financial success. It was subsistence living. You had to really love what you were doing, and you had to be very confident. I think a lot of people who lived that life and who pursued that path did so because that's what spoke to them. That's who they were. It was hand to mouth all the time, unless you had a side talent like doing lighting at the Arts and Culture Centre. People picked up gigs in the film industry and television. Anybody from this community had to sort of wear multiple hats, and a lot of them got the hell out. Some of us got an education, and now we're pushing pencils all day long. Our asses are getting flat and wide from sitting down all day long.

You can't stay true to the scene if it doesn't give back at some point.

Jon Whalen: Bar None made money the first month we were open and the last month we were open. We started doing multi-band nights with Bung, Lizband, Potbelly, and Hardship Post, and we turned the corner.

But I had been dodging the tax man and the suppliers, the landlord, and everybody for months. It had become stupid. I should have gotten out of there six or eight months earlier. Then those bands did the same thing at the LSPU Hall and the Loft and packed those places. That's when our generation of the scene really got going.

Fred Gamberg *(from "'Good gig,' said Fred. Potbelly, Whodafunkit, Hardship Post, Bung: LSPU Hall, October 9, 1992." The* Muse, *October 23, 1992)*: I only found out about this gig because I asked a member of Hardship Post when he was going to play next. I was surprised because there were no plans for any gigs just two days before. In any case, I have to hand it to the organizers for a successful and quick promotion because the very next day there were more concert posters around town than you could shake a stick at, and this performance was the talk of the town. I made the definite plans to go, and that I did.

When I walked through the door, I expected to see a few people (there hasn't been a show of this sort for a while). This show boasted the largest turnout for any live club performance-type thing in at least a year. Successful promotion, indeed.

Geoff Younghusband: We were never allowed to soundcheck properly at the Loft because there was a restaurant downstairs. We had a deal with them so that we could soundcheck at [...] five-thirty before their dinner people arrived, and then we weren't allowed to make noise until ten o'clock, when business petered off.

Fred Gamberg *(from "Bung, Whodafunkit, Potbelly, Hardship Post. The Loft, November 13 and 14." The* Muse; *November 20, 1992)*: Some people might not have wanted to see these bands again in the space of a month, but I figured that since they have been writing new material and one band (Whodafunkit) had a recent lineup change, I just had to be there.

Bung, who have been together for about a year, played first on Friday and second on Saturday night. This is a bit different but it gave people who normally leave early a chance to hear them before the midnight hour. The sound was not to the Gambergian quality level, as singer Jon Whalen's voice was barely audible. Phil Winters' guitar work seemed to drown out the others onstage. Apart from this, they played well on Friday, though Saturday was a lot better because the sound problems were fixed.

Phil Winters: The Loft would have been '92. The first gig we played down there we rented out the space. We were all playing at the Hall pretty often. I was technical director [there] then.

The core bands were Bung, Lizband, Potbelly, and Hardship Post. It expanded to Ditch and Potatobug. Dead Red and Darshiva were also active. There was this family of musicians playing shows together. As a matter of fact, me and Barry both played in Lizband up until mid-'93.

Bob Dicks (*musician*): Ditch lasted two and a half years. It wasn't a long time. We're surprised people still remember.

Ritche Perez (*musician*): When John Rowe joined [Potatobug], he played mandolin through a Marshall amp. Jamie Tucker joined, and Peter Harbin left. We had established our band members, and we were starting to write.

Our first gig was a fundraiser at Capricorn's Bar on George Street. We were doing traditional music because that was John Rowe's background. O'Brien's Music is his family's business. We did a set of traditional songs, and then we broke into the heavy grunge drop-D tuning. I'm not sure how well that went over.

Natalie Spracklin: The Loft was one of the first times that groups came together en masse for a fixed price. We shared the cost of rental equipment; we paid for whoever was doing sound. I remember the first gig we played there. We charged five bucks. People were paying three dollars cover. We had increased it slightly just so the bands could get paid. I think, generally, it was three bucks anywhere in town to see a band. But that's all anybody would pay. If people were going to George Street, they'd pay three bucks cover. A drink was probably a dollar.

The Loft was an opportunity to play a much bigger venue than Bar None. Although we didn't know who was running the place, and they didn't care who we were, they treated us in a professional way. We were treated as though we were an actual commodity. Back then, if you tried to get a gig on George Street, they'd laugh right in your face. They didn't hire anyone who wasn't playing covers. If you were doing original material, they would never hire you in a million years, even if you were just taking in the door.

What we did at the Loft was a real shift. Those shows were packed. People were hanging off the ceiling.

I recall that when Whodafunkit played, we were mostly sandwiched in between other bands. Bung would hardly ever open a show because the audience would shoot their wad and go home. I loved Bung, but it was a big-boy mosh-pit scene. With Whodafunkit, there was a space to dance.

Pressure Drop asked us to open for them. The first night the place was full. And then Pressure Drop offered us two dozen beer as payment. First off, we had never agreed to play with them, but they had already advertised the bill. I said, "We'll play the first night, but you're going to have to let people know we're not playing the second night." In many ways, they weren't part of our community. They just wanted to take the proceeds from the door for themselves. I thought, *That's not how we do things*. We had a more communal approach to booking gigs.

Money was an afterthought. We never did it for money. We never did it to get rich. In fact, more often than not, we did benefit gigs and loved doing those every bit as much as walking out with a couple hundred bucks in our pockets. It wasn't about money. But it's just the thought and the sentiment that goes behind it. We didn't want to be treated like we were an afterthought.

Doug Jones: Potbelly opened for Sloan at Bar None. They did Canada Day at Quidi Vidi and got booed off the stage.

Jon Whalen: I booked Sloan sight unseen. It was one of the last things I did of any consequence before Bar None shut down.

Rennie Squires: Nobody really knew who Sloan were.

Geoff Younghusband: They had just released their *Peppermint* EP on Murderecords. At that time, Sloan was a lot noisier [...]. It was a swirling, loud mass. Chris Murphy and Patrick Pentland [of Sloan] both had Kustom amps with the heads and cabinets wrapped in glossy vinyl and glitter. They were everything they continued to be. Chris was crawling around the stage, over and under the band's equipment.

Doug Jones: Shortly thereafter, we did the *Slagroom* tape with Ward Pike. Potbelly played with the Privateers at the Loft. Ward was an awesome guitar player and is still a fantastic guy, but he was standing on a table wearing a pirate shirt. The Privateers were a different kind of thing.

Rennie Squires: I had never even laid eyes on a four-track before. Ward Pike had a studio out in the west end. I thought the place was like something off of TV. It was an actual studio. It had proper faders and an isolation room. That was my first introduction to recording.

Doug Jones: Things didn't really start going [with Potbelly] until Ren and Stirling left and Tony Tucker joined the band. [...] We needed another guitar player. We went to Sebastian Lippa's house and jammed. He said, "You guys sound fine as a three-piece."

There was a consensus: "Okay. Let's try that."

Geoff Younghusband: The first sort of tour was the 1993 ECMAs in Halifax. Hardship Post, Bung, Lizband, and Potbelly played the Double Deuce and then did a mini-tour with Eric's Trip through St. John, Moncton, and Charlottetown. The bands were packed into two minivans. There was a minivan for the smokers, and there was a fifteen-person passenger van with the back seats pulled out for the gear and the non-smokers. I drove that van for most of the tour because everyone else was too freaked out to drive. Basically, it was Lizband and Bung in the smoking van. There was me, most of Potbelly and Hardship Post, and Don Ellis, who came to do sound, in our van.

Marcel Levandier: There was always this undercurrent: *Maybe we got a chance of making it*. With Tough Justice and those bands, they never had a fucking thing. They knew there was no chance of "making it." They didn't want to make it. They wanted to put out a demo and sell it to their friends.

With Sloan getting signed to Geffen, all of a sudden, Halifax was popular. It was dubbed "Seattle of the East." Thus, Newfoundland was trying to ride its coattails.

Natalie Spracklin: People might tell you that they never had aspirations, but I think they did. I don't think they wanted to be superstars on the radio like Nirvana, but I think they wanted some recognition. It was a measure of success. If you don't tour, you're not going to have a following. You're not going to have success. It was hard for a lot of people to get out of here. No one had the dough for that.

Phil Winters: The Fredericton show was an all-ages at a farmers' market. That city was all one-way streets and stop lights. And it smelled bad. That's my impression of it anyway.

Arthur Haynes: A kid got stabbed. Walking away from that experience, we thought, *Was there an already pre-existing beef? Or did we incite them to violence?*

Phil Winters:. We found out that the last ferry back home left at midnight. Everyone was playing super fast. Get through the set. Get everything down, and get the next band up. Eric's Trip was closing out the night, and they were using our gear. *C'mon, c'mon, c'mon.* Looking at the watch. *C'mon, c'mon, c'mon.* Looking at the watch. We loaded everything into the vans and burned it to the ferry terminal. We got there just in the nick of time; I think they were about to put up the gate.

Geoff Younghusband: Potbelly released our second album, *Glid*, through Duckworth Distribution.

Robert Buck *(promoter)*: Music was going in a different direction, and tourism was really beginning to evolve. So the whole idea of developing a music-distribution company—as much as we wanted to get Newfoundland and Labrador music out to the province, the real goal was to get it out to everybody else. During the early '90s, the music industry was in a fiery growth stage.

From a creative perspective, there was a great melting pot here. The indie scene started, and we were receptive to it. I mean, obviously, the bread-and-butter money was traditional music. And that was the national flavour, but we had some great successes with alternative music, too. Thomas Trio and the Red Albino were coming along. They showed the most promise. Bung and Hardship Post were a little more in line with Sloan and what was happening worldwide.

The indie music was really good, really innovative, but sales was a challenge. That's probably why artists move to Toronto or larger centres. You need a certain tipping point in order to make it work. And as much as St. John's is a great creative place, it doesn't provide the financial resources to support those kinds of niche markets. That's why traditional music was easier. You need to reach out nationally and internationally to attract enough revenue.

Natalie Spracklin: I was in Montreal studying. I went to see Potbelly play at some weird sports bar. Whodafunkit didn't tour. We didn't record. We didn't do anything like that.

Geoff Younghusband: I can't determine if that tour was a positive or a negative. Tony was underage. I thought he had his parents sign off on a waiver to get him into bars, but he told me recently that he forged the letter saying that I was his temporary guardian.

Doug Jones: We received a box of tapes and the inserts on the road. I probably had a hundred bucks in my pocket. We were supposed to do a showcase for a subsidiary of Warner. The showcase was booked at a sports bar. The label liked us, but it wasn't really the best place to showcase our music.

We met up with Grasshopper in Moncton; a lot of the shows were with local bands. We stayed with Grasshopper in Toronto in an industrial warehouse. They lived on the second floor. Everything was painted black, and it was the middle of summer. It was as hot as hell. We played a recreation centre, which was a tiny room, and it was almost like doing the old punk rock shows back home where we rented a space and a PA.

Geoff Younghusband: Grasshopper were a very difficult band. They were just as likely to get up there and make a racket and scream and try and drive everybody out of the bar. You read stories about bands in the early New York scene: "We got up there and emptied the place. We tried to end up with nobody left." Grasshopper were one of those bands. Yet they had this weird following in Toronto of kids who loved them. They were like Potbelly in that they had these big noisy sections in their songs. Sometimes those noisy sections would overwhelm the songs, and they would never come back from it. Potbelly was about losing ourselves in the noise but bringing the control back. Grasshopper were mostly about the noise. They'd get up and make a racket and scream and hope that the bar would turn them off.

Doug Jones: Someone from Capital Records showed up to watch us at an ECMA showcase, but I never really put much stock into that. If you got some attention, especially around that time, because of the Nirvana thing and Seattle-of-the-East stuff, if you let someone blow smoke up your ass, pretty soon you're going to start to believe it yourself.

Mike Kean *(musician)*: If we had actually lived in a place that was closer to the mainland and attached by a fixed link, or if we'd made our capital city closer to the ferry terminal in Port aux Basques, we wouldn't die trying to get across Canada. If you don't know what you're doing, you get screwed by renting a vehicle. These days it's just as cheap to fly as it is to drive to the mainland. By the time [Lizband] played our last shows in Halifax and

Toronto, we figured out how to not lose money. We could do it with a little bit of help from government funding and planning.

Marcel Levandier: We didn't understand the music industry. I don't think we understood just how dog-eat-dog and horrible it actually was. There was this magazine, *Impact Magazine*. It was a Canadian magazine that Ken Tizzard worked for. They had this list: "Top 10 Unsigned Bands in Canada." We were all on it. Lizband was on it. Hardship Post was on it. Bung was on it. Moist and I Mother Earth [were on it]. None of them are really anywhere today.

Robert Buck: Duckworth Distribution lasted about eight or nine years, from about 1989 or '90 to about 1997 or '98. It ended because we got overexposed. You know, one thing about Fred [Brokenshire], he was a great sales guy, a great promoter, a great talker with great ideas. But he wasn't that good with the numbers. He wasn't that good with the books. And that was the biggest downside. That wasn't his forte. In hindsight, we would have been better off having a business manager. I mean, we did have a good accountant. But we would have been better off with someone who actually saw the numbers on a daily basis and who could suggest where and when to pivot.

In his heyday, Fred Brokenshire was clever. He was sharp as a tack. As an innovator, his ideas were always larger than life. To some people, that was a detriment. But I just saw what he did with the music industry. I don't know if he ever really got the recognition that he deserved. When a business fails, people talk about the losses. They don't talk about what it took to get there. I thought that he went out on a limb for the artists here. Even though it didn't necessarily work out the way everybody wanted, I think he opened a lot of doors. There was a lot of artists that are successful now that probably wouldn't have been without those doors being open. There's people in Atlantic Canada who did something similar. Chip Sutherland, Brookes Diamond, and Sherry Jones were all very innovative people who helped move the industry forward. There's a group of us who have been around for like thirty years. You can count on one hand the number of industry people and musicians who have been in this industry that long.

HALFWAY TO HELL

Doug Rowe: Our rehearsal space was at 333 Duckworth Street. It was called "Halfway to Hell." I came up with that. But I'm sure other people will take credit for it.

Geoff Younghusband: I'm not going to say he's lying, but I think it was more of a collective thing. I don't think I could attribute it to just one person. Certainly, the My Dog Popper album we listened to in high school was called *668: Neighbor of the Beast*. This idea existed of numbers being related to the [devil], but not specifically 666. I wouldn't be surprised if Phil Winters laid claim to it.

Phil Winters: Maybe Geoff's right. I was the meddler. I was always into 666 and devil stuff.

Doug Rowe: Me and Bob Dicks were on the beer, walking down the steps by the Duke. I said, "We just escaped from Halfway to Hell." Maybe that's where it came from.

Natalie Spracklin: What I remember most is that we were a community.

Phil Winters: It was a family.

Geoff Younghusband: Every scene breeds its own core group of people.

Natalie Spracklin: We came together as a unit, and we shared a rehearsal space at 333 Duckworth Street. We shared equipment. Geoff was really instrumental in managing all of that. He found that space, got us organized, and collected rent.

Geoff Younghusband: That's where that whole early '90s scene began.

Phil Winters: Bung started jamming at 333 Duckworth, which was right around the corner from Bar None. It couldn't have been more perfect. There was a family of bands in there. That's another story, finding jam spaces. Empty buildings—whatever you could find. Geoff was always on the hunt looking around.

Geoff Younghusband: I sort of became that driving force for bands finding rehearsal spaces, making posters, and booking gigs. I was actively looking for a spot because when Stirling left Potbelly, we weren't jamming at his place. I lived in downtown rental apartments. We had reached the age where no one was living home. We wanted the space to be downtown. We needed to start our own place where we were free to smoke pot and cigarettes and drink beer, stuff we weren't allowed to do in our parents' garages and basements.

Through Pam Hall I got directed to Strat Canning, who owned 333 Duckworth Street, an empty office space at the bottom of Church Hill. Pam was an art director for some of the first films that I worked on.

Barry Newhook: Ron Hynes had a spot there. I think he could have bought the building, or he was interested in it at some point.

Doug Jones: There was a time when the front room and the back room were rented out. There was nothing upstairs.

Arthur Haynes: I lived on the third floor in an abandoned room. I wasn't homeless because I had a key and a sleeping bag. There was no shower and no bed, but I had a roof over my head.

Doug Jones: Initially, there was Potbelly, Bung, Whodafunkit, Lizband, and Hardship Post rehearsing in there.

Jon Swyers: We were there, one way or another, for three or four years. Wouldn't it be nice to have such a resource centre now?

Bob Dicks: Every time I walk by 333 Duckworth Street, I cross myself. There was a heavy locked door in front for security and another that you could jimmy with a credit card if you didn't have the keys.

Paul Gruchy: There was old furniture, somewhere to sit down, a maggoty love seat with the legs beat off. The wallpaper was peeling, and the ceiling was sagging. The industrial carpet was threadbare.

It's weird that everyone decided to jam in the back room, come to think of it, because the other rooms were nicer, especially the larger room out front. The room in the back was built onto the building, which is kind of typical for St. John's. It had a seven-foot ceiling. The rest of the ceilings were quite high.

Johnny Fisher: It was uninhabitable for a normal human being.

Geoff Younghusband: Between four bands, it was three hundred bucks a month. We had a drum kit in each corner, amps stacked between them, and a calendar on the wall.

Johnny Fisher: Darshiva, which eventually morphed into Potmaster, jammed in the back. The middle room is where people stored their gear. The only time anyone made use of the front room was when there was recording going on.

Geoff Younghusband: We were doing a lot of LSD and experimenting with psychedelic metal. We [Potbelly/Potmaster] had an absolutely astounding drummer in Tony Tucker. He's a self-taught drummer who went on to learn African hand drumming at astounding levels. [Then there was] Johnny Fisher, who was sort of the master at bizarre, psychedelic swirling guitar noise, and Natalie Noseworthy, who was the sexpot metal fiend with a voice to die for.

Natalie Noseworthy: My musical tastes weren't that sophisticated. I became obsessed with Metallica and After Forever. I dated Dan Moore for a while. Then I got a big metal guitar, a Flying V, and covered it in silver sparkles.

My parents were musicians. My mom is Phyllis Morrissey. She was kind of like a local folk performer. I don't like to say "celebrity," but she was on TV and radio. I'd done backups on some of her recordings. I'd been in the CBC studio before. She had three recordings and done a bunch of TV specials. I was familiar with the milieu. Being around musicians was not foreign to me.

Ritche Perez: The building was in a commercial zone. I don't remember police going there or any real trouble. The only issue was guitar pedals and patch cables going missing, and that's why there wasn't much partying. There were strict rules about friends coming over. People were always leaving beer bottles and garbage on the floor.

Geoff Younghusband: There were constant rackets about the mess.

Mike Kean: You can make the place great and take care of it, or you can make it barebones and just worry about getting the garbage out and not burning the place down. It was a shithole, but it had to be that way. It was exactly what we needed.

Jon Swyers: On Friday nights, people would come out of the Zone and fight in the alleyway. We put microphones out the windows and recorded them: "Good luck getting your fucking jeans back, you bitch!"

Jon Whalen: Everyone who shared the rent on that room put off shows together. The first three hundred dollars would go to pay the rent, and the rest would get divvied up among everyone equally. It was only later when we discovered that if [Bung] headlined a show that we'd get 75 per cent of the crowd. That's when the payment system became more structured. But when we shared that space, we all had a common cause. If a band was going off to do some gig and they needed to borrow a bass, or they needed to borrow an amp, or a drum kit, or a mic, everybody shared. You'd never think of saying, "No, you can't use my Shure 58 microphone." We were all supporting each other creatively, too. No one went around badmouthing anyone else's band. It mightn't be the kind of music you would make yourself, but you'd show respect and appreciation for it.

Natalie Spracklin: Geoff had a very specific sort of way of organizing his life and everything around him. He's still like that. If it wasn't for him and his skills, I don't think any of us would have had those opportunities. It took four bands to be able to rent that rehearsal space and share the cost. And who the hell else would have been able to organize us like that? Nobody. That era changed how people perceived musicians who were writing their own music.

Geoff found that space. He got us organized. He collected rent. He brought us together as a unit.

A SCRAPPY ESTHETIC

Peter Rowan *(promoter)*: In those early days, I had something to do with the ECMAs. I don't remember exactly what it was. Bands were submitting for performances. Sherry Jones came into my space. I didn't have an office; I just had a space. She said, "I don't know what to make of this. You might like it." I remember putting on this tape from Hardship Post. The first song was called "Sugarcane." I got four bars in, pressed stop, took the tape out and went home because I didn't want anyone else to hear it.

Every label in the world was looking for the next Nirvana. Obviously, there could only be one Nirvana. But I heard "Sugarcane" and thought, *Yes, it's kind of a Nirvana song, but it's the best Nirvana song that Nirvana hasn't recorded yet.* Back then, I had some juice, as they say. I guess that's when I started talking to Sebastian Lippa. I persuaded somebody, maybe somebody at Warner Brothers, to come to St. John's and watch Hardship Post play. They were amazing. And, of course, the audience was so completely into them.

My vision for Hardship Post was world domination. I managed Eric's Trip. Eric's Trip was never about that. Eric's Trip was always about flying under the radar. Sub Pop was really the only place for them. That was the appropriate label. Sebastian Lippa wrote incredible pop songs. You could produce them and mix them and put whatever haircut you wanted on them. I believed that they could be huge. I believed that through them I could actually make a living and succeed financially. I thought Hardship Post could have ruled the world if they wanted to. And that's the key. If Sebastian Lippa had wanted to, he could have become a giant rock star. He could have been as big a rock star as there possibly could be.

Sebastian Lippa *(musician)*: In Grade 8 or 9, I met Matt Clarke through some mutual friends, and we started a two-piece band. He was the drummer, I played guitar, and we jammed at my house. You'd think that it would make more sense to set up at his place, but his mother taught music classes and couldn't have the noise. We played in the basement, and we called ourselves the Angry Tea Men. Mom would pick us up from school and drive out to our place on the Boulevard. We would have tea, and jam in the basement. I guess it was kind of punk inspired. That was when I first got into alternative music—the Dead Milkmen, the Smiths, and more underground stuff.

Matt Clarke *(musician)*: Sebastian grew up across from Quidi Vidi Lake. John Roche introduced us. John said, "I know a guy who plays guitar." Sebastian and I [...] started hanging around together outside of playing music. I would say that we became pretty good friends and quite enjoyed one another's company.

Sebastian Lippa: Our first show was a fundraiser at the LSPU Hall. Rick Mercer was the emcee. I want to say it was for nuclear disarmament. It might've been put together by some girls from my high school. Youth for Social Justice is a name that hasn't crossed my mind in a long time. We were called the Bottom Dogs, and Noah Hansen was the singer. I think it was through Matt that we found Mike Pick. He was a skateboarder and played bass. We didn't mind being scrappy. That's always helpful when you can't really play.

Matt Clarke: Noah was involved in various kinds of music lessons and was a strong singer. The only problem with Noah was that he could never remember song lyrics. He would have all these little pieces of paper with the words written down on them strewn across the front of the stage.

Woody Whelan *(promoter)*: I was at my cousin's house listening to music before we all went down to Bounders. We didn't even know what bands were playing. I had already bought the Firehose record. It was ex-Minutemen, and it was raging. We walked into Bounders and this young band was up onstage playing "Brave Captain." That was the Bottom Dogs.

Sebastian Lippa: Mike Pick moved to Jasper, and we somehow convinced Don Ellis to join the band. I don't know how we managed that one because Don had a lot more experience than us. He'd actually been to Toronto and Montreal. Dave Sweetapple was the vocalist.

Dave Sweetapple: I kind of got the intensity of being young and into hardcore out of my system moshing at Gang Green shows in Toronto. Going back to St. John's was more about working. My father and grandfather were both longshoremen. A lot of my time was spent on the cargo ship *Sanderling*. There'd be four hundred new cars, a hundred and twenty tractor trailers on the mid-deck, and two hundred containers on the top deck. You'd be either driving cars or lashing trailers—stuff like that. I'd get two days of work, which would be enough to go down to Bar None and drink for the rest of the week. I really wasn't thinking about music. Noah Hansen was going away to school, and Don said, "These guys got this thing, and they've done a bunch of shows, but their singer is leaving. Do you want to give it a try?"

I look back at that era from '87 through to '91. Music had this weird thing going on that was post-punk and pre-grunge. We were still listening to Discord records, and bands like Dinosaur Jr. and the Pixies were coming along. The Meat Puppets and the later-period SST Records influenced us, too. With Infradig, I wrote the lyrics, and Sebastian wrote the music. It didn't have the same kind of intensity as playing stupid covers with the Riot. It was more about having something to do on the weekends.

Sebastian Lippa: And it didn't last long. It might've ended when I went away on a youth exchange. When I got back, Crackwillow came together. Becky Moyes was the singer.

Becky Moyes: When I was in my early twenties, Seb and I hung out with the same sort of guys—Chris Darlington, John Roche, Noah Hansen. Seb had just come back from Canada World Youth, and Dana Warren said he wanted a female singer in his band. This is my memory. "Why don't you have lunch with him? You could talk about international development."

Matt Clarke: I'd gone out west for a year to work, got back playing with Sebastian, and started university. Crackwillow probably lasted a winter term—something like that. It was long enough to get a set's worth of music together. I think most of that was original. There was a sense of trying to find the right people.

Becky Moyes: Crackwillow was probably my favourite time performing onstage because I had the lead. Crackwillow hit me right in the guts. It felt powerful. I still drive by Seb's parents' house, where we jammed in the basement. His mother would have cookies and milk for us. She loved doting on the youngsters.

Matt Clarke: Don Ellis set up a console in the garage, and we did a recording live off the floor. I seem to remember that Becky never showed up for that session.

Becky Moyes: Sebastian decided that his voice was good enough. I always said to him, "Your voice is great. You don't actually need me. You can just do your own thing." I sang with them for a year and off they went to Halifax.

Sebastian Lippa: Crackwillow and Hardship Post were basically the same band except without Becky. I don't know if she kept doing music or not, or if you've seen her perform, but she had a bold feminine persona. Sometimes she'd wear this long velvet dress, and she had great projection to her voice. But to be honest, it wasn't really the image I had in mind.

This was around the time when Nirvana's *Nevermind* came out. To me, Kurt Cobain wasn't the best singer in the world, but he had turned his shortcomings into a plus. Like I was saying—a scrappy esthetic. I thought, *I'm starting a new band. It's going to be a three-piece, and I'll sing.* That was Hardship Post.

Matt Clarke: We were looking for a band name. Reading through the dictionary, I came across this term, "hardship post." It's someone who's in an isolated military or diplomatic posting. It struck me that it was a little like being in St. John's sometimes when you're twenty years old, feeling like you're out on the edge of the Earth, removed from all the exciting things happening.

Hardship Post was heavily guitar focused. We were experimenting with our instruments and trying to stretch our legs.

Sebastian Lippa: I had written a bunch of stuff on that youth exchange. "Colourblind" was the only song that we kept playing.

Matt Clarke: My sense is that Sebastian had reached the point where he wanted to sing his own songs. I think that's how we went from the four-piece with Mike Pick and Becky Moyes to a three-piece with Mike Kean.

Mike Kean: We learned fifteen songs, played two or three times, and then Seb went tree planting. We thought the band was over. He called me and

Matt when he got back in September. He said that he wanted to start again and write new material.

Sebastian Lippa: The songs were coming fast and easy. Those first few months were probably the most fun I've ever had playing music. It was totally unselfconscious. It didn't cross anyone's mind that we could make any sort of career out of it.

Matt Clarke: We'd outgrown the basement. We were doing enough gigs to scrounge up our contribution to a shared downtown practice space.

Sebastian Lippa: I was going to university, and it was just the worst combination. I ended up getting kicked out because I wasn't going to classes. Instead, I was sleeping in and writing songs. The choice was clear and very easy to make.

Mike Kean: The first two shows were at Bar None. Our first kind of real recording was on reel-to-reel. By the time it was finished, we had a whole bunch of new songs that were twice as good as far as we were concerned.

Sebastian Lippa: *The NewMusic* [MuchMusic TV show] was in town, and they did a spot on the St. John's scene. They had their film crew come into 333 Duckworth Street. Sloan had signed to Geffen; Eric's Trip had signed to Sub Pop. Nirvana had just gone from obscurity to multi-platinum superstars. We knew there was interest in what we were doing.

Matt Clarke: *The NewMusic* piece featured Hardship Post, Bung, and Potbelly. Soon after, we had industry people phoning us: "We'd like to represent you as management." It was something we had never experienced before. That would have been 1992.

Sheffia Samuelson *(activist/scene supporter)*: Getting your band on Much-Music used to be a major big deal. There were really two shows which featured indie and alternative bands. *City Limits* was the first one. If you wanted to watch a Cure video, or if you wanted to see Morrissey or the Smiths, that's what you watched. Then there was *The NewMusic*.

Sebastian Lippa: Things happened pretty quickly. All of a sudden, we were doing these shows, and they were kind of popular. We'd play the Loft, and there would actually be a lot of people coming out. That was definitely a new thing.

Matt Clarke: I first met Peter Rowan when Sloan played the Great Canadian Party in July 1992. Then they played back-to-back nights at Bar None. Peter was already co-managing Sloan and Eric's Trip. There had been some interest from other music managers, at least one from Toronto, but we weren't convinced that they were necessarily on the same page as us. Peter certainly had the credentials.

Peter Rowan: St. John's was obviously a strong and supportive community, and that's what Halifax had, too. You were challenged and motivated by your peers' successes. You were happy for them, but it was also a challenge. It was like John Lennon and Paul McCartney trying to one-up each other. While you were blown away by what someone had done, you felt that you could do better.

Sebastian Lippa: I knew what was happening in Halifax through *Brave New Waves*. Then I heard Eric's Trip had just been signed to Sub Pop. Then Jale, who didn't even have a record, had also signed to Sub Pop. Peter called me when he got his hands on our demo and said that he would like us to come and play the East Coast Music Awards in Halifax. During that February trip, we definitely played the Double Deuce and the Flamingo. We did a Newfoundland night and a show with some up-and-coming Halifax bands. I don't have any particularly strong memories—we never lit anyone on fire—but people saw potential.

Peter Rowan was the guy who drew me away from St. John's. He became like a big brother figure. He wasn't just some guy running a festival. He was like another member of the band. I remember on the first or second call, he said, "I'd like to represent you." He was very forward in that way. This was also in the context that he had started out co-representing Sloan with Chip. But they had parted ways, and Peter was no longer representing Sloan. I think he was looking for bands to manage.

Peter Rowan: There were tons of great bands in Moncton. There were tons of great bands in Halifax. There were tons of great bands in St. John's. But those three bands—Sloan, Eric's Trip, and Hardship Post—were one step above. I'm motivated by pop songs. That's what makes me want to dance; that's what makes me smile. Again, I'm not in this for the money.

I'm doing it because every once in a while, I get this visceral feeling. I don't think I was arrogant, but I was pretty confident about Hardship Post's abilities. I had been doing music long enough to know what was real and what wasn't.

Sebastian Lippa: It had been on my mind to move out of the house. I could be out of my parents' house and be in Halifax. Peter was there, and Sloan was there. It just felt like one step closer to the action. I probably came back from Halifax that February thinking I'd like to move there. I think we were back in Halifax by April. Matt was into it. Mike Pick was in Jasper, and he was into it, too. We were looking for a change, to get out of St. John's and experience something different.

Right off the bat, Peter was trying to set up some tours. The first one might've been to New York for the CMJ Music Festival [College of Music Journalists] with Jale and Bubaiskull. That was the pitch I made to my parents: "We're going to Halifax, and we're going on tour. We got stuff lined up for the spring and the summer."

Mike Kean: In a very uncomfortable way that sort of made Matt squirm in his seat, Seb said, "You've worked hard in the band, but we've got to move to Halifax. If you think you can pull it off, maybe we can talk about you coming, too." But I wouldn't have been able to move to Halifax. I just wasn't mature enough.

Peter Rowan: I'm sure it wasn't any fun for Mike. But I think it was a fairly mutual decision. It's one of the hardest things about being a manager. I've almost lost all ability to enjoy a band for the sake of enjoying a band. I'm always looking for the weakest link.

Sebastian Lippa: Mike is such a retiring guy. He's probably still the same way. He's really super mellow and self-effacing. I want to say there's something in his playing that's kind of reflective of that. In a three-piece, you've really got to bring your stuff to the table. He was a root note, follow-the-chords kind of guy. I don't remember having any conflict whatsoever with him. I can't imagine anyone having a conflict with Mike. I don't think it was as much a personality thing as maybe just needing more. It was also an opportunity to get back to playing with Mike Pick. Mike was playing in Rocktopus. They put out at least one record, and they got airplay on *Brave New Waves*. This was before we had any sort of inclination that we could go on to bigger and better things, career-wise. Even still, we knew Mike Pick could bring us up a level.

Mike Kean: Mike was the guy who got me the gig with Hardship Post. At the same time, Lizband and the folks in Bung were the people I hung out with. Those were my friends. Leaving Hardship Post to play with Lizband wasn't a difficult decision.

Just getting out of Newfoundland was so hard. But it was just as hard to get bands to come here. That meant that nobody met travelling bands who they could hook up with for a couple of shows on the mainland. If you lived in Halifax, and there wasn't an ocean in between you and the rest of the country, once in a while, a band would come through. Network, network, network. For us, getting somebody to take a chance on coming all this way and spending all this money to have a show bomb was just about impossible. People cut Newfoundland out. Canada was from Vancouver to Halifax.

It didn't occur to a lot of us to leave Newfoundland, because the opportunities weren't there. Sloan was drawing a lot of attention. Halifax had their own record labels. Hardship Post figured, "We'll move up there and make a record." I can totally understand that. I think a lot more bands would have tried to get to Halifax if they'd had the chance. Bravo to them for actually doing it.

Matt Clarke: The main place to play was the Double Deuce, which was kind of like the Bar None of Halifax. That was really where the scene was centred out of. We became friends with the staff, and Mike and I both ended up working there. The crowds were into what we were doing, and we got good turnouts right from the start. I'm not sure if that was because we were working with Peter Rowan. We already knew Sloan, and they were the big kids on campus. Even though they were Moncton-based, Eric's Trip were often associated with Halifax because they played there [so much]. All of that gave us a smoother introduction than we might have had otherwise.

Sebastian Lippa: St. John's was vibrant, but Halifax was more of what I was looking for. The music scene had more infrastructure. There were people like Peter. Sloan had done a lot of path-breaking. There were booking agents getting bands out to North American and the worldwide market. Colin MacKenzie was managing Murderecords. There was Cinnamon Toast Records. There was No Records. You want to be close to those kinds of people.

Dave Sweetapple: Hardship Post had been recording stuff, and Seb was sending me cassettes and flyers. I remember thinking, *This sounds just like what is going on in Seattle right now. I have to put this out. This can't be released somewhere else. I'm too close to them for it not to happen.* The band sent down the tapes and artwork. They had it all pieced together, and we pressed them.

The one thing about St. John's that I regret is not putting out records. It was always a money issue. There were no pressing plants on the island, and the concept of sending away to World Records in Toronto was just alien. Da Slyme did it, and Bob did it with Schizoid, him and Rod Wills. I always wanted to do a label. When I got to the United States, I realized I finally could.

The first time I met Woody Whelan was at an Infradig show at the Corner Stone. I believe it was Earth Day 1990. Within a year, I had moved to the States, and we started putting out singles together. The first one was Ken Chambers, a guy from the Moving Targets. Then there was a band called Smack Mellon. Then there was Hardship Post and "Sugarcane." I started working for a management company, and we stopped doing the label together.

Woody Whelan: When it comes down to it, Magwheel Records was Dave's idea. The guy from Big Chief, Mark Dancy, did the logo for fifty bucks. It was around the time of Soundgarden's *Badmotorfinger*, which he did the cover for. Me and Dave were buying his artwork, and somewhere along the line, we just decided to contact him. Again, it was the whole do-it-yourself motto. One thing always leads to another.

We put out the Hardship Post single in May or June 1993, and I left Newfoundland in late July. It wasn't that long after "Sugarcane" came out that they got all the media attention in Nova Scotia. I can't remember them ever doing "Sugarcane" after that. I don't think they ever played it again.

Peter Rowan: The *Moodring* cassette had made the rounds, and people were pretty excited when Hardship Post moved over here. I knew those guys admired Eric's Trip. I was kind of the hub for all of these incredible people. I said, "Maybe we could go up to Rick's freaky basement, and we'll record you?" It was the right time, the right place, the right people.

Sebastian Lippa: *Hack* didn't really work because we never came to any sort of cohesive vision on what we wanted to do. But that's probably the difference in the bands. Eric's Trip was Rick's brainchild, whereas Hardship Post was a collection of songs.

Matt Clarke: I have no idea how many CDs we sold. I certainly never got a cheque for any royalties. I assume there were probably three thousand pressed. It was in record stores and got distributed by one of the major labels that Murderecords had an arrangement with.

We went out to Vancouver for a showcase or a Canada Music Week event. We'd also done some touring to New York and Rhode Island. We did a tour with Jale through Ontario and Quebec.

Sebastian Lippa: We were getting interest from labels pretty quickly, starting with Canada and then the United States. By the fall of '94, we had signed.

Peter Rowan: I remember going in to meet Mike McCarty at EMI Publishing. I played them "Sugarcane." I think I asked for half a million dollars for a publishing advance on that song. We didn't get it, but that's the level we're talking about.

Matt Clarke: I think we actually held off from encouraging the big labels from tabling an offer. I know Sebastian was certainly feeling that he really didn't relate to them. When it started to appear that maybe Sub Pop was interested, there was a lot more enthusiasm to go that route.

Peter Rowan: Chip and I were in LA, and I got the call that Sub Pop wanted to make an offer for Eric's Trip. We just couldn't believe it. We're in LA, and we're hanging with Geffen for Sloan, and the only thing cooler than Geffen was Sub Pop. Here we were with the two bands. We were kings of the world. A year later, we got a call from Sub Pop telling me that they were going to make an offer for Hardship Post. It was the most depressing phone call that I've ever had because I knew Seb was going to take the Sub Pop deal.

At that time, we were in the process of starting to work out what would have been a six-figure deal from Sony Records. We were looking at a six hundred thousand dollar advance, or whatever ridiculous amount it was. We were looking at life-changing money. Instead, we took twenty thousand dollars from Sub Pop, which didn't pay anybody's bills. It didn't pay off any of the debt that had accumulated.

Sebastian Lippa: I remember going out to dinner in Halifax with Bruce Pavitt and Jonathan Poneman. […] We signed the deal right there at the table.

Peter Rowan: I'm sure that I said that we were aiming really low. We were definitely aiming low in terms of being rock stars. But Sebastian wasn't interested in that. As a manager, I've always believed that my job was to do what a band wanted. The guys wanted to sign with Sub Pop. I'd already been working with them for a year, and I knew just how little money they had. Could they hype things? Yes. Could they pay for things, or would they pay for things? No. What Sub Pop brought to the equation was an immediate stamp of approval. It's not a question of the band being cool. Of course, they're cool. They're on Sub Pop, you moron.

Sebastian Lippa: [The music] became so much more self-aware and self-conscious compared to the early days. I was trying to make music that didn't sound so much like my influences. I don't think I was that successful, at least on the record. Some of the ideas worked, but it was definitely about turning the distortion down. There was a move towards more commercial-sounding alternative music, but we wanted to maintain a kind of low-fi esthetic.

I can't really comment on how we were perceived by Newfoundland bands. I know some people felt like we had left them behind and didn't look back. My own take on it was that it fed into a bigger Newfoundland narrative. St. John's was a small scene. As a community, it was much smaller and insular than many other places where people coming and going is taken for granted. In St. John's, it's a bit more painful to see people leave. It was a small scene struggling for recognition. There were scarce opportunities, and you wanted to see somebody make it and stay. But when you saw somebody leave as soon as they had the chance, it reinforced the idea that it's impossible to do anything there. It told the rest of the world that you couldn't wait to get away.

My folks are not Newfoundlanders; I don't have extended family there. I didn't grow up with Newfoundland being part of my identity. It just wasn't part of my family history. My parents are from Toronto, and they both left their families behind, much to their shock and horror. I never thought twice about leaving.

Matt Clarke: There were whisperings I heard that we had sold out. But no one really says that stuff to your face. You just hear that so-and-so said something.

Peter Rowan: During a show at the LSPU Hall, someone in the audience was yelling, "Go back to the mainland." Success is a funny thing. I often find that on the East Coast there's a desire to drag people back down. It was hard on everybody to hear those kinds of comments. They had to move to Halifax. They'd outgrown St. John's.

Geoff Younghusband: A lot of people sort of felt like they'd abandoned us. At the same time, we all knew that they were striving to get to the next level. Maybe everyone was jealous that they had made an attempt to go for it. They had their Sub Pop deal, and there was some animosity in that they never pulled anyone along with them. They sort of immediately amalgamated into and became part of the Halifax scene and were identified as a Halifax band. Certainly, in my young state of mind, I felt like I had put a lot of effort into helping them create the scene that was following them. Of course, they were their own band. They attracted their own fans. But I was there booking shows and doing posters and was friends with all of them. In hindsight, I'm like, "Why was I upset? I should have been happy that my friends were playing on Sub Pop Records."

Sebastian Lippa: Al Sutton [Rustbelt Studios] produced the record. We might've been the first Sub Pop band to record with him. It was three weeks in Detroit. The label put us up in a downtown hotel, and we would get up and walk to the studio in the morning, record all day, and come back for dinner. There wasn't a lot going on, and we had no money, either. The label took us out to dinner and showed us around. Mostly it was just the three of us hanging out in the hotel.

At some point, Kid Rock came into the studio. I thought he was the biggest idiot. He was working on one particular track: "Balls in Your Mouth."

We didn't have a lot of ideas floating around, other than trying to keep the songs really simple and clean. Other than that, it was not a complex process. There wasn't a lot of talk or experimentation. There was a lot of work that went into capturing performances. Mike had two songs on the album. He wrote lots of others.

The record came out in May. Right before we went out on tour, we kicked Matt out of the band. Talk about career self-destruction. Instead, we went out as a half-baked two-piece with Mike on drums. Matt wasn't pleasant to tour with, and I don't think he enjoyed that aspect of being in a band. On a personal level, we had really drifted apart.

Woody Whelan: There was an ill-fated Montreal show, and Matt basically decided that he was going to leave the band. I brought a bunch of friends out to see them. I went up to Seb after the show, and I told him how disappointed I was in the musical direction that they had taken.

We all went to get something to eat. When I got there, Seb and Mike were sitting alone, being grumpy. Maybe it was the whole situation. Maybe something had happened that night. I don't know. I was like, "Hey, where's Matt?" They just pointed [in his direction]. Matt was sitting with his back turned and his arms folded, staring out the window.

I asked him, "What's going on?"

He said, "I'm fucking done."

Matt Clarke: To some extent, I was having difficulty understanding what Seb was looking for. There was an artistic disconnect in terms of what he wanted and what I thought the music called for. That's probably a large part of it. Maybe we were burned out from spending too much time together in vans. Generally speaking, I think we weren't having as much fun playing music together anymore. Time passes and people grow apart.

Sebastian Lippa: The road did not help, but there were underlying personality differences that became more pronounced. Music-wise we couldn't see eye to eye. There was a move towards simplicity. I didn't know it at the time, but the sound I was trying to tap into was the kind of calculated amateur approach of the Velvet Underground and Wire. Matt could always do way more on the drums than the songs needed. It would drive me insane. I'm very conflict-averse. For much of the band, we found a happy medium. But at a certain point, the compromise became unworkable. Matt no longer enjoyed playing in the band and started to resent me. And it showed. Obviously, I didn't see his strengths as a drummer, and I felt that he didn't appreciate my vision. After a tour in the spring of 1995, I was tired of it. What I didn't realize was that Mike felt the same way, too. Those guys stayed friends although Matt was pretty upset about being kicked out of the band.

You're just becoming an adult. You have no idea how to negotiate the complex relationships in a band. They're unlike those in the work world. You're creating art, and you don't have a boss who can say, "Matt, play the fucking beat like Seb said. Seb, stop being a pretentious asshole." Someone like that could have really helped. You hear stories of big superstars with these strong managers who act like parents telling them what to do. With young bands, you're doing it all yourself. You don't have the language to talk about what you're trying to accomplish. At least, I certainly didn't. That was always the weakness of my approach. I never really thought through what I was trying to do. I simply couldn't express it or explain it.

Matt Clarke: The sound of the band had changed. We didn't sound anything like the *Moodring* cassette that Don Ellis recorded at 333 Duckworth, with the Kurt Cobain-style growling and the angry guitar tone. The music was starting to get stripped down. The guitar was pulled back, and it was more about the songwriting. If people had been familiar with *Moodring* and *Hack, Somebody Spoke* wouldn't necessarily have been the record you were expecting to hear.

Mike Pick *(musician)*: It was a completely conscious decision. We had an idea for the sound that we wanted, so we tried to move towards it. In doing so, we kind of dropped the older sound, which was okay because it was pretty derivative anyway. It was so much like Hüsker Dü and Nirvana that we weren't really our own band. By developing the newer sound on the record, I think we became fairly distinct.

Matt Clarke: The way things unfolded, the record came out—we recorded it in November '94, and it came out spring of '95—and Seb and Mike decided to go ahead and tour the album themselves. Mike was not a drummer, but he could function behind a drum kit. Sebastian had great songs—interesting lyrics and melodies—but Mike and I had real presence as a rhythm section. Combined with Seb's strong pop sensibility, we were a good live band. When Mike and Seb went out on tour, it was maybe a bit anticlimactic.

Sebastian Lippa: The timing was ill-advised, but that's where being young and stupid comes in. Peter, Joyce, and Sub Pop were not about to force us to go out on the road together. We toured in support of the album with Zumpano and Six Finger Satellite. That was meant to be a triple headliner, especially in Canada. Going out as a two-piece, we were slotted in as the opener every night. We weren't playing to the same number of people as we normally would. The people we did perform for were probably left wondering what the hell they'd just heard. People would come up to us and say, "What were you guys thinking?"

Me, I thought our new music sounded great because Mike got what I was trying to do. He had the simple approach that I was looking for. Obviously, it sounded nothing like the record without bass. This was before there was any successful guitar-and-drums model out there that I was aware of. I didn't understand the dynamics that were required.

As soon as we got back from the road, we were performing and trying to find a drummer. The word was out that we were looking. We held try-outs for different players. The final incarnation of Hardship Post was me, Mike, and Alyson MacLeod of Jale. But that wasn't really working because Mike didn't want to be the drummer. We recorded almost a full album on four-track in our rehearsal space, which we gave to Sub Pop. They seemed to like it a lot. I think it was our best stuff. But that's easy enough to say when no one has heard it.

Peter Rowan: Seb just didn't want to be part of the star-making machine. He pulled a Joni Mitchell. He wasn't interested in what he had to give of himself to succeed. It's a very unhealthy lifestyle, this rock and roll world. You meet interesting people who also live very unhealthy lives. There are a lot of things that aren't attractive about the business. I think there was a lot of pressure on Seb, whether that was from me or other people or the record label. At the time, he just wanted to make music. As someone who doesn't make music, him walking away was mind-blowing. It's not that he was just writing songs; he was writing amazing songs.

It was a hard time, but there were lots of good times. I've been very lucky, not necessarily at making a career out of this, but I've been fortunate enough to work with some really exceptional people, whether it was Sloan or Eric's Trip or Hardship Post. We were very lucky to be at a certain time and a certain place.

Fur Packed Action broke up in the middle of a record—classic band stuff—and I was working with them at the time. Five or six years later, they did a reunion show. Out of nowhere, an envelope arrived in the mail with a wad of bills and a bunch of change. The letter said, "We thought we should send you a little commission. Here's enough money for dinner, a bag of weed, and a bottle of booze." It was so sweet. Not many bands do stuff like that. When Jody and I talked about doing stuff together again, he said, "Let's have some times." I had some times with Hardship Post. There are bands that I would never talk about again, but those guys are not one of them.

Sebastian Lippa: Hardship Post was my last proper band. I haven't come close to anything like that since. I did a one-off show in Halifax as my final goodbye to music. I put together a band with Joel Plaskett and Drew Yamada, and we performed a batch of new songs. That was in '96.

BLOWING SMOKE (UP YOUR ASS)

A SCRAPPY ESTHETIC

The last Hardship Post show of me, Mike, and Alyson was as a T-Rex cover band. I think it was part of the Halifax Pop Explosion. The second-last show we did was as Mike and the Balls. We performed Mike's stuff, and I played drums.

Clearly, we had no direction whatsoever. It was all up in the air at that point. That's why we broke up: we didn't know what we wanted to be. We just ran out of gas. I wish there was a recording or a video of that T-Rex gig. We wore top hats and had long curly hair. We were nailing all those high background vocals. As Mike and the Balls, we opened up for the band Cracker. David Lowery had some success as the guy from Camper Van Beethoven. He wanted to record us. He loved Mike's deep baritone voice; he thought he sounded like Leonard Cohen. That was something we could have pursued if we had had a bit more legs under us. But you need the drive. It's not just about having good ideas.

DANGER: FALLING ROCK

Geoff Younghusband: I heard that Fred Gamberg and Jon Swyers were doing a compilation of local bands. I have to admit, being the cocky guy that I was, I sort forced myself into the project. I said to some close friends, "I don't want them fucking this up. I'm going to go and make sure that it's done right." But Fred and Jon quite willingly let me come on board.

They had the basic framework before I got involved. Bands paid a hundred dollars, and we didn't say no to anybody. We set up in 333 Duckworth with Wallace Hammond and an ADAT [Alesis Digital Audio Tape recorder]. Bands would come in and within two hours record maybe three songs. But they could do whatever they wanted. If they wanted to spend their two hours laying down bed tracks and then guitar overdubs, they could do that. If they wanted to come in and play live off the floor, they could do that, too. The bands owned all the songs. We were going to take one song [from each band] and mix them. If the bands wanted the rest of the stuff mixed, they could barter with Wallace. That being said, I'm still in possession of the master tapes of *Danger: Falling Rock*, and no one has ever come looking to mix another song from their session. [Once the sessions were finished], we sat down with Wallace and picked out the best stuff. If you paid your hundred dollars, showed up, and recorded, then your one song got released on the tape.

Karmella Perez: In my twenties, I majored in English literature and women's studies and had a zine, *No Name Brand*. I was into the Riot Grrl movement and read a lot about what was going on in Washington in the early '90s. I would get my friends to write random articles about whatever was on their mind.

A lot of other zines were doing tapes. We were kind of throwing around the idea of having a cassette to go with each zine. "How about we do one with Newfoundland bands?"

I was dating Jon Swyers. Jon got talking to Fred Gamberg about the idea of putting together a compilation.

Jon Swyers: Fred's love of music drove him so hard that he felt he needed to support the rest of the community. Fred had a CHMR show, *On the Edge*. He was an advocate of Brent Bambury's *Brave New Waves*, CBC's late-night music program. He turned me onto that, which was a way, before the internet, to access good up-and-coming music without having to share tapes with somebody. Arbitrarily finding music was a little more difficult then.

We were becoming more interested in recording and making viable demos that we could use for commercial purposes. Part of it was being collectively motivated to access digital recording equipment prior to the advent of computer software. But we needed a larger base of funds. We were using ADATs when they were pretty expensive. I think they cost five thousand dollars for eight tracks of digital recording. Now you can buy eight tracks of digital recording for two hundred and fifty dollars.

Jim Fidler loaned us the ADAT device. Wallace had the mics and the console. We had a pretty rigid schedule. We worked seven or eight hours a day over two weeks. There wasn't much down time. It was a full-time operation to make that recording.

Geoff Younghusband: I remember it being a bit of a whirlwind. We were overwhelmed and sort of amazed at how many bands were eventually involved.

Jon Swyers: We wanted them to sound better than a cassette demo or board tape. We thought that a compilation would generate more interest amongst a wider group of people.

Phil van Ulden *(musician)*: We cobbled together used instruments. My brother, Leo, bought a cheap drum kit [...] that was kind of put together haphazardly. He had no cymbal stand, so he took a milk crate and stuck a broomstick in it with a screw in the top.

This all happened in our basement on Circular Road, which would flood [when it rained]. It was our bedroom, which had a door to the outside so we wouldn't disturb Mom when our friends were coming over.

Leo was hanging around with Ivan Coffin. He played bass for Darshiva and a band called Dropkick Jesus. When talk of a [compilation] of local bands started, Ivan, Leo, and Ted put together a song. But Ivan didn't really commit. He might have been recording with another band. At the last minute, a day or two before the recording was supposed to happen, he bailed on the whole thing. We replaced him with Chris Hanlon, who perpetually lived in our basement.

Chris had a riff and some lyrics. The song was called "My Cricket Eater." It went, "I'm climbing the wall. I'm climbing the wall." At the time, my family was trying to launch Wallnuts [climbing gym]. Maybe there was some connection.

Geoff Younghusband: *Danger: Falling Rock* included eighteen bands, and it did show that St. John's had a bit of everything. There's sHeavy and Dreadheavy, which were stoner rock and reggae. The Cabmen was an acoustic duo, and Jon Swyers's Resisterhead was electronic. After Forever was metal, and Giver was kind of esoteric punk. Bung and Lizband gave us songs that were already recorded.

Phil Winters: "Powerful" was a Lizband song that Barry and I wrote. "Found" was recorded during the *Whole* [recording] sessions at 333 Duckworth and ended up on the album backwards. We gave the unedited version to Best Dressed Records.

Karmella Perez: There used to be this sign in front of the LSPU Hall where Fred's mural is now. It said "Danger: Falling Rock" because the concrete wall was crumbling. It was a bit of a hazard. Jon and I were walking by; I looked at him and said, "That would be a wicked name for the compilation."

Jon Swyers: I think the first time, we pressed maybe a few hundred cassettes. We sold almost all of them that first night [at the release show]. CBC Radio had us into the studio to talk about the overwhelming success of our small enterprise, and the *Evening Telegram* interviewed us, ironically enough, at the Family Barbershop on Duckworth Street. The image was in direct juxtaposition to the Best Dressed theme. We weren't very well dressed, with our long hair and dirty boots.

Doug Rowe: Ditch were together for three years. Outside of "Autumn Eyes" on Danger: Falling Rock, that's all that exists. [...] I think people have this memory that we were better than we were. But I don't know because there are no studio recordings kicking around. There are board tapes, but decades have passed, and the cassettes are deteriorating.

Geoff Younghusband: The label took a bit of backlash that the bands didn't get money back and that we used the funds to start a record label [Best Dressed Records]. We put out the Potmaster record [*Freak Me Out to the Deluxe*, 1995]. Then we put money into a record by Lizband [*I've Been Here Before*, 1998] and Fur Packed Action [*The Dull Thud of Fur*, 1998].

Best Dressed Records struggled. We tried to get Potatobug involved [in the label], but they didn't want anything to do with us. I think they saw the money as kind of tainted. We offered them a straight-up, dollar-for-dollar investment: "We'll loan you the money to get your CD pressed. We got our logo on it, and you can pay us back the money." That was basically the deal we offered them, but they just weren't interested.

The comp and the label were great ways to keep cash flowing into the community. The basic idea was to be a community label promoting local music. But I don't think any of us understood how to run a record label.

THE QUEEN OF PUNK ROCK

Geoff Seymour: Liz Pickard was playing folk music around town. I remember going to see her and Ed Kavanagh play at the Grad House. The two of them were doing stuff like Simon and Garfunkel covers. Then Liz took that beautiful voice of hers and mixed it up with some really heavy music.

Marcel Levandier: Pat Janes started bringing bands to St. John's during the late '80s. The first time I ever saw Liz play was with Red Scare, opening for Deja Voodoo at the Nickel Theatre.

Barry Newhook: The Riot went through a bunch of different incarnations. Duncan didn't want to sing anymore. He wanted to play guitar, and I went back to playing bass. The band had sort of simmered down to nothing; it was just me and Duncan.

Liz was interested in being in a proper band, and I liked the idea of getting someone of her calibre. That's when the Riot morphed into Red Scare.

Steve Hussey: Liz was loved and hated. Some people don't like women singing about stuff like guys jerking off to porn rags and then kissing their wives on the cheek. It's offensive. But Minnie White [Newfoundland musician and the "First Lady of the Accordion"] thought Liz was great. Liz is a smart woman and a wonderful singer. She's crafty with words. A lot of people dislike her music, but a lot of people dislike Bob Dylan and Jimi Hendrix, too.

Marcel Levandier: Liz got asked to play in Halifax for the '93 East Coast Music Awards. So did Bung, Hardship Post, and Potbelly. We put together a band with me and her and Paul Curnew. Phil and Barry played with us then, too. We were called The Liz Pickard Band.

Mike Kean: When the Lizband first got going, it was a different sort of element than Red Scare. Duncan wasn't in the band anymore, and Liz was writing her own songs. She wrote most of the songs on our first record, like "Complacency Song." Connie and Ron Hynes wrote "Mary Got a Baby." Ron Hynes and Liz did a bunch of shows together. "Johnny" was a song they used to perform together. Some of that material came out on the *11:11: Newfoundland Women Sing [Songs by Ron and Connie Hynes]* compilation [1996]. Probably 60 per cent of the music was written by Liz and interpreted by the band.

Lizband got me involved as soon as I left Hardship Post. Then we heard about Steve Hussey. Coincidentally, I'd met him many years ago. Do you remember Pete's Subs, [...] next to Holiday Lanes bowling alley on Elizabeth Avenue? I had a four-hour conversation with this dude who had hair down to his waist and wore eye makeup. Apparently, it was Steve Hussey.

Steve Hussey: I joined Lizband on the suggestion of Phil.

Mike Kean: We went to see Steve play at the Fat Cat [St. John's blues bar]. He seemed so nervous. He played the whole set with his back to the audience.

Steve Hussey: I would go see everybody who played the blues: Bill Rose, Lou Skinner, and Ralph Walker. Anything that was jazz: Jimmy Thompson and Nelson Giles.

Mike Kean: It was the only time that we had someone who could really play guitar.

Steve Hussey: Everyone just assumed that I was good because I hung out with Roger Howse and Denis Parker.

Lizband was really Marcel and Liz. I only added colour and texture. Liz came up with the words; Marcel came up with the hooks. The better Liz got at playing guitar, the more the music became about the stuff that she was writing.

Marcel Levandier: *Six Songs*, our first EP, came out in 1994.

Mike Kean: Don Ellis engineered that recording at NIFCO [Newfoundland Independent Filmmakers Co-operative].

Lois Brown: I asked Liz to help out with a song for a theatre show that I was working on. I wrote all of these words, and me, Liz, and Ann Troake [Newfoundland filmmaker] manipulated them into something that she could sing. The song ended up being "Queen of Swords."

Steve Hussey: With Liz, you had to be creative.

Mike Kean: Some of her earlier songs came from theatre shows and some songs she'd written on an acoustic guitar.

Steve Hussey: I remember all of Liz's words. If you really pay attention to what she's saying there's some outright shame-on-you kind of stuff directed at Frank Sobey, the guy who owned the Sobeys empire. Then there was one about pregnant girls, "Portion to Abortion." She had this song about being afraid to fly called "Lone Star" [that was released in 1998 on *I've Been Here Before*]. She wrote "Lone Star" coming back from either Nova Scotia or New Brunswick, when every musician from Newfoundland was on the plane. Everyone was there: the Fables, the Irish Descendants. I think it was February; we were coming back, and it was fucking stormy. Liz lost it. "Lone Star" was about that experience. She's looking out the window, and all she can see is one star. "Lone star, tell me how far can I fall from here. / It's been a long night, and it's a hard flight, and I just don't feel secure."

Marcel Levandier: We did a lot of stuff for the first couple of years. We played the Halifax Pop Explosion. We went to Toronto for Canada Music Week. Bob Wiseman recorded us, but it didn't work out.

Steve Hussey: Bob was an avant-garde Canadian musician who played with Blue Rodeo for a long time. He's on their first six albums.

Marcel Levandier: He wanted to be a music producer, but we were too cool for that: "You can't tell us how to play our music!"

Steve Hussey: There were all kinds of label interest in Lizband. Louis Thomas took us on [with Sonic Entertainment], and we were supposed to play *Breakfast Television* or something. I think we didn't make it, and that was a bit of a no-no. At Canadian Music Week, we got a good time slot, but we turned it down because it was too early. It was like, "You got to call this guy and do a radio interview. You got to tie your shoes, clap your hands three times, and pat your belly."

Marcel Levandier: There was always this sentiment that Liz could make it on her own if she wanted to sing other people's music. But that's not what Liz is about. She would be perfectly happy with sleeping on floors, touring, and playing original music.

Steve Hussey: We all went to Canadian Music Week in Toronto. Bob Wiseman was with us. During that time, there was that Ten Canadian Bands to Watch list. Hardship Post was signed to Sub Pop and Warner. Bung were briefly signed to MCA. All the other bands got a record deal, and we never did.

We were slackers; we changed our sound. We went from sounding somewhere between Soundgarden and Smashing Pumpkins to the kind of pop punk that was popular in the late '90s.

During our first trip to Canadian Music Week, we played some shows at the Phoenix. That was kind of funny because we got booed off the stage by all of these homesick Newfoundlanders who came out and saw this aggressive and weird fem-band. Liz was really confrontational, and the audience was really confrontational—"One step closer and you're getting a Strat across the head." It was that kind of thing. We were on the same bill as Pam Morgan and the Irish Descendants. It's okay to maybe do that here [in Newfoundland], but it was not a good thing to do up there [on the mainland].

Louise Moyes: I think it needs to be said how very important Liz was to us. She was this incredible female lead in a band singing about feminist themes—stuff like "Motherfucker" and "Gynecologist's Dream." There's never enough female lead singers.

Becky Moyes: She was so strong. She was our queen of punk rock.

Natalie Spracklin: I think about some of the things that she's managed to accomplish and sustain for a long period of time. She had the Rock Can Roll Festival. She had the Rock School for Girls. She facilitated that whole movement. She was instrumental in bringing more women into the underground music scene in St. John's because she was a mentor and continues to be a mentor to young women.

That's something you can see now. There's a lot more young women playing music. Despite the size of this town and the size of the scene, that demographic has emerged.

THE MOST DANGEROUS BAND IN THE WORLD
BUNG PART 2

Johnny Fisher: It seemed like with every Bung performance, something would happen. People would get naked. People would go-go dance on the sides of the stage. There would be brawls. There would be insane mosh pits. Always a sold-out room, no matter where they played.

Rick Power (*showgoer*): They were the stuff of legend.

Jon Whalen: Music Quest '93 was definitely one of those shows.

Liz Pickard (*singer*): It was very educational because we really came to learn a lot about the kinds of events and venues that you do not play. Number one: music competitions. Don't do it to yourself. Number two: any venue that has a bunch of bouncers and which needs that kind of policing, you don't want to have anything to do with.

A rock show is a conversation. It's a pagan ritual. It's freedom. There's a relationship between who is on the stage and the people who are listening and dancing and moving. I don't play venues anymore where that is interfered with. I now control how I am presented. I don't want to be presented behind a bunch of big assholes with their arms crossed.

Arthur Haynes: Music Quest was on my birthday, June 19, 1993. Dave Carver [Tenth Avenue Productions] and his goons. It was the second last night of a battle of the bands at the Curling Club, which Carver promoted.

We were scheduled to go on at 12:30. The event was very well publicized, and at 11:30 the place was a ghost town. By quarter after 12, maybe six hundred people poured in through the doors in less than fifteen minutes.

You're also talking about the beginning of Dave Carver's promotional life. It almost ruined him. Carver had hired security from the Breezeway, the red shirts from the university. At that point in time, they were infamous for beating the fuck out of people. MUN shows back then weren't worth going to if you looked any bit different, because you were singled out.

Three or four numbers into our set, things started getting out of hand. The crowd was getting jostled. Security had all formed a line across the front of the stage, pushing the crowd back. Liz Pickard was Barry's partner. She had a child with Jon and a child with Justin. To combat the pushing and shoving, she took her shirt off and stood there with her breasts exposed.

Barry Newhook: At shows, there'd be all kinds of women taking off their tops. Maybe other people felt different, but I felt it was part of the scene, and it really fit in with my egalitarian point of view of what I felt punk rock was all about. To me, it was empowerment. Bung was definitely sort of embracing rock-star decadence, too. You don't have to be so politically minded.

Sheffia Samuelson: I stood in front of the stage wearing nothing but a bra. We all did that. But I was never liberated enough to get rid of the bra. I remember it was a Sam Shades show. A lot of those shows were hot and sweaty. Again, you're surrounded by people you know. You want to feel like a strong woman. You got women dancing around in bras and men dancing around in their underwear. I'm surprised there's not more photos of that stuff around.

Arthur Haynes: Liz was screaming at this guy, and he's screaming at her. He somehow managed to turn her around and put her in a chokehold. Barry walked three or four steps out and put his foot up the side of the guy's head. As Jon so eloquently put it in the *Evening Telegram*, "It wasn't like a furious kick to the head. It was kind of a get-his-attention kick in the head." And then the room went kapow. It erupted into a full-on fist fight with strangling, punching, and kicking.

Carver came onstage with his biggest goon. This guy must've been about 400 pounds. He pointed at me. I was drunk, and I was stoned. My only thought was, *I'm about to get pulverized*. I put my guitar over my shoulder like a baseball bat, and I stood there in front of him screaming. I might've been 130 pounds. I was wearing my fourteen-year-old sister's cut-off jean shorts and a pair of combat boots. My hair was down to my waist. I was soaking wet and covered in shitty tattoos, with the Squire Stratocaster I'd borrowed from somebody over my shoulder, screaming, "Is it worth it? Because I'm going to knock your fucking teeth out if you take one more step."

Phil Winters: A couple of other bands played that night with no problem. We got up onstage, and Carver sent five or six beefy security guys to stand in front of the stage. There wasn't going to be any fucking around during this show. We couldn't understand it. People moshing and dancing is all good, clean fun. To us, the fix was in.

Liz got up onstage to dance with Barry because Liz and Barry were together. They'd been together for years. Nobody thought anything of it except for the security guards who started grabbing her and physically trying to remove her from the stage. Then a couple more women took their shirts off to defuse the situation. Marcel threw a beer can from the audience and hit me in the head.

Marcel Levandier: I didn't mean to hit Phil. I threw it at one of the bouncers, but it ended up hitting Phil because I'm not a baseball player.

Phil Winters: What's not so funny was Torquil Colbo being terrorized by the security guards. Girls were being manhandled. The security guards came out in front almost right after the first note, and there was this offensive energy. In [that] day and age, crowd surfing [was] de rigueur. I saw Soundgarden at the Concert Hall in 1992. There were people dropping off the walls onto the crowd from the balcony, and nobody got hurt.

Geoff Seymour: David Carver came up to me behind the lighting console and said, "Turn the lights off. Turn the lights off." Instead, I cranked them up to full. Johnny Fisher was a pretty mild-mannered guy. They took both Johnny and Torquil Colbo out of the building in a full nelson. The band kept going, and they shut down the main sound. I cranked the lights up so everybody could see what was going on. I knew that my friends were in trouble. I wasn't going to let David Carver and the security whitewash what was happening. Everyone was at least going to see it for themselves.

Arthur Haynes: The security started massing at the doors, and we snuck Barry out the back. Carver and his red shirts were waiting at the two main doors until the building was empty. In my opinion, they were going to put Barry in the hospital.

Marcel Levandier: The next night they weren't letting Bung in through the doors. Carver took me and Liz to the upstairs office because he wanted to "talk with us," and all these big security guards were standing around with their arms crossed like in some gangster movie. It was intimidation—pure and simple. Then Carver was going around saying none of us would ever work in this town again.

Arthur Haynes: The next night they announced that the Fowler brothers, Barry and Ken—Albert Fayth—had won the battle of the bands. They won the best band in Newfoundland doing a Joe Cocker cover. I'm not saying they weren't good, but they won best band in Newfoundland doing "A Little Help from My Friends."

On our first album, there's a "no thanks" section, and Carver's name was in there. We wrote "Doganfaced Motherfucker" about "asshole Dave." Some of those quotes are right out of his mouth. Carver said, "Don't you know who I am? I bring all the big bands to Newfoundland. You'll never play in this town again."

Barry Newhook: Needless to say, Bung didn't play any Tenth Avenue [events] after that.

Phil Winters: We recorded our first album early the next year [1994] at 333 Duckworth. Ross Murray and Don Ellis did the engineering.

Barry Newhook: Bung definitely played those songs to death. For the most part, the ones that we could rely on were stuck on the record.

Phil Winters: When Wallace Hammond recorded the Schizoid demo in Don's basement, it was very rudimentary, low-tech, and low-fi. Doing the first Bung album, we had limited resources, and we were all still learning.

Fred Brokenshire and Duckworth Distribution put up the money. I don't think we came up with any of it on our own. As far as I know, it was a payback situation, a recoupable thing. *Whole* probably took us a week to record. It wasn't a long-drawn-out process.

Geoff Younghusband: I was an amateur photographer who took a lot of pictures. Sometimes they got used for tape covers, and I was sort of into graphic design. I worked in a photo lab, and I started printing posters using Electrocet. As a twenty-three-year-old, I dropped four thousand bucks of hard-earned money on a 486 computer with eight megabytes of RAM and a three-pass colour scanner. I started laying out records, and my first immediate job was designing Bung's album art.

Jon Whalen: Nineteen ninety-four was the big year. We put out an album. We toured. We went to New York. That's when things really kicked in. All this stuff kind of came together and was right there for the taking.

Arthur Haynes: You hear stories about bands signing contracts over beer in dark bars without reading it over, and you wonder how anybody does that. But we did. We signed a distribution deal during the [1994] Juno Awards. It was also Canadian Music Week. Jodie Ferneyhough approached us and picked us up under his management company. Him and Cam Carpenter were fairly tight. They decided they were going to manage Bung together. Cam Carpenter was an A&R guy for MCA. What we got from MCA was two days at Metalworks Studios in Mississauga.

Jon Whalen: We did the ECMAs here in St. John's [1994], and then we were invited to Canadian Music Week. The buzz was really starting to pick up, and that's when MCA got us to sign a right of first refusal.

Barry Newhook: Looking back, I think record companies only ask you to do stuff like make a demo recording just to see if they can work with you. I think Cam Carpenter might have even implied that we could have had something [more substantial] with MCA if we pursued it.

We looked at a contract. We would get 12 per cent of record sales. You get a loan, basically, enough money to record an album and to fund a tour. You're always in debt to the record company. You're constantly touring. If I was presented with that when I was twenty, I would have jumped on it. But at that point in my life, it just didn't seem that appealing to me.

Phil Winters: I have the contract here somewhere that MCA wanted us to sign, but there were opposing views. We couldn't come together. I'm sure that if we had vigorously pursued Cam Carpenter and MCA, they would have played ball.

We did this little mini-tour up to Toronto and back. We played with some great bands. We played with some not-so-great bands. We smoked some crack and drank a lot of rum. There was good times and bad times. There was a lot of pressure started coming from Jodie, the manager, and Duckworth Distribution was still there as part of our record.

We played in Toronto and then drove to a hotel in Mississauga. We got there probably 4:30 in the morning. We had to be at Metalworks at 7:30. We played our gig, drove to Mississauga, got to the hotel, crashed, got up, checked out, went to Metalworks, recorded all day, and then drove back to Toronto. "The Legend of Sleepy Demo" is what we called it. All that was over two days in late March. We did three songs: "Scumtribe," "Charmed," and "Wankfest."

Arthur Haynes: Graham Stairs was working for EMI. He was fishing around St. John's, too. We were offered a five-album deal with EMI, which we couldn't accept because of the agreement we had signed with MCA.

When the EMI deal came across the table, it was the first time in my life where I actually had to stand up and say, "I think we need to speak with our lawyer."

Jonny got all pissed off and upset. "What are you talking about?"

I was like, "We're legally bound to another contract. We can't sign this deal. I know you want to, but we can't." I don't know if he ever got over it. Jon was born to be a rock star, and he came pretty close. He was a pen stroke away.

Jon Whalen: We were invited down to New York for the College of Music Journalists Festival. But Justin didn't get into the United States. As his replacement, we could have had Ani DiFranco's drummer for a hundred dollars a show, but the boys didn't want to do that. We had taken out a seven-thousand-dollar bank loan just to get to this thing, and we're going to be paying it off for a year anyway. It was two fucking shows. We could've signed for the United States. The whole push wasn't to get a Canadian record deal but to get an international record deal.

Barry Newhook: The organizer's lawyers asked if anyone had a criminal record. Justin said he did. We went over to the RCMP office, and the officer there looked for three separate charges or convictions. But there was only one on the computer. Justin asked, "Where did they go?"

"They sometimes get lost when they're transferred over to computers. They're never going to show up. If they don't show up on my computer, they're not going to show up on theirs. There's this one thing. It was from so long ago, and it was such a small thing."

It was a possession charge. The cop asked him all these questions about his personal history. Justin is from British Hong Kong. He lived in Carbonear when his parents first came over, and then he moved into town. His father worked with the consulate or something. He told them how long he was living here and that he had a house in St. John's. The officer wrote up a fantastic letter: "He has a family here. We've never had any trouble from him. He's an upstanding citizen. He owns property here and has no intention of staying in your country. He's invited to this event, will be leaving on this date and returning on this date."

The RCMP officer said, "Don't worry. This letter will get you into the country."

As soon as we got there, they looked Justin up and said, "Nope. You got a drug conviction. Zero tolerance."

"But I have this letter."

"Forget the letter. Can you get out of the line? Do you understand what 'zero tolerance' means? It means you are not allowed in our country. You have a drug conviction. I don't want to see the letter from the police. You're talking to the authority here."

So that was that.

Phil Winters: I wasn't working at the LSPU Hall anymore. I was still doing stage-managing, and I probably did more lighting then, too. I was working on films as a grip. There was a couple of productions on the go, but not a whole hell of a lot of work.

I don't know if the band was all on the same page. I think we all wanted to play music and get paid for it, but there were certain things that we didn't want to compromise on and certain realities of being a touring band that were probably not acceptable.

We got to New York. Of course, Justin wasn't there, and we had a showcase the next day. We went out with MCA and our manager. We were talking about getting a session drummer to play with us instead, but it was unimportant to me because it wasn't Justin. Our groove came from him. Our sound was built over several years of being together. I'm sure the session guy was a fine musician. Looking back, I'm sure he could have done it no problem, lick for lick, tap for tap. At the time, it [the argument] was actually vicious. Me and Jon were barking at each other in front of these two ladies who wanted to take the band to Australia. After that, they didn't want to take the band anywhere. Junkhouse went to Australia instead.

We didn't play our showcase, either. If only Justin had made it.

Arthur Haynes: I don't know what would have happened. Life goes on, man. We came close, as close as anybody I know. We were right there, but the band started to implode. Justin didn't want to leave his kids; he didn't want to tour. Then we flew in Jodie from Ontario for the signing of the MCA contract.

Phil Winters: When he got here, we asked him if these rumours about Cam [leaving MCA] were true. He said, "Yes, it's true. There's no deal."

We were like, "Why didn't you tell us that on the goddamn phone? Why did we have to fly you in here from Toronto to tell us that?"

Jon Whalen: After our deal went south, Arthur left, and we played as a four-piece for a while. We still drew a crowd, but it wasn't the same. There was a general disenchantment. I always liked Arthur's creative influence. It's a much heavier, fuller, and chaotic sound when he's involved. The songwriting pretty much stopped, too. At one point, Barry wanted Phil to work around a bass line, and Phil was just being a jerk about it. I can't remember his exact words, but it was something like, "I'm not going to fool around with your stupid little riff."

Barry said to me, "Man, if this is the way it's going to be, I can't deal with it. This has been dead for two years anyway."

When it looked like we were going to get a record deal, Justin quit the band, and we tried a couple of other drummers. Then the record deal went south, and he rejoined. We were seven thousand dollars in debt with no record deal on the horizon.

Arthur Haynes: Jon's old man co-signed a seven-thousand-dollar loan with the Hong Kong Bank for us to go to New York, which is why the Sam Shades shows continued. We played there every Thursday for like two months to pay him back. The last two or three shows were not good. We weren't there because we wanted to be. Crowds were waning, and most of our crew wouldn't even go to George Street. There was a lot of rowdy skeets and baymen who weren't interested in what we were doing. We covered "L.A. Woman" and some Johnny Cash. We did some AC/DC. But we only had three or four of those numbers. It's hard to fill up two hours and twenty minutes with people standing in front of you with their arms crossed looking like they're going to punch you in the face.

Jon Whalen: We played a few shows for that brief period with other people. But it wasn't the same. Paul Curnew was probably a better drummer than Justin in a lot of ways, but it still didn't work quite right. He probably would've become our drummer if things had continued on that way. Once it looked like we weren't touring, Justin rejoined. He felt that he could play around St. John's once a month.

We just kind of drifted apart.

Arthur made it to our final show. That would've been 1996 or 1997. I remember the drummer for Bad Religion was there. He came backstage and said, "You guys shouldn't quit, man. You're really good. You should come down to California. Blah, blah, blah."

I consider Bung a band to have broken up, but we put out a record since then. There was a four-year period where we didn't play at all. We played a show at Junctions [Rockcanroll Festival, 2004] and that was sort of our first time back. We probably managed to do a show once a year since then. That's not really a band. That's kind of getting the cobwebs out of your brain.

Phil Winters: I was tired of doing everything for Bung. I was setting up the shows. I was doing the posters. I was calling rehearsals and trying to get us all together. There was apathy on Jon's part because he wanted to go for it, and we weren't going for it. I totally understand his point of view. Barry had been away in Toronto to work. So we had a couple of different bass players. Geoff Younghusband played bass with us for a gig, and Aneirin Thomas played bass with us for a gig. Don Ellis played bass with us for a gig. There was film work going on. The band just wasn't fun anymore. It was a chore and a pain in the ass.

We were going to play one last show the night before my birthday. It was a long day and a late night, and I had to work on a film shoot the next morning. I'd done acid, I was loaded, and I'd smoked a lot of pot. When I got home, I was supposed to be ready to work at like six in the morning. I got back home at probably 3:30 or 4:00. I was in no shape to go to work, but I woke up with my boss standing over the bed: "How are you doing, Phil?"

Arthur Haynes: The last show, for me, was at Junctions, before they expanded and tore out the ceiling. Myself and Phil were butting heads quite a lot. My drinking problem was more of a problem for other people. I never really had a problem with it myself. But I was saucy and unreliable. We were full-on bickering and fighting. I don't know what it was that Phil said to me, but it was over the microphone. It was something like, "You sucked tonight, and you're going to come to rehearsal tomorrow." He was shaking his finger at me and scolding me over the microphone while there was still fifteen or twenty people still milling about.

I snapped. "That's it—this is done for me. For what it used to be, it has turned into a lot of shattered dreams and busted egos."

I was out west for twelve years. It was literally two weeks after I moved back home that Bung was ready to record the second record. There was no plan; I hadn't heard anything from them. There were the scattered phone calls and letters. During that time away, I think I was home three times. There was a funeral, a wedding, and a national tour with a Celtic band that I used to play with. We did the Newfoundland and Labrador Folk Festival in 2004. When my grandmother died, I came back for the funeral. Bung happened to be doing a show at the LSPU Hall, and I played with them then.

Where we are now, I'd play with those guys any time on any stage. The songs are still poignant. The music is still as good as it ever was. I think we're a better band now, too. Maybe we're more grateful for what it is, as opposed to shrugging it off like it's just this thing that we're involved in.

It was twenty-five years ago, but it seems like it was yesterday. None of us grew up. We're getting old—don't get me wrong. Everybody is growing older. There are children and marriages involved. But something stopped back then, and not many of us managed to evolve beyond that point. Some of us have been stuck back there and haven't been able to go on with their lives because of it. As far as the way that I look at the world and the way that I live my life, it hasn't changed one bit. I'm not motivated by money. I'm not motivated by social status. I still believe that there's a chance for me to be a musician. It's never gone away.

If somebody came to me tomorrow and said they could offer us the same deal we got offered twenty-five years ago, I'd sign it in a flash. That's saying something for a guy with a mortgage and a family. I really believe that there's still potential for this band. I guess I feel like I still have potential, too.

SCRUFFY-LOOKING TEENAGERS PLAYING PUNK ROCK IN THE PARK
PEACE-A-CHORD PART 2

Bruce Gilbert: To a cynic, Peace-A-Chord was a naive, ragtag, homemade peace-and-love festival, whereas the Folk Festival was aspiring to be an organized, corporate-sponsored event.

Andrea Cooper: The year Joel Plaskett played the Folk Festival [2013], they sold out of beer tickets within the first hour for the entire weekend. The Folk Festival supports the folk arts and celebrates culture. Peace-A-Chord celebrated diversity. That's the difference.

Sheffia Samuelson: My dad was a musician. For a long time, he was in charge of the Folk Festival. All those people who everyone now worships used to sit at my kitchen table. My dad was a musician, a drummer, but I never really saw him playing much growing up. I would see him with his bodhran every once in a while, but that's about it. Sandy Morris sent me a link a few years ago of my father in 1981 introducing Figgy Duff at the Folk Festival in Pippy Park. I don't ever remember it being in Pippy Park.

The Folk Festival was good clean music. Look what it's become. When my dad did it, there was almost no admission. Everything was donated. Now everything costs an arm and a leg. The Folk Festival is a cash cow.

Peace-A-Chord was [a bunch of] scruffy-looking teenagers playing punk rock in the park and hippies giving speeches. The city never wanted that.

Karmella Perez: By 1990, the festival had grown from a half-day to two full days. The committee had kind of transformed Peace-A-Chord into a music festival.

Lesley Thompson: Our formula was to get guest speakers on in between bands. They were people from organizations like the Women's Centre and OXFAM. Maybe we did a bad job at putting the issues more front and centre. There was enough programming happening during the day that you could come with your family and not get smashed by a mosh pit.

Andrea Cooper: I started volunteering when I was twelve. The first few years I kind of watched what Tina and Dana were doing.

Most of us were Type A personalities who worked hard to pull off the Youth for Social Justice camps and the festival, and half the time we never really knew what we were doing. But we wanted to create something worthwhile for the community.

Peter Harbin *(musician/organizer)*: My first Peace-A-Chord was in 1990. I got snagged into going with my brother, a totally conservative type of guy. Him and his girlfriend were volunteering with Helping Hands, doing face painting.

Sheffia Samuelson: I can't remember how I got involved. I think it came about through hanging out with Karmella Perez and her friends. This was '89 or '90. The festival was still being run under the banner of Ploughshares Youth. We used to meet in the back room of OXFAM on Duckworth Street.

Tiffany Martin *(coordinator, Peace-A-Chord)*: Not everybody really wanted the job of coordinator. There was a natural evolution of people filling it. There was no process or vote. You sort of volunteered for two or three years and then put your name forward.

Lesley Thompson: Peace-A-Chord was probably on my mind every waking hour. I remember there being some tension between me and Diana Daly. Of course, there's going to be some tension. Knowing me, I probably thought she wasn't putting in enough effort. Knowing me, that was probably really unfair.

Andrea Cooper: When I took over, we were able to get some real money for office space at 333 Duckworth Street for a hundred dollars a month.

Lesley Thompson: There was a history in St. John's of funding these types of social justice projects. We got grants from the Sisters of Mercy. Every year, we would have the most fucked-up bands play at Peace-A-Chord with the most offensive names, and the Sisters of Mercy would give us money.

We weren't just sort of wagging the dog and organizing some bands for our friends. It was good community-based work.

Andrea Cooper: I was at Duckworth Lunch and heard that the canopy wasn't going up over the stage. It was like a Friday or something. Andy Wells [former mayor of St. John's] was eating there. I have no idea how I did this, being as shy as I was, but I went up to him and explained the situation. He called somebody and made things happen. It was a time when communication was harder. Tracking down the right people was harder. Trying to figure out how to get funding was harder.

Lesley Thompson: Peace-A-Chord '94 cost fifty-eight hundred dollars. We were already in debt nineteen hundred dollars. We probably got Natalie Spracklin's dad to donate a canopy to go over the top of the stage. There was always the threat of rain. All of a sudden, on the morning of the festival, someone showed up with military-style tents. It was probably George Thorne and a bunch of his friends who set it up.

Sheffia Samuelson: In 1991, Peace-A-Chord got rained out. We moved to the Curling Club [on Bonaventure Avenue]. That's the one Me, Mom and Morgentaler played. Every year, we used to try and bring in two bands from away. I remember seeing Spirit of the West for the first time at Peace-A-Chord. I remember seeing Jane Siberry. Before that, there was Deja Voodoo from Montreal and the Gruesomes.

Andrea Cooper: It was something like a thousand dollars to rent the Curling Club. By the time I started running the festival (1994), we couldn't afford a rain venue. It's a lot of work to pick up and move. The Folk Festival can't do that because it takes days to set up.

The year it rained, I cried. You work so hard, and then it starts raining. I was devastated. And then I was kind of embarrassed because I was crying.

Karmella Perez: Someone said, "Billy Bragg is in town." He'd gone on a whale-watching tour, or something. A bunch of people went into Duckworth Lunch and sat down to have coffee, and there he was. I don't know who asked him or who spoke to him about playing a benefit show. They told him we were in debt.

Andrea Cooper: Sheffia saw him on the street. "Would you play a fundraiser for us?"

Karmella Perez: It was ten bucks at the Star of the Sea. Billy Bragg borrowed a guitar. It was a totally makeshift event. He didn't even have a set list. He got up and said, "I don't know what to play. What do you guys want to hear?" There was a little girl dancing in the front, so he started singing children's songs.

Peace-A-Chord died in 1992. We were so broke that no one could get it together. Most of the people who had organized had moved away to school or just didn't want to have anything to do with it because they were burned out. The next year, it came back with a vengeance.

Andrea Cooper: Programming was so hard. We didn't have to go looking for bands. The worst part was calling people and telling them that they couldn't play. There were only so many hours in a day. Nobody wanted to play ten-minute sets; nobody wanted the afternoon slot. Everybody wanted to play at night.

Eleven o'clock we shut everything down. I don't think that was a good idea. It used to stop at nine. Going on until eleven brought out the bottle smashers. For us, going later in the evening was just an effort to try and fit more bands onto the schedule.

Karmella Perez: Peace-A-Chord was definitely the number one social event of the summer.

Peter Harbin: I saw ads for the '93 organizing committee. I basically spent the next ten years working on the festival full-time. I coordinated in '98 and stage-managed right up until the end.

Every year, Wallace [Hammond] did sound. I always gave him a hand. I got a great satisfaction working myself to exhaustion from being awake for twenty-something hours, getting a few hours' sleep, working another day of Peace-A-Chord, and then breaking it all down until seven o'clock in the morning.

Erin Whitney *(coordinator, Peace-A-Chord)*: I've never been good at counting crowds. We had no mechanism for doing that. At night, the area around the stage would be packed. I guess there would be a thousand people in the park over the weekend.

There was a remarkable sense of community surrounding the all-ages scene and Peace-A-Chord. Those certainly fed into each other. There was never any trouble finding volunteers. We would have volunteer meetings where we couldn't fit everyone into the office.

Karmella Perez: Nineteen ninety-three was the first Peace-A-Chord [my brother] Ritche played with Potatobug. At the time, I'd never seen him sing. I was almost embarrassed. I thought, *People are going to hate this*. I didn't want to have to tell him that his band sucked. I didn't have the heart for that. But they got up onstage, and everyone went crazy. I don't know if Ritche remembers this. I was helping him put his gear into the car, and he shook my hand. He was like, "I did that because of you. I've always wanted to play Peace-A-Chord."

To this day, he claims that if I hadn't helped organize Peace-A-Chord that he wouldn't have been in a band. He didn't go to shows as much as I did, but I used to make him go to Peace-A-Chord every year.

Lesley Thompson: At that time, St. John's was going through a love affair with Halifax. A lot of people were listening to Halifax bands. St. John's musicians were moving to Halifax as opposed to Toronto or Montreal.

Andrea Cooper: The whole female rock thing was going on, and there was a group of us women who really wanted to bring in Jale. I played in a band called Snatch with Jocelyne Thomas. Peace-A-Chord was our first and only performance.

Natalie Noseworthy: The boys from Bung were there, and that gave us some confidence. We invited Phil and Arthur up onstage to do the official Snatch salute, which was them putting their hands down their pants and out through their zipper.

Andrea Cooper: We couldn't get Jale, so we got Thrush Hermit instead. It was Joel Plaskett's first time in Newfoundland.

Karmella Perez: We were no longer involved. I couldn't organize because I was attending MUN. I wasn't a teenager anymore. There were all of these kids—swarms of kids—at the festival. Nineteen ninety-four was the first year that they kind of made it more about music rather than social justice. I don't remember any speakers; I don't remember any workshops. That isn't to say there weren't any. I just don't remember them.

Lesley Thompson: There were always the concerns that we were going to get shut down. The neighbourhood had put up with us for such a long time, and we were always treading on thin ice.

A really interesting discussion was going on around town, the concept of indecency and why women's bodies are considered indecent. We had agreed that Bung would close out one of the nights. At some point in time, [Jon Whalen] said something unbelievably inappropriate like "Can all the ladies show us their titties?" It was something like that.

It definitely wasn't, "I'm a smart guy, and I'm a feminist. I really support my women friends taking their shirts off." It was more about taking advantage of the conversation that was happening. It was a public festival in Bannerman Park called "Peace-A-Chord." It was a stupid thing to do.

I remember going backstage and challenging him on it. Some dude shouldn't be asking the ladies in the audience to shake their titties, especially since there was police around, and the noise complaints a problem, too.

Erin Whitney: I was living in the neighbourhood, and someone came to my door with a petition to ban the festival. I said, "I'm not going to sign that. Have you actually talked to the people at Peace-A-Chord? If you have a problem with them, maybe you guys can work it out."

Andrea Cooper: Public relations wasn't even something we thought about.

Erin Whitney: The festival was loud, and it sometimes attracted a kind of a rough crowd. It was a free outdoor music festival. There were always assholes who wanted to show up and smash beer bottles.

Lesley Thompson: It was probably 1995 when Diana Daly and I coordinated. The committee started talking about the tension between the freedom of speech and our mandate. It was a really kind of intense conversation for a bunch of young volunteers to have with each other. It was sparked by André Samuelson's band [Stigma]. Their lyrics were kind of misogynist. We had to get a guarantee from Stigma to tone it down, and the band ultimately respected the process. I remember being surprised. In previous years, we had metal bands saying crazy stuff, but it kind of flew under the radar.

Dan Moore: Festered Corpse played the Peace-A-Chord at like eleven o'clock in the morning. It was at the Curling Club that year because it was raining outside. There was mostly only eight-year-old kids there. Everyone else was sat back forty feet from the stage. Maybe three or four punks were up front [to watch us]. All these little kids with balloons were running around with their faces painted while we played "Sweet Slut of Mine."

Andrea Cooper: The city thought the Peace-A-Chord crowd were nuisances. Instead of seeing us as being empowered, all they saw was us using the city's labour, the city's staff; then there were the concerns for the noise and dirtying the park. The city could be quite hard on us. We would ask for certain things, and they would fight us. I don't think they were sad when Peace-A-Chord finally stopped.

Erin Whitney: There were always a few dudes out in the back drinking beer. In 1997, they set fire to one of our banners. That fed into a general decline of the social justice aspect of the festival. The social justice groups that would come and do presentations and have tables and speakers on the main stage in between bands stopped wanting to do it because they felt like nobody was listening and everybody was there for a big rock show. That was always disheartening.

Lesley Thompson: In 1997, we added a second stage. That year, I coordinated the second stage and did the newsletter.

Tiffany Martin: There were dance pieces, comedy sketches, and acoustic acts. Workshops finally had a dedicated space.

Erin Whitney: We were trying to accommodate as many people as we could. That was probably part of an attempt to make the festival more family friendly.

Tiffany Martin: We always had cops walk through the park, and there was never a problem. There was always a kind of understanding that smoking weed wasn't going to lead to physical altercations. It was going to lead to pizza. But you can't have underage drinking en masse at the park. It got to a point where people were coming down at night just to get loaded. And they weren't respectful.

After the banner was burned, I had a fit, and I left the park going, "It should never happen again. Peace-A-Chord should be over. Choose to organize a music festival and let the social justice stuff take a back seat. But acknowledge what you're doing. Call it something else. Rebrand it."

What the festival was and what it had become were two totally different things.

Lesley Thompson: Something that was facilitated by OXFAM was a group called Puppets for Change. A small group of people took a summer-long workshop with this Montreal puppeteer who was with a puppet group in Vermont called the Bread and Puppet Group. She trained us for six weeks in puppet-building and scriptwriting. In 1996, after I finished high school, we went on tour.

I think at that point I really separated myself from Peace-A-Chord. I felt like it was probably time to leave the festival behind. And I don't really remember exactly why that was. I hope that when I passed the files on that I was gracious in doing it. For some reason, I feel like I left with a bad taste in my mouth.

Erin Whitney: In 1998, we sort of had less volunteers. At the same time, the city was being difficult and a little less supportive. It was harder to get money together. [In '99], me and Melissa Parsons and Tiffany Martin coordinated. It was disheartening enough that we were kind of happy to leave it behind.

Dana Warren: Peace-A-Chord didn't change for a long time, in that it held pretty tightly to the theme of promoting peace. But the organizing group became more and more marginalized by the authorities. What destroyed them was booze and alcohol and the suspicions from adults. By that time, Peace-A-Chord were further removed from OXFAM. It slowly made a turn for the worse, and I don't know if anybody even noticed.

I saw Bill Hynd a little while ago, and he said, "Dana, you got to come down to the OXFAM building and get this picture of you and Evelyn [Riggs] at Peace-A-Chord." I was constantly the person with the peace symbol painted on my face. I had a braid in my hair with feathers all through it.

We were total hippies. But the OXFAM office on Duckworth Street and the archives are all gone now. The building burned to the ground [in September 2013].

Erin Whitney: After the petition went around and it was sent to city council, Peace-A-Chord was kicked out of the park. I don't know who approached me, but myself and Tiffany Martin, Liz Pickard, Sean Murray, and maybe Melissa Parsons got together and formed an advisory committee to try and convince the city to let Peace-A-Chord continue. We went through all kinds of public meetings with the Special Events Advisory Committee, who were a really dour bunch. They ended up letting it go ahead in the park. Evening concerts were at the LSPU Hall. That Peace-A-Chord was called "Police-A-Chord" because the city made us put up snow fencing and hire security to check bags. They paid for it all, which cost about ten thousand dollars.

I don't know if that was really worth fighting for.

The next year [2006], which was the last, we did it inside the LSPU Hall. I was working at the Hall then, which was how I convinced them to let Peace-A-Chord happen. As Operations Manager, I was in charge of the rentals and box office and stuff like that. The LSPU Hall stopped having all-ages shows there because they didn't want a bunch of kids crawling all over their nice new chairs.

Bruce Gilbert: My daughter and her buddies are in bands. They had meetings with Sheilagh O'Leary and a few other people, and there was some talk about bringing Peace-A-Chord back. Of course, they didn't have the wherewithal, the capacity, the time, or the space. It's a mammoth undertaking for a bunch of teenagers.

Erin Whitney: Arts administration is not something that I ever trained for. It absolutely comes from what I was doing when I was fifteen and sixteen years old trying to make a festival happen. Thinking back, I'm amazed at the work that kids would put into Peace-A-Chord and what we could accomplish. I think the grown-up world should provide those opportunities to young people more often. Maybe they could learn a thing or two themselves.

A HARD-VOLUME EXPERIENCE
OR, THE END OF THE CENTURY

Paul Ryan *(Fred Gamberg's best friend)*: I used to dream of Fred. I don't remember the details, but I remember dreaming of him. It was kind of nice because it was almost like he was still around, but then I would wake up.

I don't dream of him anymore, but I remember thinking, only a few years ago, that I'll never speak to him again—he's gone.

Aileen O'Keefe *(Fred Gamberg's sister. Interviewed by Leslie Pierce, February 11, 2009)*: Fred's full name was Frederick Gerard Gamberg. His family called him "Freddie." He was born on March 23, 1971, in St. John's. He was twenty-four when he died [July 10, 1995]. He grew up here. We moved to 44 Poplar Avenue when he was a year old, and he lived there all his life. He attended St. Pius X and Brother Rice back when they were Catholic boys' schools. He wasn't super athletic, but he did play on the Brother Rice rugby team.

He discovered music at maybe thirteen or fourteen.

Fred Gamberg *(interviewed by Paul Ryan, October 1, 1994)*: When was the first time I went to a show? It was at the Grad House. It was 1985 or '86. It's almost ten years ago when you think about it. The first time I went to an all-ages show was Halloween at the 301 Club.

Paul Ryan: I spoke to Fred at that show. Dog Meat BBQ, Tough Justice, and Schizoid played. Fred was being Fred. He had on a trench coat and his hair was all messy. He had the same Sid Vicious T-shirt as me, and we started talking because we recognized one another from school.

We clicked pretty quickly. We were fifteen and in a school with a bunch of jocks. We kind of banded together.

Ritche Perez: He was a mall rat, like me and my sister. Hanging out at the arcade, I would see him going around with his combat boots and his army jacket. We used to think he was a Nazi because he had his head shaved. One day, I came home, and he was there with my sister.

Karmella Perez: That's how you met anyone—the Mall. Kids who wore black talked to each other. It's as simple as that.
   At the time, we were hanging out at OXFAM. Fred was maybe volunteering with Peace-A-Chord. Maybe he was in Ploughshares Youth or Youth for Social Justice. We were all connected in that way. When Mom opened the café [Coco Manga], it became a hangout for a large group of young people. Fred would drop in for coffee, and he eventually became good friends with my brother. Fred bought Ritche a Clash tape and had him over to his house for spaghetti. They basically became friends for life at that point.

Frank Nolan *(musician)*: I met Fred at Funland Games Arcade. My God, he could talk. It was actually a little hard to deal with him sometimes. You had to constantly tell him to shut up. Once he came off of the Ritalin, there was nothing holding him back.

Jon Swyers: Fred was, in retrospect, like a cartoon. He had a very unusual personality, and he was driven. He had a love of music that was unparalleled by most. His skill set in terms of music-making was very rudimentary. But his passion drove him to support the rest of the community. I think in this marvellous era of medical science, Fred ranked very high on the Asperger's spectrum. I mean that in no negative sense. I have a number of friends who fit that description.

Paul Ryan: We were listening to whatever was on the radio and trying to figure this stuff out, and Fred already had records and was listening to *Brave New Waves*. Fred sent Touch and Go Records an order for a Butthole Surfers tape, *Rembrandt Pussyhorse*. For them to figure out what it was that he wanted, they had to read this page-long letter that he had written them. It was like some kind of puzzle that they had to decode. That's classic Fred Gamberg for you.

Dave Andrews *(musician)*: He always had strong opinions. My girlfriend used to do an acoustic thing with Bob Dicks. Fred gave her a letter, a big, long letter, about things they could do to improve, the important aspects, and the ins and outs of playing live.

Karmella Perez: He always wrote in a little notebook. You'd meet him once and have a conversation with him. The next time you saw him, even if it was weeks or months later, he would remember you because of what he'd written in this notebook.

Aileen O'Keefe *(from Leslie Pierce interview)*: He was a true individual. He had ADHD [Attention Deficit Hyperactivity Disorder] as a child and was kind of an underachiever at school but he was very gregarious and could talk to anyone. He didn't drive. He never saw the need to, when he could walk or take the bus. He was always out and about, especially downtown. Everyone knew Fred. We were astonished at how many people came forward after his death to tell us they had known him.

Dave Andrews: When it came to talking to your parents, he was always charming. He used to call at like one in the morning. He would never say, "Is Dave there?" He would have a chat with my mom or dad instead.

Paul Ryan: Fred was also a listener. If I broke up with a girlfriend, I used to call him, and he would listen for hours. I guess when you're younger, things like breakups can affect you more. I remember him at a party standing up with a beer, listening and enjoying the conversation.

That's probably what I miss most, that I don't have his ear.

Geoff Younghusband: I guess I met him at CHMR when I was doing my radio show in 1990 or '91. He would show up in the middle of the night and take over from me. If you weren't going to make your show, Fred would fill in. If you were late for your show, Fred would start spinning records. He was always there.

Fred Gamberg *(from Paul Ryan interview)*: It all started when I was managing Ditch, helping out, putting gigs together. Geoff Younghusband used to organize virtually all the gigs in town. I helped out behind the scenes, moving gear and trying to figure out scheduling, and I started to get an inkling of how to do things.

December 17, 1993, was the first gig I truly organized from start to finish. It required playing in the Bishops College gym, and that place seats about seven hundred. We had three hundred–odd people show up for the all-ages show. Those are the shows for the younger crowd downtown. There's no worry about IDing for liquor. It was a concert with Potatobug; Ditch; my old band, Noon Day Gun; and a couple of other bands—I believe, Necropolis and Dropkick Jesus.

It required getting a sound system and a sound person. We rented a cube van, and it also meant spending some money on postering and doing a lot of publicity work and phoning radio stations and getting public service announcements on the air. It was a fundraising effort. We were trying to come up with some money for the school's foster child.

That formula is essentially the formula I continue to use. Since then, I've organized numerous concerts at the LSPU Hall. It requires bringing in a smaller sound system, finding volunteers to help do the door or security to make sure people don't smoke in there because it's a non-smoking building. Finding the bands and looking after promotion, which comes down to posters and handing out flyers.

Ritche Perez: With the all-ages shows at the LSPU Hall, Fred would find high school bands out of nowhere.

Jon Swyers: Punk rock culture comes with an implied air of negativity. It's sort of "fuck the system." That's the motivation and backdrop to that subculture. Fred was one of those people who saw beyond that.

Doug Rowe: He was a networker. He was constantly rallying the troops.

Fred Gamberg *(from Paul Ryan interview)*: Not only was I managing Ditch, but I had started my own band. I was singing for Noon Day Gun. We played at Peace-A-Chord. That was our first live gig.

Dave Andrews: Darryl Grace was the bassist, and Gina Ryan was the drummer. Gina was definitely the most accomplished musician, and she was only like fifteen.

We recorded an EP with Brian Downton in the main studio room at CHMR. Of course, we had to use it after the station had gone off the air, so we were up there at like one in the morning and spent the whole night.

A HARD-VOLUME EXPERIENCE

Karmella Perez: At first, his band was called Nail Gun. I remember seeing them play, and Fred was singing through a megaphone. I was like, "Fred, you don't need a megaphone. You don't even need a microphone. That's how loud you are."

Peter Harbin: My favourite thought of him is wearing a Rollins [Band] shirt that said, "I AM A HARD-VOLUME EXPERIENCE." That was Fred, a hard-volume experience.

Dave Andrews: Henry Rollins was definitely a big influence on him as far as his vocal performance went. Fred quit smoking because he wanted to save his voice. At the time, he was a pretty heavy smoker. He quit cold turkey and started drinking a lot of strong black coffee.

The last song we worked on was called "Ritalin." Fred wrote the lyrics. We never actually played it live. He was writing about having to take Ritalin in school. We weren't together much longer after that.

Paul Ryan: When Noon Day Gun broke up, he formed Giver with Rene Rubia and Frankie Paul Nolan. Fred played drums. I think he started practising drums on a snare. He wholeheartedly adopted a philosophy of do-it-yourself punk rock. He didn't care if he couldn't sing—he got up and sang. He didn't care if he wasn't the best drummer—he got up and played. That's how a lot of bands got started, kids who couldn't play a note but who didn't care either way.

Ray Walsh *(musician)*: Giver was kind of a train wreck. They were this strange punk entity with Rene's really weird stage presence and lyrics and Frankie Paul's equally weird bass lines and sound. Fred could hardly keep a beat. At the same time, it had this odd charm. They were, by far, the most unique thing on the scene. It was almost performance art.

Frank Nolan: I listened to Crass. They were an art collective and industrial punk band. I also listened to Front 242, early Yellow, Frank Zappa, and a lot of obscure music.

The original concept for Giver was two basses, a drum kit made from steel oil drums, and dual combative vocals through gas masks rigged with microphones. That was the general concept. We couldn't find any oil drums. We had a Roland organ that was given to me by Geoff Panting. I also had a beat-up old accordion and half a drum kit. I had a loan of Graham Howcroft's

250-watt Kustom bass cabinet and his Electro-Voice 18-inch folded speaker with a 27-inch mid-range horn that was bolted onto the top.

The day Giver was formed, we'd been at Rene's trying different things, with the two of us trading off one another. I got bored and decided I was going to go and find a drummer. Rene was living on Military Road. I walked down to Coco Manga and Fred [...] was finishing his last few sips of coffee. He was tapping on the table and keeping a good beat. I walked over, grabbed him by the arm, and marched him out the door. His CDs and stuff were all left behind on the table. I dragged him kicking and screaming up to Rene's place and sat him behind the drums. I picked up the bass and started playing something—anything. Fred listened and began tapping out a beat. We played non-stop for about forty-five minutes.

Fred had an opening for an upcoming show. There was about ten minutes where we were talking about what we were going to call ourselves. I said, "As soon as you stopped playing, you said 'give 'er.' That sounds like a good band name to me. I think we should go with that."

Peter Harbin: I sold Fred my Stewart drum set, the ones I had grown up playing. I think he gave me eighty bucks. You might as well have had a garbage can for a ride cymbal. The drums were total trash. But they were perfect for Giver. He upgraded to Noel Dinn's Tama drums after Noel died.

Frank Nolan: We had to fill a forty-minute slot. We put together six songs. A week before the gig, we were still trying to figure out how to make the songs slower to fill time. As it turned out, we played them all in fifteen minutes.

Paul Ryan: There was another benefit concert, and Fred was one of the organizers. They needed an extra band, and he called me up and said, "Do you want to play at this show?"

I had my cousin's guitar; I never had an amp.

We called ourselves the Shitz. There was Ritche Perez, Darryl Grace, Matt Clarke, Dave Andrews, me, and Fred. We never rehearsed. We got together right before we went on. "We kind of know some Ramones. We might be able to play some Dead Kennedys." I came up with a riff, and Fred wrote some lyrics.

People loved it. They were like, "When are you playing again?"

I don't think it was good music. It was just the feeling that it gave them.

Fred never thought he was some visionary who was going to change the world. It was nothing like that. He played music for pure enjoyment: Let's get up onstage and play a few songs. Let's have a laugh and go for it.

Ray Walsh: Fred never stopped. He was always trying to organize shows, no matter what obstacles were in his way. It seemed like he had this boundless energy. Mind you, he lost a lot of money on shows. That was one of the reasons why the LSPU Hall stopped having them. It got to a point where we couldn't pay them back.

In the early days, it was cheaper. You only had to pay the Hall a couple hundred bucks. But then they were asking five hundred dollars and a thousand dollars, or something like that. There's no way you can make that kind of money. It wasn't financially feasible. Fred started to run into a bit of that, but it didn't seem to matter. He'd put in as much of his own money as he could.

One time at the Loft, Fred was just cleaning up, and I was helping him. I kind of got a little glimpse into him then. He really cared about putting in the effort. That was when I truly got a sense of just how much work he put into these shows. He was cleaning bathrooms at that point just to make sure that he could get the next gig.

Sometimes he could be difficult to deal with, in the sense that he was forceful. Little did we know that's what you have to do keep the ship sailing. Sometimes you got to be a little bit of a dictator. Some of us didn't appreciate him maybe as much as we should have. I certainly never realized the amount of pressure that he was putting on himself.

When it came right down to it, half the shows wouldn't have happened if he wasn't directly involved with them. He was a driving [force] making things happen.

Fred Gamberg *(from Paul Ryan interview)*: The LSPU Hall is the best venue, and it's the easiest to look after. They have it worked out to a science. When I'm not running the show, the Hall will get me there to supervise. They like to have someone there representing the Hall upstairs to keep an eye on everything and make sure the rules are being followed. They usually have me do it. I volunteer at the LSPU Hall anyway. The Hall knows that I get the job done right. I've never had any problems with my gigs. Some people leave their gear overnight and not tell the technical director or the night manager. The next day you come in to set up for a play, and you've got band gear on centre stage. That's not cool. At the end of my gigs, I have the bands drive their gear home and usually work arrangements with cars.

I organized a gig on January 14; we were sold out, and there was an additional 250 people outside. That obviously shows the popularity of the three bands who performed: Noon Day Gun, Ditch, and Dead Red from Corner Brook. That was three bands for $5.25. We sold out that evening, and our costs worked out perfectly. We managed to avoid a catastrophe.

Another thing I've come up with is selling tickets in advance. When you do that, it's such an easy method of picking them up. At first, I was doing them through the LSPU Hall's box office. Now I'm doing them myself because I'll be on the street. You can run your own box, as opposed to the LSPU Hall looking after the money, which is an additional administrative charge. Probably the best thing is you don't have a big crowd of people outside the front door all at once, pushing in to get their tickets.

In the summer, there seems to be less demand to go to all-ages shows. There are things to do in the evening for young people. We were getting less than a hundred people at gigs. That's painful because you're playing for absolutely no money at all. It's costing money, and I'm the one signing the papers.

It gets scary at the end of the night if we don't get enough people through the front door. That actually happened twice this summer, where I owed money to the sound man. There was supposed to be a festival in Victoria Park. Because that was cancelled, I lost a hundred dollars. I was supposed to look after the equipment overnight, and I was getting paid a hundred dollars. Wallace, who was the sound person for the show at the Hall, felt really bad and let the cost ride. The second time, I was shy like ten bucks.

Geoff Younghusband: I found Fred to be a bit of problem in the all-ages scene. Because he was so open and eager to do anything, he over-saturated the market. He didn't grasp the concept of over-saturation. There was just more bands to listen to. It didn't matter how good they were or how bad they were or whether they could fill the room at the LSPU Hall. Whether he lost his shirt or not, he still put on a show the next week.

But some of us thought, *We don't have an audience anymore because they've been spread so thin*. There was so much stuff to go to in this small city that, at times, it felt like he wasn't giving anything time to blossom. But I'm pretty sure that if you talked to a lot of those people who never aspired to be professional musicians, [they] would have never played a gig if it wasn't for Fred Gamberg. He gave that dream to many people.

Phil van Ulden: We grew up in the centre of the city, the Rabbittown area. Eventually, my parents decided that they were splitting up, and Dad moved off to New Brunswick. We stayed in St. John's with Mom.

We went into city housing and moved across from the Molson Brewery on Circular Road. There was a pathway by our place that went to Empire Avenue and eventually onto Churchill Square. That path was used by a lot of people who lived in the area. One of them was Fred Gamberg.

The final incarnation of Ched hadn't happened yet. We hadn't played a show. We didn't really have much of a connection to the music scene, other than through Ritche and Ivan. We weren't anywhere near ready to play, because we only had one song. I remember jamming in the basement, making a pile of noise, and there was a knock at the door. It was Fred.

We'd seen him around before. He said, "I always hear you guys playing. You should play a show. I can get some other bands."

The show happened at the LSPU Hall. I think it was Halloween. We took a few months to put some songs together. Chris Hanlon was a little bit wild at times. At the end of the set, he smashed his guitar on the stage.

Fred Gamberg *(from Paul Ryan interview)*: There was a concert we had in the Not Broken Crockery installation, the former MUN Extension building. Ten bands performed over a seven-hour time period. It was from 3:30 in the afternoon until 10:30 at night. It was a long concert. It was the last all-ages show that Ditch ever played. It was their farewell show. Bob Dicks and Nicole Rousseau opened with an acoustic set. We had more bands show up to play while the concert was in progress.

Doug Rowe: It was called The Last Thrash.

Paul Gruchy: Fred passed out handbills to anyone and everyone. [...] As word trickled out, bands were showing up with their gear. Potatobug, After Forever, Sheavy, and Giver all played. It was a great send-off for Bob and a way to close out the whole Ditch chapter.

Bob Dicks: I moved to Calgary because I wanted to start a career. I wasn't making any money in St. John's.

Fred Gamberg *(from Paul Ryan interview)*: We had a room that could hold possibly a hundred people. In the audience, we had ninety-four with less than a day's notice—no posters and one PSA at the MUN radio station. Through word of mouth and handing out flyers, we managed to get ninety-four people at a concert. That was with just a thirty-dollar overhead.

Karmella Perez: Just before he passed away, Fred went to Corner Brook with Dead Red. He showed up at the café and said, "I just got off a plane, and I came straight downtown." He was talking about how his life had changed.

We were like, "Come on, Fred. You just went to Corner Brook. It's not anything."

Aileen O'Keefe (from *Leslie Pierce interview*): A strange fact is that Fred never left the island of Newfoundland, not even for a holiday. It just worked out that way.

Karmella Perez: Jon Swyers said that he had seen notes in Fred's book that he had ideas of bigger things to come. Shortly after that, he passed away.

Karmella Perez: Holly Jackson's parents bought a house on the road that leads to Big River in Flatrock. The person who owned it before them said that they couldn't handle the noise from all the kids swimming there.

I haven't gone to Big River since Fred passed away. When I first got my licence, we used to hang out there a lot. There are photos of us sitting on the rocks writing and just hanging out. The place never felt dangerous; it was beautiful.

The night Fred died, I remember it was so hot and humid outside. There was a show at Junctions, and I was standing outside with a bunch of people. Fred came over and asked if we were going to Flatrock, because he needed a ride.

Paul Ryan: Earlier that night, we were sat at the War Memorial talking and Fred came by. "I'm going swimming with a few friends."

Karmella Perez: I went to Cape Spear with Jon Swyers. For years, we claimed that we saw a UFO. But it was just some weird lights in the sky. I dropped Jon off and came home.

The next morning, someone called and asked if Ritche had seen Fred. It became kind of a panic: "Where is Fred? Who was the last person to see him?"

Ritche Perez: I got a call at like four in the morning, and I was half asleep. My mom opened the door and said, "Constable so-and-so is on the phone."

He was like, "Do you know where Fred Gamberg is? His mother's looking for him, and he hasn't shown up."

Paul Ryan: His cousin, Dave, called me at home. "Were you talking to Fred today?"

It was a rainy kind of night. I remember looking out my bedroom window and thinking, *Jesus, Fred, what are you after doing? Where are you after going?*

Seven o'clock the next morning, I got the phone call. Fred had drowned.

Ray Walsh: There was a lot of rumours going around. Some people said he fell off a cliff. Some people said he went off on his own, slipped, and hit his head. Then others said he went for a swim, there was nobody around, and he drowned.

Aileen O'Keefe (*from Leslie Pierce interview*): Fred wasn't a strong swimmer. We didn't learn to swim as children. Apparently, he was last seen sitting by himself while the others went on ahead. We believe he stumbled and struck his head on a rock and tumbled into the water.

Ritche Perez: I was at Wilderness Software. It was my first multimedia position after Cabot College. I got a call from my mom, and she said, "Fred's gone."

Karmella Perez: I was having lunch with my dad. He was working at St. Clare's. I called Jon. He said, "You might want to sit down. I have to tell you something. They found Fred today at Flatrock." I walked downtown completely numb. Fred was in a stage production of *Breakfast Club*. The posters were all over the light poles. At the café, people were really in shock and crying. I thought, *Oh, fuck. It's real.*

Aileen O'Keefe (*from Leslie Pierce interview*): Of course, [we were devastated]. My father was in Corner Brook attending a Boy Scout Jamboree, and meeting him at the airport the next day was the hardest thing I've ever done. I don't think my mother ever got over his death. She passed away October 6, 2005 of brain cancer.

Karmella Perez: There were two benefit shows for Fred, one at the LSPU Hall and one at the Loft.

Peter Harbin: George Thorne and Frankie Paul were pretty much spearheading the LSPU Hall show. I was their second-in-command, I guess. Everything we raised went to the food bank. The day before the show, we took apart the first three rows of seating and built this huge drum riser.

We spent until like nine in the morning building this drum riser and taking apart all the staging. Then we got three hours sleep and went back to do security for the twelve-hour all-ages show.

Ritche Perez: The benefit show at the Loft was to help his family pay for a headstone.

Geoff Younghusband: The show poster read "A Monumental Concert."

Peter Harbin: There was such a sombre mood at the Loft. I didn't cry until they started playing excerpts of Fred's radio show. I was like, *I'm never going to hear that voice again*. One thing about Fred, you always remember the voice.

Karmella Perez: It was really intense, because people started getting up and speaking about him. I'm pretty good friends with Paul Ryan. Somebody got up and made some crude remark about Fred. Paul kind of flipped. I said, "Everyone has different memories. You get up there, and you say what you need to say. If this is what people are going to remember about him, then that's their problem. You got something to say, so you get up and say it."

Paul Ryan: I really didn't want to, because I was shy. By that time, all of our older friends had moved to the mainland. I was just about the only one left, and I wanted to say something about Fred from when he was younger. "Everyone knows Fred liked to talk. In his kindergarten picture, his head is turned, and his hand is covering his mouth because he's talking to the kid next to him."

Geoff Younghusband: Every band got twenty minutes, and there was five minutes in between sets. A band would finish playing their four songs, they wouldn't even be off the stage, and the next band was ready to go. It was a night of everyone blasting through.

Peter Harbin: The Loft sold out of beer not once, not twice, but three times. They completely sold out of beer, went to a corner store, and bought more.

Paul Ryan: I don't think his parents truly knew what he was doing downtown. I don't think they thought much of it. They had no idea so many people cared about their son. I mean, the church was full at the funeral. I went outside and people were gathered there, too.

His father asked me, "Do you know what he was going to do with himself? Did he plan on leaving Newfoundland?"

As far as I knew, he was going to keep putting off shows. That's what I told him.

Paul Gruchy: With Fred's death there was a lull in the scene. The air was sort of sucked out of the room.

Ritche Perez: The games arcade deteriorated. I just didn't want to be part of it anymore. My mom ended up taking care of it with a few other people. It closed shortly after, because it was being neglected. Then Mom got sick, the café closed, and she went home to the Philippines. Potatobug broke up. It felt like the end of the century.

Ray Walsh: Losing a family member is not the same as losing your buddy. That's a much more shocking experience. Fred was so idealistic and created a lot of energy. He left an obvious and apparent void. Once the grief wasn't so constant, people talked about who was going to replace Fred as a promoter. Who was going to step up to the plate? Some people tried, but it was never quite the same. No one had the same level of commitment.

Johnny Fisher: No story about the underground St. John's music scene would be complete without Fred Gamberg. He was a cornerstone.

Jon Swyers: A huge change had happened to the music community. When Kurt Cobain died, it affected music across the board, especially youth culture. Then Fred died. We didn't have the same enthusiasm to continue on.

Geoff Younghusband: For our scene, the core group of people who grew up in the late '80s and early '90s era of punk rock in St. John's, I don't think it would be wrong to say Fred's death was a sort of marker for the endpoint.

At the same time, maybe it's a marker for adulthood beginning. I owned a house and was renovating it. People had girlfriends for more than two or three months. We were done with four-track recordings. Computers and the internet had arrived. Digital recordings were beginning. The scene just moved to new places.

EPILOGUE
A MOVING TARGET

Jody Richardson: I came back to St. John's [from Toronto], and I worked for CBC. I was doing commentary stuff and different things. I got involved in theatre again. I wanted to start a new band, something that didn't have the same level of responsibility as the Thomas Trio.

Geoff Younghusband: This was in 1995. It was the first summer that Fur Packed Action played. Jon Whalen was running the Loft. Rock Fight was the battle of the bands that he put off. Fur Packed Action formed because we said, "We're going to play in Rock Fight, and we're going to win."

There was one point that summer where we saw Potatobug. Maybe it was at Peace-A-Chord. They were at the height of their awesomeness. We were like, "Whatever happens, Potatobug has to win."

Jody Richardson: I wrote a song called "Don't Vote for Us," which was all about Potatobug being a much better band than Fur Packed Action. It went, "Don't vote for us because we know Potatobug outscore us."

Fur Packed Action's first gig was at MUN, and we wore dresses. What a stupid thing. The original Fur Packed Action stuff was completely nutty. I was ready then, at that point. I had gone through the whole process with the Trio, and I didn't care how things were perceived.

Fur Packed Action was like a complete rebirth.

We went up to play Gobblefest in Sydney, and I played naked. Except I put a condom on.

I came out onstage and played with my guitar in front of my crotch. Afterwards, the guy cleaning off the stage came over with the condom. "I think this is yours."

"Oh, sorry about that."

Barry and Geoff laughed. It was excellent times with the boys.

Mike Kean: Liz and Jody have been a writing team for a long time. They did four or five shows together. A lot of them were comedies. *The Birth of Theatre* [RCA Theatre, 2005] told the history of [theatre] through human evolution. [Before that, there was] *Domestic Bliss* and *Our Religion* [RCA Theatre, 1997]. Some of these shows were a bit of a stinker, but they did a lot of great work together.

Jody Richardson: *The Comedy Is Killing Me* was a cabaret-style comedy show to help pay off some debts. Liz Pickard is a dear friend of mine. She brought Crispin Glover to town to perform his spoken word show [*Crispin Hellion Glover's Big Slide Show*], and it bombed. Then she was on the hook for three thousand dollars. For the first *The Comedy Is Killing Me*, we had a bake sale. The headline read "Liz and Chuck's Big Slideshow. Midnight set by Lizband. Special appearance by Steve Lush." That was the first time myself and Liz wrote together.

We thought, *Why don't we write a play about that experience of bringing Crispin Glover to St. John's?* It told the story of Liz's failed promotional endeavour. I played Crispin Glover. Phil Winters played Liz. Alison Carter played me. Liz played Crispin's road manager. The real character was his road manager. He was this LA pretty boy asshole. At one point, Liz actually called him "pretty boy."

He said, "That's totally what I call myself. How did you know?"

When I say Crispin's show bombed, I mean nobody turned up whatsoever. Crispin said, "It's the only show I've ever done that has not made money."

Liz goes, "I feel so lucky to have that distinction."

Move forward to us trying to figure out a way to make money to pay for the debt. We did our first *The Comedy Is Killing Me* as a variety show with a bake sale. Grown-ass people having a bake sale.

We didn't have a director; we did it ourselves. Fur Packed Action was the band. The thing started with a song: "Hello, all you beautiful people. Welcome to this evening's entertaining night of comedy. It has to be funny with a little twist of despair. Can't you see the comedy in the air?"

Phil came out as Liz. "Do you know who Crispin Glover is?"

Then we went to a song. "Crispin Glover, he's an actor living down in Hollywood. He made some movies on the big screen. He got bored and decided to rewrite some old books. Crispin Glover was so interesting that everyone wanted a reading. Oh, Crispin, you're so interesting."

Then I did my version of Crispin's slide show. Crispin has got a very interesting and particular brain. I made up a whole slide show of images from the book. I have a copy of the book. He signed it. "Thanks for the help, Jody. I stole my best lines from you." I asked him to write that.

Geoff Younghusband: The show poster said, "Music, slide show, strong plot. Hollywood stars and safe cozy environment." It was performed it in two or three bars. It was a rotating cast of the whole punk rock scene. Anyone involved with Jody and Liz were in it at some point.

Geoff Younghusband: The year Fur Packed Action started, all I saw was audiences grow. We ramped up Fur Packed Action for five years, and it kept getting bigger and bigger. The all-ages scene we were part of certainly died. The all-ages shows that came out of the Riverdale Tennis Club and that were part of the late '90s and early 2000s had huge turnouts. I didn't even know that they were happening. I was completely immersed in the bar scene.

Jody Richardson: I was making music when the current generation of musicians were in diapers, and I'll be making music when they're in Depends. Every generation has to tear down their elders. You have this great young band, and they really liked Fur Packed Action. After two years, they get a little success, and they're not really talking to you anymore. Then you're just a joke. "You had this great band, and you never did anything with it." Then they go to university or they start working as a cook, and they're not doing music anymore, or they do continue with music, and they go out into the world, and it doesn't work out. They all come back. Then they're sitting next to me at the bar, and they don't hate you so much anymore.

After the first few times it happened, I realized what was going on. "Look at you! You're going through your little arc. I love it." That's happened to me so many times. Now I just find it cute and funny.

Jody Richardson: The Trio first got back together in 1997 for our friend John Lush, who had multiple sclerosis. We did a big benefit to get him a swank motorized wheelchair.

Lil Thomas: It might've been Tim Angel's idea. I'm not 100 per cent sure. Basically, John Lush was someone who we all grew up with and who was a very good friend of ours. He was diagnosed with multiple sclerosis, and he basically tried a whole bunch of therapeutic stuff to mitigate the symptoms and ended up moving outside of town. Obviously, he was trying to cope with a life-changing issue. All he wanted to do was to go up to the lake and walk his dog, but his mobility was really challenging at the time. The whole idea of the benefit was to raise money to purchase a scooter for him.

I remember that night at the Delta very clearly. The look on John's face, knowing that all of those people were coming together for him, was an incredible and inspiring feeling. With all the adversity that he had to deal with, it was pretty moving to see.

Jody Richardson: The next Trio reunion [in 2012] came about because of the Fur Packed Action reunion [in 2011]. With Fur Packed, there was a weekend of benefit shows that happened for Tiffany Martin. When we got together and did those two nights, it was just so joyful. I thought, *This is something that will be good for me, for [the Thomas brothers], and we'll move forward into the future.*

The Trio experience was over by the time I was twenty-six or twenty-seven, and it didn't end under the best circumstances. Your forties is the time in your life when you look back at where you have been, where you thought you would be, and where you think you're going. Time has moved on, and here you are. You're older. You realize it's easy to love, but hate takes energy. I've always said, "You never know why you love somebody. But you know exactly why you hate somebody." Hate is always so exhausting. I knew that it would be good to be around each other as adults and to not deny that part of our life.

I emailed Louis and told him I was thinking about a reunion. I got an email back right away. "Let's start talking about this."

I think Danny replied to the email before I had actually sent it. And Lil was in. Then we started thinking about the logistics.

I wanted to make sure that we'd play as well as we could. As the front man, I was under a lot of pressure. The Thomases could have done it, honest to God, after the first practice. They just sunk back into it. Louis was playing as well as he ever did. Lil was still the monster, and Danny was frapping the bass.

Lil Thomas: I still play all the time, but Danny and Louis haven't played in years. I was more worried about them than anything else. I know Jody stayed fairly active as well. I figured, for me, I'd just have to remember the parts and go through the motions. I'd say we were 70 per cent there without doing anything. Danny and Louis worked really hard to get themselves into shape. Drumming for two hours is not easy, especially with Louis. During a show, Louis would lose gallons of water. He pounded the piss out of the drums.

Jody Richardson: The reunion started with two nights at the Ship and two nights at the Delta. The Delta cost us so much money because of all the production stuff that we weren't going to make that much profit. The George Street Association got in touch with Louis when we were doing our preparations: "We're looking for a band."

Louis went, "Hilariously enough, the Trio is going to be playing." We got a guarantee from the promotion, which paid us really well for our rehearsal time.

I couldn't possibly have foreseen how intense the nostalgic convergence was. What I realized—and this brings the story full circle—once again, we were a band playing for a scene.

The first night at the Ship sold out. The second night sold out. The first Delta show was almost sold out. And then we started to hear all the stories of people coming home from here and there. People came from the States. John Moyes flew in from Halifax with his girls. People were getting in touch with me going, "Me and my two sisters and my brother are all going to be there. We haven't seen each other in a really long time. All the family is so excited to be coming home." [...] All of these different people wanted to get together, and they were using the reunion shows as a good excuse to do it.

I took that responsibility pretty seriously and made sure that I was flat out the whole time. I wanted it to be the greatest show that they'd ever seen. I wanted to be non-stop. I wanted people walking away saying, "Sure, we're forty-five, forty-six, forty-seven. But we're still going."

Lil Thomas: I had to play like a son of a bitch. I was playing three times as intense as what I have to do now [with Kore and the Mellowtones]. I couldn't take my fingers off the guitar. Getting into that kind of space, both physically and mentally, was definitely a switch for me. For the first Delta show, we ended up playing for two hours and fifteen minutes straight. We were almost passing out at the end of the night. We were flying on a natural high.

Jody Richardson: When the George Street thing happened, I knew that with [...] whatever I do, I might get financial success, but I knew George Street was a once-in-a-lifetime experience.

You're going to have 4,500 people on the street. I was like, *I want to walk on the crowd like Iggy Pop*. I was talking to some other friends about my idea: "If I don't walk on the crowd, the show will not be a success."

Everything had to be ramped up. However good the Ship and the Delta were, it didn't matter, if George Street didn't pay off. I did yoga that day and calmed myself down and got my white outfit ready. The gig was going on, and I had already jumped and danced around outside the performance area in amongst the crowd and then climbed a telephone pole. I said to myself, *It's time, man—it's time.*

Tim Baker and Tom Power saw me start to walk, and they rushed over. I looked down, and this random dude was underneath me, and I motioned to him. As soon as he grabbed my foot, people realized what was going on. I thought, *I'm going to stand up and get the audience to do two-part harmonies*. I pulled it off and finished the show. It was pure magic.

* * *

Jody Richardson: As you get older, you realize everybody is in it for their own thing. I live here [in Newfoundland], and I continue to make music the way I want to make it. I get to play music with people who I really enjoy playing with. I got my house, the house I've always lived in. I don't make a lot of money—but success is a moving target.

What I do is tough because of the population; the demographic is so small here that there are not a lot of people my age who are still making music. [...] I remember when everybody moved on to families and moved into office jobs or left the province. I don't have enough fingers and toes to rail off the people who left and found excellent success. I would go to Toronto and Montreal and see all of these people who are my age who are still doing things creatively who never made a shitload of money and just did what they wanted to do. Then I would feel completely calm. I go to Montreal, I'm walking down the street, and there are tons of people like me. There's a grey-haired guy sitting in the bar with a gorgeous lady. It's important to keep a perspective on that all the time.

I just saw an interview with the great David Yow, the singer for the Jesus Lizard. How many bands would not even [have] existed without the Jesus Lizard? They were unbelievably influential. He said, "It's great to work in the arts and pay your bills. That way you're doing all right."

That made me feel amazing.

CAST OF CHARACTERS

Aileen O'Keefe: Fred Gamberg's sister
Andrea Cooper: Coordinator, Peace-A-Chord
Andrew Younghusband: Actor; co-founder of Corey and Wade's Playhouse
Andy Jones: Comedian, actor, writer, member of CODCO
Arthur Haynes: Guitarist for Malpractice, Tumblebug, Bung
Barry Newhook: Bassist for the Riot, Lizband, Bung; guitarist for the Fleming Street Massacre Blues Band, WAFUT
Becky (Rebecca) Moyes: Network coordinator for Youth for Social Justice; backup singer for Thomas Trio and the Red Albino; singer for Crackwillow
Bob Armstrong: Guitarist for Schizoid; promoter and founder of Dead Upturned Puppy Productions (D.U.P.P.); co-founder of *Wabana Riot* fanzine
Bob Dicks: Guitarist for Rubber Samuel, Ditch
Bruce Gilbert: Newfoundland and Labrador Human Rights Association Education Officer; co-founder and coordinator for Youth for Social Justice
Charlie Tomlinson: Actor, playwright, director
Chris Jerrett: Singer for Public Enemy, Schizoid, Sudden Impact
Clark Hancock: Guitarist and singer for WAFUT
Dan Moore: Guitarist for Festered Corpse, Sacrament, sHeavy; singer and guitarist for After Forever
Dana Warren: Co-founder and coordinator for Peace-A-Chord; coordinator for Youth for Social Justice
Danny Thomas: Drummer for Tough Justice; bassist for Thomas Trio and the Red Albino
Dave Andrews: Guitarist for Noon Day Gun
Dave Sweetapple: Bassist for the Riot; singer for Infradig; co-founder of Magwheel Records

David Guy: Singer and guitarist for No Fixed Address; guitarist for Stolen Bones

Dean Locke (d. 2021): Bassist, Tough Justice

Don Ellis: Recording/sound engineer; drummer for Tough Justice; bassist for Schizoid, Infradig, Rise

Doug Jones: Singer for Age of Majority; singer and guitarist for Undermine, Potbelly

Doug Rowe: Drummer for Undermine, Ditch

Erin Whitney: Coordinator, Peace-A-Chord

Frank Nolan: Bassist for Giver

Fred Gamberg (d. 1995): DJ at CHMR; singer for Noonday Gun, Nailbomb; drummer for Giver; all-ages show promoter; co-founder, Best Dressed Records

Gene Long: Peace activist; OXFAM Development Educator; Member of the House of Assembly of Newfoundland and Labrador

Geoff Seymour: Theatre technician

Geoff Younghusband: Bassist and singer for Potmaster, Jupiter Landing, Fur Packed Action; organizer for 333 Duckworth Street jam space; co-founder, Best Dressed Records

Jennifer Dick: Co-founder, Peace-A-Chord

Jody Richardson: Singer and guitarist for the Dervishes; guitarist for White Trash Compactor; singer for the Dirt Buffaloes, Thomas Trio and the Red Albino, Fur Packed Action

Johnny Fisher (d. 2020): Guitarist for the Asthmatics, Tough Justice; singer and guitarist for Fish 'n' Rod, Potmaster, Jupiter Landing

John Nolan: Singer for Malpractice, Tumblebug

John Pastore: Bassist for Public Enemy; promoter for Dead Upturned Puppy Productions (D.U.P.P.); co-founder of *Wabana Riot* zine

Jon Swyers: Drummer for Darshiva, Stirling Slacks; co-founder, Best Dressed Records

Jon Whalen: Owner, Bar None; manager, the Loft; singer for the Fleming Street Massacre Blues Band, Bung

Karmella Perez: Organizer, Peace-A-Chord

Ken Tizzard: Bassist for WAFUT, the Watchmen

Kent Noseworthy: Activist, showgoer

Lesley Thompson: Coordinator, Peace-A-Chord

Lil Thomas: Guitarist for Stolen Bones, Part-Time Reggae Club, Thomas Trio and the Red Albino

Linda Kronbergs: Keyboardist for Thomas Trio and the Red Albino

CAST OF CHARACTERS

Liz Pickard: Singer for Red Scare, Lizband
Lois Brown: Playwright and director; theatre arts teacher
Lori Cooper: Keyboardist for Thomas Trio and the Red Albino
Louis Thomas: Drummer for Stolen Bones, Part-Time Reggae Band, Thomas Trio and the Red Albino
Louise Moyes: Dancer and choreographer
Marcel Levandier: Guitarist for Rubber Samuel, Lizband
Matt Clarke: Drummer for the Bottom Dogs, Crackwillow, Infradig, Hardship Post
Mike Buhler: Showgoer, scene supporter
Mike Fisher: Singer and guitarist for the Reaction
Mike Kean: Bassist for Hardship Post, Lizband
Mike O'Brien: Singer for the Bubonic Plague, Dog Meat BBQ
Mike Pick: Singer and bass player for Hardship Post
Nadine Brothers: Bartender and manager, Bounders
Natalie Noseworthy: Singer and guitarist for Darshiva, Potmaster
Natalie Spracklin: Singer for Whodafunkit
Noel S. Goodridge: Former Chief Justice, Supreme Court of Newfoundland and Labrador
Norm Whalen: Lawyer representing Robbie Thomas in *R. v. Henrietta Roberta Thomas*
Paul Gruchy: Bassist for Undermine, Ditch, sHeavy
Paul Ryan: Fred Gamberg's best friend
Peter Harbin: Guitarist for Potatobug; Peace-A-Chord organizer
Peter Rowan: Founder, DK Records; manager of Sloan, Eric's Trip, Hardship Post; co-founder, Halifax Pop Explosion
Phil van Ulden: Singer and guitarist for Ched
Phil Winters: Guitarist for Schizoid, Bung
Ray Walsh: Bassist for Necropolis
Rennie Squires: Drummer for Age of Majority, Potbelly, sHeavy
Rhonda Pelley: Co-founder, Peace-A-Chord
Rick Mercer: Actor and playwright; founder, Corey and Wade's Playhouse
Rick Power: showgoer
Ritche Perez: Guitarist for More Damn Initials, Artificial Noise; singer and guitarist for Potatobug
Robbie (Roberta) Thomas *(d. 2010)*: Mother of Danny, Lil, and Louis Thomas; defendant in *R. v. Henrietta Roberta Thomas*
Robert Buck: Fred's Records employee; vice-president, Duckworth Distribution

Rod Wills *(d. 2020)*: Drummer for Schizoid, Sacrament, Fish 'n' Rod, the Privateers

Sean Panting: Early member of Corey and Wade's Playhouse; singer and guitarist for Joyful Noise, Drive

Sebastian Lippa: Guitarist for the Bottom Dogs, Crackwillow, Infradig; singer and guitarist for Hardship Post

Sheffia Samuelson: Activist; Peace-A-Chord organizer

Sheilagh O'Leary: Co-founder, Peace-A-Chord; bartender at Friends; photographer

Steve Hussey: Guitarist for Lizband

Terry Carter: Drummer for Da Slyme, the A-Tones, the Reaction

Thom Thorne: Singer for Part-Time Reggae Club, White Trash Compactor

Tiffany Martin: Coordinator, Peace-A-Chord

Tina Thoden: Co-founder and coordinator, Peace-A-Chord

Wallace Hammond: Sound engineer; co-founder, Vikki-Beat record label; guitarist for Da Slyme, Bubonic Plague, Dog Meat BBQ, Big Tears, A-Tones

Woody Whelan: Co-founder, Magwheel Records

ACKNOWLEDGEMENTS

Let It All Fall: Underground Music and the Culture of Rebellion in Newfoundland, 1977–'95 was supposed to profile a dozen musicians, but it quickly expanded into an extensive project that took a decade to complete. Over one hundred subjects were interviewed, and there are a lot of life stories here. The input of all participants has been of immense value; without their memories and insights, the book wouldn't have been possible.

My thanks to the special people in my life: my parents for their constant love and support; Trina, for coming into my life and for always saying the right thing at the right time; and Anja, my constant source of inspiration.

For their encouragement, my thanks to: Joan Sullivan, Craig Frances Power, Katrina Rice, Neachel Keeping, Colleen Quigley, Jason Conway, Donna Smith, Matthew Paul, John Marshall, Rick Mercer, Gerry Porter, Dwayne Whalen, Justin Kennedy, Tracy Tucker, James Langer, Leslie Pierce, Liz Worth, Mark Yarm, Christopher Ward, Tracy Barron, Geoff Younghusband, and Don Ellis.

My thanks to the photographers whose work is featured in the book: Sheilagh O'Leary, Jared Reid, Ian Vardy, Tony Moore, Geoff Younghusband, Justin Hall, and Tina Riche.

My thanks to organizations that were immensely helpful during the years of research: Arts Newfoundland and Labrador, the Provincial Court of Newfoundland and Labrador, the Gathering Place, The Rooms, the Centre for Newfoundland Studies, the St. John's City Archives, and CBC Newfoundland and Labrador.

And finally, my thanks to the team at Breakwater Books. This project switched hands many times over a long period. Your patience and belief made it happen.